S0-FIV-994

Dilemmas of Justice in Eastern Europe's Democratic Transitions

Dilemmas of Justice in Eastern Europe's Democratic Transitions

Noel Calhoun

DILEMMAS OF JUSTICE IN EASTERN EUROPE'S DEMOCRATIC TRANSITIONS

First published 2004 by
PALGRAVE MACMILLAN™
175 Fifth Avenue, New York, N.Y. 10010 and
Houndmills, Basingstoke, Hampshire, England RG21 6XS
Companies and representatives throughout the world

PALGRAVE MACMILLAN is the global academic imprint of the Palgrave Macmillan division of St. Martin's Press, LLC and of Palgrave Macmillan Ltd. Macmillan® is a registered trademark in the United States, United Kingdom and other countries. Palgrave is a registered trademark in the European Union and other countries.

ISBN 1–4039–6389–4 hardback

Library of Congress Cataloging-in-Publication Data
Calhoun, Noel.
Dilemmas of justice in Eastern Europe's democratic transitions / Noel Calhoun.
p. cm.
Includes bibliographical references and index.
ISBN 1–4039–6389–4 (alk. paper)
1. Europe, Eastern—Politics and government—1989– 2. Justice, Administration of—Europe, Eastern. 3. Human rights—Europe, Eastern. I. Title.

DJK51.C35 2004
320.943'01'1—dc22 2003064654

A catalogue record for this book is available from the British Library.

Design by Newgen Imaging Systems (P) Ltd., Chennai, India.

First edition: August 2004
10 9 8 7 6 5 4 3 2 1

Printed in the United States of America.

To Vanya

Contents

Acknowledgments

In the course of researching this book I have incurred many debts in many places. For financial support, I am grateful to the PSC-CUNY Foundation, the Krupp Foundation for European Studies, Abby and George O'Neill, the Davis Center for Russian Research, and the Foreign Language and Area Studies program. At Harvard, my advisor Prof. Timothy Colton gave me tremendous encouragement. I also thank other professors at Harvard—Grzegorz Ekiert, Samuel Huntington, Henry Steiner, Theda Skocpol—for their assistance at key points.

In Germany, I received ready assistance from the staff at the library of the Free University of Berlin and at the Archiv des 15. Januar. Christiane Lemke and Gero Neugebauer gave useful direction. My appreciation goes out to the American Church in Berlin for being a lovely community of support, and to Mark Duckenfield who provided entertaining distractions.

In Poland, the staff of the Sejm library helped me to locate parliamentary materials, while the Institute for Political Studies provided an academic home away from home. For their advice I thank Jerzy Holzer, Jacek Wasilewski, Sergiusz Kowalski, Aleksander Herzog, Jan Ordynski, and Adam Kieruj. Several friends in Poland were always ready to drag me from the library—thanks to Polina Zdziech, Ann Dentry, Father Dariusz Sambora, and the late Wioletta Boguslawska.

In the last few years, Russia has become my home. Here too I have found many people willing to put aside their daily concerns to help an American researcher. At Memorial, the Sakharov Library, and *Za Pravo Cheloveka*, staff persons were willing to talk long and hard about the problems of coming to terms with the Soviet past. I am especially thankful to Lev Ponomarev who provided me with a corner in which to pore over documents along with ample amounts of tea. Special thanks also to Maria Tarasova, Aleksander Kostinsky, and Tatiana Gromova. In Moscow wonderful friends—especially parishioners from the Moscow Protestant Chaplaincy and colleagues at work—have always been ready with an encouraging word.

Finally, I would like to thank my family and friends for giving me the benefit of their love, patience, and good humor. They made it possible to live with joy, even while spending long months—often in chilly East European capitals—thinking about the human rights abuses of communism. I especially thank my parents Michael and Roxine Hild and my in-laws Merrell and Constance Calhoun. Thanks also to dear friends John and Barbara Melin, Abraham and Larisa Waya, Nancy AntonJensen and Benjamin Frommer. My husband John Calhoun has helped me immensely in this project—from beginning to end. I remember the project's inception during a long conversation we had about political reconciliation. That evening we walked from East Jerusalem to the West and back again. Those were the days when reconciliation still seemed possible in the Middle East. Now we live on a different continent in what seems like a different age, but John is still there, proofreading my footnotes. That is loyalty. And, finally, my deepest gratitude for the gift of our son Nicholas Moses Calhoun, who gives us hope.

Abbreviations

CDU – Christian Democratic Union (Germany)
CPSU – Communist Party of the Soviet Union
FSB – Federal Security Service (Russia)
IW – Military Intelligence (Poland)
KGB – Committee for State Security (Soviet Union)
KLD – Congress of Liberal Democrats (Poland)
KPN – Confederation for an Independent Poland
NKVD – People's Commissariat of Internal Affairs
OKP – Citizen's Parliamentary Club (Poland)
PC – Center Alliance (Poland)
PDS – Party of Democratic Socialism (Germany)
PSL – Polish Peasants' Party (Poland)
PZPR – Polish United Workers' Party
RSFSR – Russian Soviet Federated Socialist Republic
SB – Security Service (Poland)
SED – Socialist Unity Party of Germany (East Germany)
SLD – Union of Leftist Democrats (Poland)
SPD – Social Democratic Party (Germany)
UB – Security Department (Poland)
UD – Democratic Union (Poland)
UOP – Department of Protection of the State (Poland)
UP – Labor Union (Poland)
UW – Freedom Union (Poland)

Introduction

While murder and mayhem have plagued humankind through the centuries, the bloody twentieth century proved that the state with its unrivaled power to organize the use of force has a particularly horrifying potential for inflicting violence. Vladimir Lenin's militaristic definition of the state—"special bodies of armed men"—was sadly prophetic.[1] Strong states like Hitler's Germany and Stalin's Russia pulled together an overwhelming array of military, bureaucratic, and police resources to organize murder on an unimaginable scale. Even weak states like Rwanda were able to compile lists of Tutsis to be massacred and order the machetes needed to carry out the gruesome genocide of 1994.[2] The historian of the twentieth century can recite a long list of states' crimes against their own citizens, ranging from the genocides in Europe, Cambodia, and Rwanda, to the "disappearance" of opposition activists in Latin America, to the brutal repression of dissidents throughout the Soviet bloc.

It is a very unequal battle, this struggle between the individual and the state, and there is very little justice to be had when the state decides on a policy of violence against its own citizens. The state can close off nearly all channels of assistance, leaving citizens with nowhere to turn: The police and courts are in the grip of the hostile state; the press will not risk printing their stories; even friends and neighbors may be reluctant to get involved. By mobilizing the full armory of violence and terror, the state can ensure not only its impunity, but the secrecy of its crimes as well. Victims can be rendered utterly powerless.

Political leaders whose rule is mired in a long history of crimes are particularly jealous of their power because power is the only guarantee of their own physical security. Once power begins to slip away, however, leaders with bloody hands begin to squirm in contemplation of their just desserts. What happens after an era of state crimes and impunity? Should the new regime seek vengeance, perhaps by quickly executing the former leaders or arranging for show trials? Or if this would risk backlash or chaos, perhaps it is better to forget the past altogether. Is there any middle ground between these unpalatable extremes?

The twentieth century has provided a range of experience in grappling with these questions. The century was not just one of state crimes, but also one in which new regimes tried to meet the challenge of overcoming the legacy of past abuses. No one has found any easy answers to the dilemmas of justice during regime transitions, where questions of moral, legal, and political significance arise. As we shall see, the moral desire to punish the guilty often conflicts with the political necessity of maintaining national unity and the legal requirements of a liberal democratic state. It is easier for a new regime to win power than to win justice.

This book examines the dilemmas of justice in the context of democratic transitions in Easter Europe, looking at how three countries—Poland, East Germany, and Russia—dealt with the legacy of human rights abuses committed under communist rule. The experience of the twentieth century shows that there are three general approaches a new regime can choose from in coming to terms with the crimes of the past: violent retribution, forgetting, or policies of truth and justice.[3] This book argues that liberal democratic ideology plays a significant role in encouraging new democracies to implement policies of truth and justice, and that this option, though highly imperfect in delivering substantive justice, can contribute to the prospects for democratic consolidation.

Violent Retribution

Violent retribution is one way to seek justice for gross crimes. When people who have long been under the thumb of oppressive rule are hurtled into power during great political upheavals, they seize the opportunity to punish their former oppressors and eliminate all pretenders to their new ascendancy. We often think of retribution as a stage of revolutionary change—the Terror. Angered by the injustices and crimes of the *ancien regime*, revolutionaries violently overthrow the old order and exact extralegal punishment for the whole catalogue of misdeeds committed in the past. The new leaders decimate the old guard. A mountain of gruesome evidence shows how common this outcome is: the cruel annihilation of the Tsar's family in the aftermath of the Russian revolution; the disappearance of members of the Ethiopian royal court as Mengistu ascended to power; the guillotine's infamous association with the French Revolution. Violent retribution is a barbaric, crude instrument. Revolutionaries do not pause to weigh the evidence of individual guilt, so the Tsar's daughters had to perish alongside those who were directly responsible for the old regime's crimes.

Not all retributive violence occurs in the context of revolution; sometimes disorder and widespread anger can lead to a groundswell of violent activity. Such was the case at the end of the Second World War, when across the continent people took advantage of the general disorder to punish those who had collaborated with the fascist regimes that had spread such misery. It is estimated that this "wild justice" claimed 10,000 victims in France, and a similar number of suspected fascists in northern Italy during the winter months of 1944–45.[4] After the transitions to democracy in Central and Eastern Europe, we might have expected a similar wave of retributive violence. With the foe defanged by the relentless progress of revolution, former dissidents and the oppressed masses might have expressed their anger in a fierce crushing of the communists. However, with the notable exception of Romania, the regime changes proceeded without violent attacks on the former communist leadership. Today former communists continue to live in peace, integrated into their respective societies.

Violent retribution—however morally repugnant—serves powerful political interests. The main interest is the one the revolutionaries so assiduously pursue—that of sweeping away their political opponents in the old regime. Those who formerly committed serious crimes against their own people are not only stripped of power, but also permanently removed from politics so that they cannot threaten political stability any longer. A period of violent retribution can also, arguably, be an emotional catharsis, giving people a sense of justice being done. This popular satisfaction at seeing former oppressors laid low may offer the new regime a surge of legitimacy.

Nevertheless, retributive violence is a costly means of achieving emotional satisfaction. Violence too often turns into the dreaded spiral, begetting only new acts of violence. Rwanda, for example, has experienced this cycle far too often: Authoritarian rule by the Tutsis led the Hutus to drive their oppressors into exile; when the Tutsis returned to Rwanda and took up arms against the Hutus, the Tutsis were ultimately murdered.[5] Another act of violence cannot possibly bring a solution to Rwanda's political problems; violence there, as elsewhere, would beget only more violence and instability.

Instead of offering widespread legitimacy, violence may split society sharply. The murdered representatives of the old regime can become beloved martyrs. Or the revolutionary bloodbath may sicken decent citizens, making the new regime, which represented a new hope for moral authority, start its life with weak legitimacy as citizens dispiritedly realize there is no goodness to be found in either the old or the new regimes. Such was the case in post-communist Romania, where the violence accompanying the regime change led to a deep cynicism about the new government's intentions and choice of means.[6]

Ironically, though violent retribution may be an effort to obtain justice for past crimes, it may ultimately sow the seeds of forgetting the past, or reimagining it in a less embarrassing way. After violence and chaos have left most political groups with dirt on their hands, all sides may be ready for a compromise of silence or myth. Weary of wild justice, purges, and trials, the French were ready in the 1950s to believe de Gaulle's happy resistancialist myth: that the real France had bravely resisted the Nazi onslaught and was thus innocent of the stain of collaboration.[7] Other European countries embraced similar myths in the mid-1950s to usher in an "era of good feelings," which for a generation allowed Europeans to forget the historical complexities and guilt of wartime collaboration.[8]

Forgetting the Past

Forgetting is primarily a way of avoiding controversy about the past, so it may assist in preserving social peace and forging national unity. After a period in which one group in society brutalized another, forgetting may seem like the only way that the groups can avoid a cycle of violent revenge. To an exhausted society, forgetting the past may seem an attractive solution. This may be especially true after a war. The Second World War, which followed so soon on the heels of the butchery of the First, left Europe worn out by its past. To try to come to account with those who were responsible risked unleashing new attacks against the fascists and their collaborators, which would only weaken the state and social unity.[9] Similarly, Americans after their war were in a hurry to forget the issue of slavery that had divided the North and South. Forgetting can have painful long-term consequences, however. This attempt to forge national unity between North and South in the United States succeeded at the expense of carving an enduring divide between black and white.[10]

Even if there is little fear that controversy about the past would turn into violence, political leaders may have other incentives to keep the issue off the political agenda. They may wish to avoid undertaking costly efforts to compensate the victims of past abuses. Compensating former slaves in the United States, for example, would have been a great financial burden for the respective states. Forgetting makes financial sense.

Forgetting also serves to remove a highly emotional and controversial issue from the political agenda during a regime transition that may be crowded with other serious priorities. For example, Spain's political leadership during its democratization in the 1970s focused on preparing the country for entry into the European Community. This overriding concern meant that discussing the internal conflicts of the past would be a painful and possibly risky distraction.[11] It also seems that former communist countries in the midst of a complex triple transition—political, social, and economic—could easily have chosen to avoid the issue of past injustices as an irrelevant detail. Surprisingly, though, this approach prevailed only in the former Soviet republics, particularly in the Russian Federation.

Finally, forgetting may also serve the personal interests of politicians whose own past is compromised, though this fact is likely to be cloaked in more public-minded justifications for setting the past aside. No one may know for sure whether public goals or the desire for personal political survival really lies behind a decision to forget the past. This is an uncertainty about Russia's transition—one that the available files do not help us to dissect. Was the forgetting of the past during Russia's democratic transition crucial for ensuring social peace or merely a means for assuring the survival of a political elite that was implicated to varying degrees in the abuses of the communist system?

In many cases, forgetting is not permanent. It assists in forging a temporary political compromise, but ultimately new political actors—often from a younger generation—may raise the issues that were deemed taboo. This delay may have the advantage of allowing sensitive debates to be carried out by people who were not directly involved in the abuses, facilitating a more dispassionate, objective handling of the issue. Young historians can examine past crimes from all angles. With the passage of time, violent revenge is less likely, as victims and perpetrators age and become less likely to thrash out in anger. Meanwhile, the disorder of regime transition has given way to a stable legal and political order that can adjudicate crimes in a way broadly perceived to be fair.

We have often heard the warning that those who forget the past are doomed to repeat it. In part, this is simply the familiar theory of criminal punishment. Punishment deters crime by removing known criminals from society and protecting society against their future actions. The trials at Nuremburg, for example, protected the new West German democracy against any Nazi attempt to rally again around popular public figures. Similarly, the trial of Slobodan Milosevic hopefully will remove him permanently from the Yugoslav political scene, where he has caused so much damage. There may also be consequences—though this involves considerable guesswork—of not putting people on trial. We know, for example, that postwar France included in high positions a number of individuals who worked closely with the Vichy regime, which obligingly sent Jews to the German gas chambers. Years later some of the same individuals were involved in the brutal war against Algerian independence. Was the failure to punish one era's abuses a cause of further crimes in another?[12] Similarly we might draw a connection between the lack of personnel changes in post-communist Russia's military and state security apparatus and the ongoing human rights abuses committed by those bodies, especially in Chechnya.[13]

Criminal punishment is also designed to deter others from committing similar crimes. It is very difficult to measure the success of punishment in deterring state crimes. We must peer behind a curtain of counter-factuals, speculating at what might have happened if these officials were left unpunished. Without Nuremburg, might there have been a fascist renaissance in Germany and perhaps even throughout Europe? Will the Milosevic trial prevent future ethnic massacres in the Balkans? Might it even deter nationalists leaders elsewhere from organizing a genocide? Though it is difficult to measure the deterrent effect of punishment, which if successful results in a nonevent, the consequences of amnesty are clearer. When the U.S. government granted an amnesty to Southern rebels and ignored former slaves' calls for justice after the Civil War, the leaders of Southern states received the clear message that there would be no punishment for oppressing blacks. This impunity permitted the Ku Klux Klan, lynchings and Jim Crow laws—a legacy of racism the country still struggles to overcome.[14]

Furthermore, while forgetting serves the political interest of some, it may harm that of others. During a transition, opponents of the old regime will draw legitimacy and public support from punishing the crimes of the past, especially if people are out on the streets demanding that the criminal old regime be brought to account. Politicians from the opposition can draw on this anger to propel themselves into power. Such was the case in South Africa where the African National Congress could count on blacks' hatred of apartheid's injustices to guarantee them success in the first democratic elections. A party winning a crucial election on the issue of condemning past crimes will not wish to simply forget them.

Policies of Truth and Justice

Countries that have recently made a transition to democracy face common challenges in dealing with the crimes of the previous regime.

Democracy sets forth an array of principles to be used in evaluating the state's behavior. All of the former regime's nasty violations of human rights—the police's unbridled use of force, the judiciary's clampdown on dissident behavior, and the oppression of religious and ethnic minorities—deserve round condemnation. The people may be out on the streets filled with anger at what they have suffered and those who are responsible. Democracy sets up a new system for assessing the state's behavior and calls on the political community to take responsibility for governing itself. At the same time, democracy establishes limitations on a new government's policies for dealing with past evils: banning extrajudicial punishment and lawless violence; calling for universal participation and equal rights; and erecting the system of the rule of law. The demand for justice explodes at the same time as legal limitations are introduced, creating the dilemmas of justice at the heart of this book.

During the third wave of democratization in the late twentieth century when so many countries had to face the dilemmas of justice in democratic transitions, a trend began to emerge. New democracies from Latin America to South Africa to Eastern Europe crafted policies of truth and justice, focusing on a mixture of limited legal redress and official truth-telling. Policies of truth and justice hold great promise as an alternative to the opposite extremes of violent retribution and forgetting the past. Rather than wild justice or no justice, this approach offers some justice—not a perfect solution (which is anyway infeasible in the real world of rough-and-tumble politics), but one that is politically feasible and morally defensible.

Legal Redress

Legal redress in the late twentieth century included much more than a set of trials to point out a few prominent scapegoats. Post-communist countries have adopted a variety of policies of legal redress aimed at apportioning blame for state crimes. To understand the different tools of legal redress, Offe constructs a useful typology, differentiating between the use of civil or criminal law as applied to victims or perpetrators.[15] Table 0.1 contains a revised version of this typology.[16] It is significant that in this approach to transitional justice, a wide range of legal tools can be used to come to terms with past injustices. Despite the availability of several legal tools, however, this form of redress is limited by both the procedural guarantees of the rule of law and the necessity of political compromise in a new democracy.

Trials—Criminal Law/Perpetrator Criminal trials of individuals who abused their authority or violated human rights under the old regime are

Table 0.1 Forms of legal redness

	Criminal law	*Civil law*
Perpetrator	Trials	Lustration
Victim	Rehabilitation	Compensation

prime examples of legal redress. During transitions to democracy, however, trials of former violators are relatively rare because they entail knotty legal and political problems. Who in the political or military hierarchy was truly responsible for the abuses of the past? Do the perpetrators or their cronies retain sufficient power to imperil the transition to democracy? Furthermore, the violators enjoy new civil protections, which ensure them the right to a fair trial, and the prosecutors face difficulties in assembling evidence of a crime sometimes long after the fact. Because of these constraints, new democracies attempting to come to terms with the past by legal redress are unlikely to succeed in holding many trials.

Lustration—Civil Law/Perpetrator A less severe form of punishment is the loss of employment or certain political rights, or lustration. Because this is a civil law measure, a lower threshold of procedural protections apply, which may make lustration less legally complicated than trials. However, because lustration may affect a group of influential and technically qualified officials, it may stimulate great political controversy. Former communist countries sometimes purged the public administration of individuals who were compromised by the old regime. Or they placed limitations on the rights of the communist party, banning it outright or confiscating its property. Such punishments do not deprive individuals of their most basic liberties; however, they do impose a lesser form of retribution.

Compensation—Civil Law/Victim A democratizing regime may decide to offer compensation to people who were victims of the previous regime's abuses. "[C]ompensation is the restoration of a good or level of well-being which someone would have enjoyed if he had not been adversely affected by another's wrong act."[17] Compensation, as Jaspers points out, is the ordinary means by which a political community atones for and takes responsibility for its past misdeeds.[18] In some countries, the amount of compensation is tiny; in others it can impact the individual's well-being. The most difficult task is deciding which groups of people deserve compensation. After the demise of an oppressive regime, almost the entire population can claim to have suffered unjustly; yet, compensation of all would be a meaningless act, as well as an economic drain. The search for a simple, limited definition of who deserves compensation is open to much political contestation.

Rehabilitation—Criminal Law/Victim The reversal of criminal sentences against victims, that is, their rehabilitation, falls in this category. Under communist rule, many people were imprisoned for expressing their beliefs, organizing clandestine groups, or simply refusing to follow the prescribed political line. A criminal record of this sort meant that the individual could not obtain employment involving a high degree of responsibility, and many avenues of educational advancement were blocked. A full rehabilitation means that the individual may reclaim all civil and political rights. Rehabilitation does not involve any punishment, and for the state it is the least expensive form of legal redress. Though rehabilitation has primarily symbolic value, it also gives the former victim a clean criminal record and the restitution of full rights. Furthermore, rehabilitation in most countries is closely linked to compensation. A criminal rehabilitation is a clear, relatively undisputed criterion that can be used to resolve the question of who is eligible for compensation.

Truth-Telling

In addition to legal redress, many new democracies of the last generation have undertaken a policy of truth-telling, using the power of the state to publicize information about the former regime's abuses. This can take various institutional forms: a parliamentary inquiry, an independent "truth commission," or the opening of archives for private and professional use. The key point is that the government takes action to help the public know the truth about past abuses.

By telling the truth about abuses committed by the state in the past, the new democracy acknowledges those who suffered. Truth-telling may pave the way for a formal state apology to the victims of human rights abuses.

The purposes of truth-telling go beyond moral restitution to include broader political goals. Truth-telling clears the fog of secrecy that enveloped politics in the past. It lays bare the institutional mechanisms that permitted cruel abuses of power. It thereby promotes greater openness in politics, a quality that may prevent similar crimes in the future. Truth-telling is ultimately the key to learning the lessons of an authoritarian past: If a society does not know what happened in its past, it cannot possibly begin to analyze why these crimes occurred.

New democracies have embraced policies of truth and justice as an approach to dealing with past injustices. They are not alone. The United Nations has intervened to establish similar solutions in post-conflict areas, such as Yugoslavia and Rwanda. After their brutal ethnic wars, the Security Council decided that those who were responsible for the massacres should be brought to justice. This was perceived as a necessary condition for the countries' future peace and stability. Political and military leaders were put on trial in procedures that complied with international legal standards. These standards meant that the trials could not be called "victor's justice"; however, they also meant that the trials dragged on for years while the alleged perpetrators of genocide enjoyed the legal protections and relative comfort that they had denied their victims.[19] Despite these imperfections, other countries have asked the United Nations to be involved in helping to bring war criminals to justice. A war crimes tribunal is functioning in Sierra Leone with strong international, as well as local, participation; a similar tribunal for Cambodia is in the planning stages.[20] In the future, these *ad hoc* responses should be less necessary as those guilty of the most serious human rights abuses may face trial at the International Criminal Court, which began to function in 2003. This court embodies the idea that those guilty of serious abuses should stand trial under fair international procedures.[21]

It is remarkable that so many countries covering such different past political contexts would choose similar approaches to dealing with the legacy of past human rights abuses. Since both forgetting the past and seeking violent revenge for it have multiple advantages, one would expect that given the wide variety of historical and political contexts in this recent wave of democratizations, we might see numerous approaches among the new democracies of the late twentieth century. Instead, policies of truth and justice have become a very common—though not all-pervasive—approach to coming to terms with the past. The explanation for this common approach lies in the spread of shared values, in particular the values of liberal democracy, which gained in legitimacy with the end of the Cold War.[22] Liberal democratic ideology shapes a new democracy's approach to dealing with the legacy of past human rights abuses. It leads to a focus on truth-telling and legal redress limited by the rule of law.

In post-communist transitions, some countries followed the international trend of policies of truth and justice, while others, primarily the former republics of the Soviet Union, did not. This makes Eastern Europe a good testing ground for looking at how liberal democratic ideology shapes transitional justice, as well as for speculating about the consequences of various approaches to dealing with the problem of transitional justice.

Chapter 1 explores the role of politics in explaining how countries have come to terms with past injustices. While regime transitions create an opportunity for punishing those who violated human rights in the past and for revealing the truth about the authoritarian regime's crimes, they also limit the new leaders in various ways. The new leaders may be constrained by agreements they made with the old regime and a precarious balance of power with the old elites. In addition, the teleology of the transition—the move toward liberal democracy—imposes constraints. The ideology of liberal democracy accords the issue of transitional justice particular salience and frames the debates and policies adopted. Ultimately, liberal democratic regimes move toward policies of truth and justice.

Chapter 2 probes more deeply into the nature of the ideology itself, teasing out its implications for transitional justice. Chapters 3 through 5 describe how three countries—East Germany/Germany, Poland, and Russia—have approached the question of transitional justice, accounting for the variation in approaches, examining legal redress, truth-telling, and forgetting.

The conclusion discusses the consequences of transitional justice for the future of democracy. It may still be too early to speculate meaningfully on this matter. After all, the transitions studied here are less than a generation old, and trials and truth-telling may yet come to be seen as a fad rather than a real solution to a complex, emotional issue. The shortfalls of this approach are clear. Perpetrators can be left unpunished because of unsatisfying legal technicalities. All the talk of truth-telling may seem to lack moral seriousness, as so much remembering is accompanied by little concrete action to help the victims of past state crimes. Future generations may reopen these issues and question the compromises that were made.

Nevertheless, while there have been many critical voices, the liberal democratic approach to transitional justice seems to have done little harm to new democracies. The crimes of the past and resulting political divisions have not risen to haunt the new regimes, which have enjoyed social peace. The liberal democratic approach ensures at least some measure of justice and legitimacy for the new regimes. Truth-telling provides the opportunity to learn lessons from the past, though whether these new democracies will learn the right lessons in the long run remains uncertain.

Chapter 1
The Politics of Transitional Justice

Why do some countries in transition collapse into violence while others try to forget the past? Why have yet others, especially in recent transitions, adopted a strategy of legal redress and truth-telling?

For the student of revolution, violence against former oppressors is the natural course. Barrington Moore's classic is memorable for its insistence that both evolutionary and revolutionary forms of political change entail the violent destruction of powerful conservative classes.[1] If left undisturbed, the conservative classes, namely the peasantry and the landed nobility, will inhibit the development of a free society, contributing instead to fascism or communism. Thus, the destruction of these classes is a progressive, albeit bloody, stage of historical development. For another student of revolution Theda Skocpol, the state institutions of the old regime, rather than the conservative classes, are the revolutionary leadership's target. The revolutionary leadership struggles to seize and transform state institutions, which provide the key resources for effecting revolutionary change in society.[2] It mobilizes the people to assist in destroying the old regime's leaders who would otherwise block the revolution's access to the state's powerful resources.

A revolution involves fundamental social, economic, and political changes. Dismantling the powerful classes and institutions that upheld the old regime is by definition an aspect of revolutionary change. Discussing the French Revolution of 1789, Dick Howard writes: "Only after the Revolution could the concept of an '*Ancien Régime*' emerge; and only then could the past and the future be opposed radically, in order to deny the ambiguities of the present."[3] In a revolution the vestiges of the past are crushed quickly and violently, as in France. The past is wiped away. Violence, or a threat to use violence, is a necessary means for breaking the old regime's stranglehold on power; the old regime's representatives will not cede power quietly and of their own accord.

"What distinguishes revolution from reform or coup d'etat is the destruction of the dominant social group. This destruction is a fundamental precondition for the innovative and positive change associated with revolution."[4] If the revolutionaries fail in their project of destruction, the old regime's supporters will threaten the legitimacy and control of the revolutionary order.

The literature on revolution suggests that when the *ancien régime* collapses and a democratic opposition seizes power, retribution is likely. This is especially true when a popular uprising accompanies the transition. In these cases, the old institutions are shattered in a violent spree, and the newly ascendant leadership utilizes the instruments of state control to reshape society. However, in post-communist Europe, Romania's bloody December was the only example of this type of violence.[5] In general, this hypothesis does not fare well in the region: It overpredicts violent retribution. Though the transitions in East Germany and Czechoslovakia did not involve much political compromise, leaving the societies ripe for retribution, violent methods were eschewed.

Students of democratization, taking as their subject less bloody periods of political change, have emphasized the role of power politics in determining a country's approach to transitional justice. In a democratic transition, moral and legal considerations are subordinate to politics. Instead, the modality of the transition and the distribution of power determine how a country will come to terms with past human rights abuses.[6]

Recent democratizations have for the most part followed one of three patterns: transformation, rupture, or negotiated transition. In a transformation, the incumbent authoritarian leaders try to transform their regime into a democracy. They inaugurate and direct the process of democratization, slowly guiding political change that culminates in free elections. In this type of transition, members of the old regime remain politically powerful even after democracy is introduced. A rupture occurs when the authoritarian regime weakens to the point of collapse, at which time the opposition seizes power. In this type of transition, power relations are inverted, but similarly imbalanced, with the opposition on top and the former government laid low. In a negotiated transition, the regime and opposition negotiate arrangements for a democratic transition.[7] Their relative powers hang in an often wobbly balance.

When a new democracy is installed by a process of transformation or negotiated transition, it is unlikely to punish members of the former

Table 1.1 Type of democratic transition and approach to transitional justice

Rupture		*Negotiated transition*	*Transformation*
Czechoslovakia	Latvia	Hungary	Bulgaria
Estonia	Lithuania	Poland	
Germany (East)	Romania		
Russia			
Retribution		*No retribution*	*No retribution*

regime. The old regime retains sufficient power to make the transition contingent upon an amnesty of past crimes. Only a rupture offers the possibility of punishing members of the old regime, since in these transitions they do not have the power to prevent this. Table 1.1 charts the predictions, which this framework generates for transitions in post-communist Europe.

How well does the evidence from post-communist Europe bear out these predictions? The answer depends on which timeframe we choose to examine. If we take a snapshot of the transition—the year 1989/90 for Central Europe and autumn 1991 for the former Soviet republics—the predictions seem fairly accurate. In those years, East Germans were storming the headquarters of the secret police, as we might expect in a country undergoing a transition by rupture. In Russia, Yeltsin was banning the country's communist party and promising to open the KGB and party archives, which would reveal the secrets of past crimes.[8] Meanwhile, in countries that experienced negotiated transitions such as Hungary and Poland, trials, as well as other retributive measures, were low on the political agenda. In Poland the government suggested a policy of forgetting the past.

During the transition and the months immediately following, the balance of power among political forces is a valuable predictor of policy choices. Opposition forces will exact retribution if they can; a mobilized populace will demand it.[9] Negotiation and compromise will lead to a quiet shelving of the past. The ground soon starts to shift, however. The strong popular mobilization and the coalescence of pacts are unlikely to survive many months, perhaps not even until the first free election. What happens then?

The distribution of power swings rapidly during a democratic transition—the old regime collapses or negotiates conditions for competitive elections; the elections yield often surprising results; the population demobilizes; and politicians grope to create a new form of ordinary politics. Unsurprisingly, the approach to transitional justice also evolves through an extended cycle.

To explain further developments, we might want to rely on an analysis of power politics.[10] Stalwarts of the old regime—former communists in this context—are very unlikely to support policies of truth and justice. They have most to fear personally from trials and purges, and keeping the tainted past in the public mind will not promote their party's good image and electoral success. We would therefore predict that the ascendance of the former communists to power, which occurred in many of the post-communist countries' second free elections, would block policies of truth and justice. If right-leaning parties dominated by former opposition activists or new nationalists later resume the reins, transitional justice may return to the political agenda. Noncommunist parties have an incentive to raise the issue of the crimes of the past, since it provides a ready weapon for tarring the reputation of the former communists. The past can become the object of political ping-pong, at least as long as the people are interested enough to pay attention to arguments over the nation's history.

While these power struggles explain the timing of many policy initiatives, the correlations are far from complete. Not all members of the former opposition embrace retributive policies, even when they are unconstrained by pacts and retribution would bring them benefits. Sometimes former communists see a tactical advantage in embracing certain policies of truth and justice. They may believe that abjuring the past will help their party become a more "normal" party of the democratic Left. Or by supporting a particular policy, they may try to shape it so that it is less damaging to their interests.

Despite its elegance and utility as an explanation, the dynamics of the quest for power do not help us answer certain broader questions about transitional justice. Why do issues of transitional justice continue to be salient long after the transition? Why has transitional justice emerged as an important issue in so many of the democratic transitions of the postwar era? Why have new democracies in diverse cultural and political contexts adopted similar policies of truth and justice, rather than simply forgetting the past?

In the third wave of democratization, debates about transitional justice have included surprising strands of continuity and commonality, for which the various power configurations of regime and opposition seem an inadequate explanation. From Argentina to Poland, arguments raged about retroactivity, collective responsibility, and the ethics of exclusion. As the dramatic changes in South Africa stirred into motion, political leaders from the country turned to the recently installed democrats in Latin America and Central Europe for guidance in dealing with the legacy of apartheid's abuses.

Effective cross-cultural borrowing requires the existence of a common political idiom, a set of mutually intelligible concepts for analyzing political experience. The shared language is liberal democratic ideology. Former South American leftists, African National Congress activists, and Central European communists rely on the concepts of liberal democracy to analyze their political situations. This newly found common ground is reinforced by international law, especially by human rights documents such as the Universal Declaration of Human Rights.[11] Furthermore, the ideas of liberal democracy, and in particular human rights, receive institutional support from a network of international organizations. Some of these are governmental organizations, such as the United Nations, which monitors human rights issues, but non-governmental organizations increasingly play a role in propagating norms, spreading information, and providing financial assistance to political groups pursuing a liberal democratic agenda.[12] The values of liberal democracy have shaped the international conversation about transitional justice and have facilitated international political communication, and the borrowing of policies.

Political actors from around the globe are looking for a way to deal with the problems of transitional justice within the context of their own political constraints. They are also examining other countries' experiences and assessing their advantages and shortcomings. As a group, the newly democratizing countries are measuring various approaches to transitional justice against the principles of liberal democracy. They appear to be groping their way to an international standard by which democratizing countries' approach to transitional justice can be evaluated. They are setting a new benchmark for how a state should exercise political responsibility for past abuses.

The great international conversation about transitional justice directs our attention to the role ideology plays in shaping policy. The goal in this book is to clarify the role ideas play in how countries come to terms with past human rights abuses. This does not mean that political power disappears from the analysis. Rather, I argue that political competition and ideology combine to explain different aspects of the dynamics of policy-making. The politics of transitional justice is in part about the struggle for power in a given institutional context; however, it also consists of people pondering how to resolve a complex problem, which has not only political, but also moral and legal implications.

The problem of evaluating the relative impact of ideal and material interests is at the heart of social inquiry. As Goldstone writes, "If social events were *always* caused by material interests or *always* by ideal ones, (or *always* by both), then we would be theorizing historical variation out of existence."[13] Disentangling the impact of material and ideal interests cannot be done once and for all time to explain all social phenomena. In different contexts we can expect the variables to play different relative roles. At most we can point to certain robust processes among various comparable contexts.

An ideology is as an "explicit, articulated, highly organized meaning system."[14] A limited number of ideologies are available in a given culture at a specific time. Although their appearance and impact on the political scene may seem sudden, ideologies develop gradually over time. They sprout out of myriad intellectual antecedents, and they grow in a particular institutional context. The individual—even a great political entrepreneur—does not fashion a novel ideology out of whole cloth; rather, he quilts the preexisting ideological scraps into a coherent pattern.[15]

People (and perhaps especially politicians) use ideology with different motivations. They may use the language of ideology to obfuscate their real interests and intentions. They may use it as a hermeneutical tool to make sense of the complex social world they experience. They may find a particular ideology congenial because it has external legitimacy and powerful backers, such as international organizations or influential countries. Politicians may also choose to use an ideology out of habit or conformity. To understand a person's motivations, one would have to peer deeply into the heart—a task the biographer may take on in a lengthy, often tentative, tome. Fortunately, however, to study the impact of ideology on policy, it matters less *why* politicians use a particular ideology and more *which* ideology they actually use.

The causal relationship between ideology and policy relies on some intermediary variable, since ideology itself cannot act. This study relies on public discourse as an intermediary factor. Political discourse is connected speech or writing that takes place within a political context, that is, in a context of ideological and power relations. The term discourse is appropriate here, rather than the simpler term "language." Discourse, with its Latin connotations of argument and conversation, denotes the use of language in an intersubjective and interactive context. In studying political discourse, the analyst looks at how communications relate to one another in substance and lexicon. The advantages of studying discourse rather than motivations are its ready availability and observability. Political discourse is everywhere and in concrete form: newspaper editorials, talk shows, stenographic records of parliamentary debates, speeches, and so on.

Ideology gives structure to discourse.[16] To use Ann Swidler's terms, ideology is a particular culture's "tool-kit" for discussing politics, while discourse refers to strategies of action, that is, how politicians actually use the "tool-kit" in political discussions.[17] Ideology provides the categories of thinking, limits the range of discussion, defines the range of problems, and fixes the roles of many political actors.

In order to appeal to others effectively, a political actor must be wise in the ways of the discourse. He must be able to draw on the discursive elements made available within his particular ideological context. Ideology affects political discourse and the course of political negotiations in two ways. First, as a set of linguistic tools, a particular ideology facilitates the identification and elaboration of certain political issues while rendering others less amenable to discussion.[18] For example, the American politician, articulate in discussing individual rights, might stand mute when called upon to define the citizen's responsibilities to his community. While in the first instance, he can draw upon the hallowed texts of American history and a long legal tradition of protecting individual rights, his political vocabulary is not nearly as rich in concepts for elaborating public responsibilities and duties.[19] This is not to say that he is disinterested in public duties; he might wish that he had the tools to speak convincingly about them. The availability of a particular ideology, not his preferences, constrains his discourse.[20]

Second, the available ideology defines what constitutes "good reasons" for supporting a particular policy.[21] The political actor defines his support or opposition to a policy within the terms available in the ideology. Unless a particularly individualistic cultural milieu so permits, political actors are unlikely to say they support a policy merely because it aids them in the maximization of power. Instead they will concoct more complex reasons that "sound good" using the ideological elements available. Since politicians use discourse to inform and persuade others, they must consider how their arguments will be received by others. Seyla Benhabib writes:

> When presenting their point of view and position to others, individuals must support them by articulating good reasons in a public context to their co-deliberators. This process of articulating good reasons in public forces the individual to think of what would count as a good reason for all others involved.[22]

These discursive tactics can have important effects. They can ease the formation of alliances, even an unlikely one between a true believer and an individual who uses ideology tactically. The prevalent ideology may require the political actor to modify his strategy subtly. He might not want to oppose a particular political goal if that goal is highly acclaimed within the prevalent ideology.

In analyzing the politics of transitional justice in post-communist Europe, I begin with a null hypothesis: that transitional justice is an aspect of the power struggle between old and new political elites. The power interests of the two groups determine the trajectory of policy-making. The alternative hypothesis explored below suggests that ideology has shaped policies of transitional justice. Liberal democratic ideology has influenced, though not determined, the approach to transitional justice in the new democracies of post-communist Europe. Its impact has varied during the different stages of the democratic transitions.[23]

Before the Transition

In the period of one-party rule that preceded democratization, the ideology of liberal democracy was a tool of critique, a call for the broad transformation of social life. In communist-controlled Europe, many highly educated people had little possibility of participating meaningfully in government and society. These marginal elites developed diverse ideological critiques of state socialist rule.[24] Some attacked the governments on nationalist grounds, saying that they paid insufficient attention to a particular ethnic group's legitimate demands. More common, though, were two other types of critique, both of which called the governments to task for failing to fulfill their promises. Some marginal elites criticized the communist governments for being insufficiently "socialist"; they pointed to the widespread poverty and the corruption of political life. Other marginal elites chose to criticize the governments for failing to implement constitutional provisions and international agreements that promised the respect of basic human rights and full participation in political life. The decision to criticize the government using its own norms was certainly a wise strategic choice, since the government could not easily repudiate the opposition's arguments without falling into self-contradiction. Nevertheless, one can still ask why the strongest opposition voices tended to use the norms of human rights and democratic participation in their criticism, rather than the socialist goals. State socialist regimes in Central and Eastern Europe were vulnerable on both counts.

Human rights and democracy were excellent ideological barbs for four reasons. First, the ideology of liberal democracy—which justifies both human rights and democratic participation—is well elaborated, while reform socialism remained a novelty. Liberal democracy has a long history, developed vocabulary, and defined institutional parameters. Using the ideology of liberal democracy, rather than that of reform socialism, was a device for intellectual economizing. Although the opposition still had to ponder how these ideas and institutions should be adapted to their own context, they did not have to engage in the more arduous task of imagining entirely new institutions and ideas. Liberal democracy's tried-and-true status was very attractive to societies tired of social experimentation.[25] Second, liberal democracy is perceived as successful. The rapid economic development, as well as the political freedoms, in Western Europe after the Second World War convinced many people east of the Oder that liberal democracy had much to recommend itself. Third, few cultural barriers stood in the way of the opposition's embrace of liberal democracy. Many opposition members, particularly in Central Europe, view themselves as members of European culture. Finally, the use of a liberal democratic ideology attracted the attention and support of Western democracies. The international attention brought greater pressure to bear on the state socialist regimes and made a crackdown on the opposition's dissent more costly.

If one analyzes the correlation of political forces during democratization, one might expect that stronger, better-organized dissident movements would be more adamant and successful in pushing for policies of truth and justice. Other things being equal, these groups are in a better position to demand concessions from the outgoing communist leaderships.[26] But in post-communist Europe, the opposite correlation is closer to the truth. Poland's regime critics, the best organized and most broadly based in the region, eschewed policies of truth and justice. Weaker opposition movements, some of which emerged only in the waning days of communist rule, demanded more retributive policies than strong ones. The East German and Bulgarian oppositions, long stifled by the ossified, harsh leadership of Stalin's men, demanded lustration and the preservation of secret police files. In Romania, where opposition was absent, blood spilled. This counterintuitive correlation can be explained by pointing out that the stronger opposition movements were likely to embrace the principles of liberal democracy, and they thereby inherited that ideology's horror of violence and support for only limited retribution. Political actors unconstrained by the liberal democratic ideology, especially the embittered communist fellow travelers, were likely to prefer harsher measures.

While the ideology of liberal democracy constituted a radical critique of real existing socialism, liberal democracy does not contain many of the usual characteristics of a radical ideology. It envisions a public space in which words, not weapons, are the means of resolving disputes.[27] It refuses to wield the mighty power of the modern state to curtail the basic liberties of even the most despised individuals, at least without due process. The characteristics of the ideology the opposition embraced helps us to comprehend its forbearance at the moment of transition.

Transition

Ideology plays a diminished role in the heady, crisis-filled days and months that accompany a democratic transition. During a crisis, material interests—one might call it a survival instinct—dominate the calculations of political actors. Theorists of revolution have pointed to the overwhelming challenges faced by the revolutionary leadership as it seizes control of the instruments of government. Organizational conundrums dominate the agenda, so the new cadres find little opportunity to reflect on the theoretical concerns that animated revolutionary discussions in the earlier stage of opposition. The imperative is to organize the exercise of state power or else the new regime may crumble.

Democratic transitions in Eastern Europe experienced a period of frenetic activity. As deals were negotiated or a graceful exit arranged, power considerations were paramount. The stronger the communist party was in the negotiation process, the more guarantees it could extract from the opposition. Where the communist party disintegrated like an ancient manuscript, the opposition was in a fine position to hasten its demise by undertaking various retributive policies.

Though ideological concerns were not central during this phase of the transition, the ideology of liberal democracy played a role in two ways: by shaping the rhetoric of regime change and the identity of political actors. First, liberal democratic ideology organized the political imagination during the rapid transition. Political scientists have stressed the great uncertainty and open-ended quality of the political transitions in Central and Eastern Europe.[28] Events in the region could conceivably have developed along many different trajectories. Indeed given the diverse power constellations in the various countries, we might have expected very different outcomes across the region. While this might seem like the ultimate experience of political freedom, human beings are not comfortable with total uncertainty and uncharted futures. They seek some device by which to exclude certain outcomes and organize their perception of social reality. Furthermore, they seek a common language with which to convey their interests to other political actors and to convince them of these interests' validity and legitimacy.

The ideas of liberal democracy—though contested in a new context—contributed to an orderly negotiating process, rather than a violent revolutionary melee. Few actors disputed that the end-result of the transition would be a more liberal and democratic regime, though they disagreed mightily on just how the regime should be organized.[29] Still, the fixing of certain parameters in the debates surely contributed to a more peaceable transition. In countries where competing political forces use entirely different ideological languages, political discussion is more difficult, and compromise is impossible without discussion. For example, in Iran the vast cultural and ideological gap between the Shah's and the Ayatollah's supporters made communication between the two groups impossible. Without the option of compromise, political events grew more radical, culminating in the violence of the Islamic revolution.[30]

Liberal democratic ideology also shaped the identity of crucial political actors. Theorists of democratic transitions have shown that the presence of a moderate opposition which is willing to negotiate with "soft-liners" within the government makes a negotiated transition more likely. The very concept of a "moderate opposition" is a new one. Fervent revolutionaries could not conceive of such a social grouping. In a revolution, the opposition usually holds a transformative ideology, that is, one that calls for ethnic solidarity or a radical redistribution of wealth.[31] The literature on democratization makes mention of this sort of radical opposition, but consigns it to the periphery of the political transformation. The radical opposition may play a pivotal role in bringing down the authoritarian regime, but they are unlikely to commit themselves to the democratic project. This is where the moderate opposition is different. Though it is clear that a moderate opposition is a real boon to democratic transitions, it is not readily apparent how it can deflect the piercing criticism of opportunism. How can such a grouping establish a rightful place in the political spectrum, maintaining the trust and allegiance of the population? Liberal democratic ideology justifies the position of the moderate opposition. Its language exalts the importance of negotiation, deliberation, and individual rights, and it is not hostile to the pragmatic necessity of compromise.

The moderate opposition inspired by liberal democratic ideology is the key to a peaceful, negotiated transition. A moderate opposition is open to talks with the government's soft-liners. Soft-liners, believing the opposition's commitment to liberal democracy, have little to fear from the negotiating process. The ideology forbids the use of force without the sanction of law, and it precludes most forms of retribution. Liberal democracy's limitations on transitional justice make the new political project less dangerous to soft-line elements in the government; therefore, they are more willing to participate in negotiations leading to democratic reform. They know the moderate opposition will not summarily throw them (or even their hard-line comrades) in jail, let alone lower the guillotine's blade. Because liberal democracy limits retribution, soft-liners are likely to find the ideology a congenial way of expressing their interests. They may also pledge allegiance to the limitations inherent in the moderate opposition's ideology. In doing so, they make themselves appear less threatening to the opposition. They acquire the opposition's trust, and increase the likelihood of an outcome more favorable to them. Soft-liners can use the language of democracy to ensure their future right to participate in government, while invoking liberalism's limitations on state powers to safeguard themselves against future retribution.

Post-Transition

The inauguration of democracy is marked by the holding of free, fair elections. What happens next seems as natural as a sunrise, but in reality requires explanation. The legislature convenes, and parties organize themselves around the poles of regime and opposition. Politicians accept the outcome of the polling of the people's will, settle down to the business of government, and attempt to better their position in anticipation of the next elections. In an established democracy, this is the ordinary course of events, but in former communist Europe it is truly extraordinary. Other outcomes seemed equally likely to occur: a coup by the losers, the losers' unwillingness to participate in the mechanisms of democratic governance, or a crackdown by the winners on the losers. Given the legacy of mutual antagonisms and often brutal repression, the low temperature of mundane democratic politics is startling. One might attribute political actors' decision to function within the parameters of the democratic system to a set of long-term calculations. A member of the opposition reasons that by following the rules he stands a good chance of prevailing in the next elections. Short-term losers can become long-term winners. Of course, the validity of this calculation depends on the assumption that the next elections will be free, fair, and regularly scheduled. It is not clear why the losers should have such trust in the winners' future adherence to the rules of democracy.[32]

After the tumult of transition ebbs, political events can develop in various ways. Students of revolution point to the ideological radicalization characteristic of a young revolutionary regime. In France, the revolutionaries splintered and pushed one another into ever more extreme positions. The Bolsheviks paused after consolidating their control of Soviet Russia, but then plunged into the extreme ideological fervor of the cultural revolution (1928–31). The very word ideology gets its pejorative connotations from these historic junctures. Ideology is associated with the inflexible, totalitarian ambitions of political radicals. Ideology ends in one-man rule, as Napoleon or Stalin appears on the political scene to hand down an orthodox interpretation of the nation's destiny.

Against this background, the placid character of early democratic politics is unusual. This might lead one to believe that the scope of change is much less radical or that cruel ideology lies in abeyance. Democratic transitions in the former Soviet bloc have led to an extensive debate about whether or not the changes there are revolutionary. On the one hand, the scope of political, legal, social, and economic change is of such a magnitude that the word "reform" seems inadequate. On the other hand, these transitions lack the violence and radical spirit of political events we are accustomed to deeming "revolutionary." The difference between Marxist and liberal democratic revolutions lies not in the degree of change or the latter's lack of ideological precepts. A liberal democratic revolution is just as dramatic and ideological as the others. After the transfer of power, the new leaders of young democracies, like other revolutionary actors, may undertake to elaborate and implement the principles that inspired the revolution. They usher in a series of profound reforms that ultimately reconfigure the social, economic, and political order.

The ideology that inspires these changes is unlike other revolutionary ideologies in that it sets limits on the means available for achieving the desired ends. In particular, the ideology of liberal democracy limits the use of state power: by protecting individual freedoms; dividing authority among various branches of government; and mandating that each use of force be provided for by law. In Poland, the opposition called the liberal democratic revolution a "self-limiting" revolution. Examining the failures of the French Revolution and the Marxist revolutions closer to home, it embraced an ideology that encouraged the development of an organized, autonomous civil society and sought to curb the use of state power.[33] A self-limiting revolution would appear to be of lesser scope, and it also lacks the romantic appeal of powerful upheavals and utopian planning. Yet in judging democratic "revolutions" by their fruits, we must conclude that they usher in at least as much change as their more eschatological Marxist equivalents.

Much ideological ferment follows revolutionary change. In post-communist Europe, communists who found themselves in the matrix of democratic institutions quickly appropriated at least the language of liberal democracy. When called upon to give an accounting of his political conversion, a formerly committed communist might claim that he had become an equally committed democrat without really repudiating his previous activities. He could say that he had not changed his mind about the ends of political community—equality, liberty, and fraternity—but only about the best means for attaining them. Or he might argue that in his youth he was overly idealistic (which seems to be a very excusable fault) or misled by those in authority. Or he can quite plausibly plead that he never believed in communism, but merely tried to eke out a comfortable living for his family within the system's constraints. The period following rapid political, social, and economic changes is likely to be one of fecund ideological development, as people work out their personal stories and imagine concepts to explain the new realities.[34]

Liberal democratic ideology deeply influences the debates over transitional justice in a new democracy and contributes to a recognizable pattern of policy outcomes. In countries where liberal democratic ideology is taking root, political discourse around issues of transitional justice utilizes themes that stem from the matrix of values advocated by liberal democratic ideology. Over time, the policies in these countries have come to resemble one another more and more. A liberal democratic approach to transitional justice means that violence is anathema. Retributive policies, such as those facilitating trials and lustration, are difficult, limited by the rule of law. Restitution and truth-telling are recommended as alternative means for a new democracy to take political responsibility for the crimes of the past.

East Germany and Poland experienced very different types of transition, leading us to expect divergent outcomes regarding transitional justice. In East Germany, democratization occurred through a full-scale rupture of the communist government. The short interregnum and negotiations did not stanch the flow of power away from the communist regime. Meanwhile, the Polish transition falls into the category of a negotiated transition; it involved lengthy negotiations between the regime and opposition. These countries exhibited the expected variation in their approaches to transitional justice during the years 1989–90: East Germany's approach was more retributive, while Poland toyed with the idea of forgetting its past. However, the gap later narrowed considerably, with both countries adopting a similar array of policies of truth and justice. The ideology of liberal democracy helped to keep the issue of transitional justice on the political agenda and to shape policy outcomes.

In Germany and Poland, politicians have slowly cobbled together policies of truth and justice, and the policies, as well as the debates surrounding them, strongly resemble each other. In other countries, transitional justice has slipped off the political agenda—no rich debates occurred and no policies were adopted. This pattern is prevalent in the republics of the former Soviet Union. The chapter on Russia examines this in depth. In Russia, some of the earliest opposition to communist-party rule came from people who demanded de-Stalinization and dared to uncover the truth about the abuses of Soviet rule. Democracy was installed in Russia by a rapid replacement of the communists after the failed 1991 coup attempt. This rupture would lead analysts to expect a strong thrust toward retribution. Indeed in late 1991, President Yeltsin outlawed the communist party, seized its assets, organized a trial of the failed putschists, and signed a law opening the KGB and party archives. Later on, though, most of these policies were reversed. Despite the significant early mobilization around the issue of past injustices, transitional justice quickly disappeared from the Russian political agenda. This trajectory of events has an ideological component. In Russia liberal democratic ideology has not shaped debates regarding transitional justice.

Pointing to the various policies of transitional justice adopted in post-communist Europe is a straightforward research task. I have identified a set of policies—trials, lustration, rehabilitation, compensation, and truth-telling—as the dependent variable. These outcomes can be (nearly) reduced to "brute data," that is, "data whose validity cannot be questioned by offering another interpretation or reading."[35]

Assessing the development and use of liberal democratic discourse in these countries is more complex and contentious.[36] The approach here is hermeneutic, seeking to find the "underlying coherence" in the text of political debates surrounding transitional justice and laying bare their "confusingly interrelated forms of meaning."[37] A reading of parliamentary debates and presidential speeches reveals recurring themes and keywords. A hermeneutic approach does not apply logical empiricist standards of verification. Admittedly, this is somewhat lamentable since logical empiricism has an enviable power to convince. Instead the approach invites other, more subjective, standards of verification. The reader is invited to assess whether this interpretation of the political debates makes sense of the original texts. Does it explain the meaning of texts that previously were puzzling or contradictory? Does it make us aware of underlying patterns, which, like familiar faces, were always there but never really seen?

This study covers a limited scope of political discourse in the former communist countries, focusing only on debates regarding transitional justice. It does not permit conclusions about whether a liberal democratic discourse affects a broad range of other policies. Furthermore, because it looks only at the political speech of elected officials, the study cannot assess the extent to which a liberal democratic discourse has deep roots in civil society.

Despite these cautionary notes about the limited scope of its conclusions, this study hints at a new approach for studying the consolidation of democracy. The standard definition says that a democracy is "consolidated" when all the major political actors accept the democratic rules of the game.[38] What constitutes evidence of this "acceptance"? Usually we look to see whether parties continue to play by the rules, even when they lose an election. This is why successful (peaceful) alterations of parties in power are seen as key to the consolidation of democracy. Perhaps a further piece of evidence is of importance. The broad use of a liberal democratic discourse is another measure of politicians' acceptance of these rules. Of course, their discourse may pay no more than "lip service" to liberal democratic ideology, but perhaps lip service is underappreciated in our cynical age. Communism, we might recall, survived hypocritical communists for a very long time.

Chapter 2
Liberal Democratic Ideology and Transitional Justice

From South Africa to Eastern Europe, in diverse contexts of democratization, societies have sought answers to the dilemmas of justice in regime transitions, analyzing their options in light of liberal democratic norms. Thus, it is worth attempting a systematic answer to the question: Is there a liberal democratic model for coming to terms with past injustices? This chapter constructs an "ideal-type" of a liberal democratic approach to transitional justice. Laying bare the central elements of this model will help us to achieve two goals. First, it will enable us to make sense of the current debates and policy decisions, exposing the assumptions that shape the debates and highlighting the common themes. Second, better theoretical explication will help us to make a principled, reasoned prescription for how countries might come to terms with the past in a way that best promotes a liberal democratic future.

The ideology of liberal democracy provides five key tools for discussing and framing the issues of transitional justice. First, the *social contract metaphor* structures the way that politicians think about the past and the responsibility of a new regime for a past regime's unjust acts. It helps them to conceive of liberal democracy as essentially a forward-looking project. Second, the *rule of law* forbids the exercise of force without legal authority. Since it places value on the limitation of state power, liberal democracy imposes many constraints on the state's right to inflict punishment on its citizens. The rule of law prohibits retroactivity, inequality before the law, and violations of due process. These protections extend even to those who committed crimes under the old regime. Third, the ideology of democracy ascribes great value to *inclusive participation*. Everyone must have the right to participate in political society; former oppressors cannot simply be banished from political life. Fourth, *openness* is a significant value. Liberal democrats believe that freedoms of speech, press, and association must be guaranteed to facilitate an open political debate, which is ultimately the key to fruitful decision-making. Finally, many people throughout the world express their desire to live under a liberal democratic regime because it holds out the promise of *justice*. They expect that such a regime will interfere minimally with their freedoms, give them an equal voice in government, and treat them fairly.

The following sections examine each of these resources, analyzing their implications for the issue of transitional justice. Drawing together these resources, we can consider liberal democracy's prescription for transitional justice.

The Social Contract

The social contract is an agreement among individuals to abandon the state of nature, enter into society, and establish rules for governing themselves.[1] It is a recipe for forming a new political society, one that new democracies have eagerly followed. It is odd, really, that the social contract has been such an enduring metaphor for a new political beginning. No one ever witnessed a real social contract, the first social stirrings of primitive humans. The whole idea represents one of liberalism's "invented traditions," rather an anachronism in an age that has celebrated scientific inquiry.

Despite being an artificial construct, social contract theory makes three important contributions to liberal democratic theory. Foremost is the rule of law. After joining together, civil society's first task is to appoint a legislature that will promulgate the laws for the new political community. Law offers protection of life, health, liberty, and property against the unreasonable, strong marauders who corrupted the state of nature. Law also places limits on the caprice of despotic government. "The Legislative, or Supream Authority, cannot assume to itself a power to Rule by extemporary Arbitrary Decrees, but is bound to dispense Justice, and decide the Rights of the Subject by promulgated standing Laws, and known Authoris'd Judges."[2] Rule of law offers consistency, predictability, and impartiality of judgment.[3] The rule of law perfects natural rights by upholding all the benefits people experienced in the state of nature, but adding the security that was so elusive in that state. Rule of law provides an escape from uncertainty, the great scourge of the state of nature.

A second major contribution of social contract theory regards the legitimate source of law. In the social contract model, law rests on the consent of the governed. People's initial consent to membership in the law-based community is the origin of their obligation to abide by the laws. Liberal theorists do not justify democracy as an end in itself.[4] Indeed generations of liberal theorists (including Spinoza and J.S. Mill) were quite fearful of what the plebeian masses would demand in a democracy. However, in beginning to see popular consent as a means to preserving liberty, they forged a link between liberty and democracy, which in tandem have influenced modern ideas of government.

A third contribution of social contract theory is its surprising model for radical, yet peaceful, political change. One can easily imagine a violent beginning for society: Brutal factions or imperious individuals force everyone else to submit to their will. This seems more natural than the peaceful assembly of all society that is envisioned by the social contract theorists.

Social contract theory contains an implicit blueprint for dealing with past injustices in the context of political change. Of course we have no examples of how nascent societies really dealt with the legacy of crimes committed in the primitive state of nature. Nevertheless, the paradigm of the social contract influences the ways in which democratizing countries contemplate the legacy of past injustices.

Social contract theory divides historical time into three distinct eras, thus organizing our thoughts about which events separate the past from the present and the future. The social contract defines exactly what is meant by the "past": The past is the time before the contract.

The period of time preceding the social contract is a pre-social state of nature, described so hauntingly by Hobbes as a state in which no authority exerts power over individuals and all people are in a perpetual state of war with one another. They live in "continuall feare, and danger of violent death; And the life of man, solitary, poore, nasty, brutish, and short."[5] Since each person is vulnerable to deadly attack, injustice is rampant and fear omnipresent. No one is entirely secure, so all share equally in the desperate plight of the state of nature.

Under these conditions, it makes no sense to ask who is responsible for unjust crimes committed in the state of nature. Any assessment of responsibility would depend on our ability to discern who acted, the intentions of the individual who acted, and the nature of that action in relationship to the moral environment. Since violence was unavoidable and expected, it was not morally relevant. It would be inappropriate to bring the standards of society to bear on the state of nature. The antidote to these poisoned relations is the social contract, which draws a thick line between the chaos of the past and the order of the future.

The second phase entails the devising of the social contract, a process later linked to constitution-writing. The social contract erases the previous state of nature and marks a new stage of historical development. People agree to live in society with one another and abide by a common set of rules. The procedures involved in drawing up the social contract inveigh against holding individuals responsible for unjust acts committed during the state of nature. The procedure for forming the social contract involves the universal, uncoerced participation of a certain population. People freely join together in order to offer themselves protection.

People may not be excluded from the social contract on the basis of their past offenses. Even those who were thieves, murderers, and rapists in the state of nature may participate in the social contract. By acceding to the social contract, individuals effect their own absolution: The promise of future obedience is sufficient atonement for all past crimes. The injustices of the past can have no practical or moral relevance under the social contract. The binding of one to all constitutes a new beginning both for the individuals involved and for the newly created political community. The tension here is immense. Though a desire for justice motivated people to establish the social contract, the only justice available is forward-looking justice.

The social contract establishes the rule of law, and this inauguration is marked in time by the drafting of a contract, which from that point on determines the nature of legal claims. The rule of law protects individuals in two ways. First, it promises equal treatment of all before the law. Everyone is treated equally regardless of his identity; thus, an individual's history as a strongman or a weakling in the state of nature is surely irrelevant under the social contract. "The notion of a hypothetical social contract . . . forces one to start afresh, stripped of historical grievances and prejudices, to reason from a moral point of view, without appeal to prior status as (victimizing) power or (powerless) victim."[6] In a twirl of circular logic, all are *assumed* to be equal in order to be *made* equal.

Second, the rule of law promises predictability. Individuals must be able to know the consequences of their actions when they are contemplating that action. They must know, for instance, that if they steal, they may be punished by imprisonment of a fixed period. Knowledge of the consequences will then figure into their calculations about whether to commit a certain act. However, if individuals commit a morally objectionable act that is not explicitly proscribed by any standing law, they may not face sanctions. Since people who committed unjust acts in the state of nature could not have known that their actions would lead to punishment, they may not be punished for those acts. This fundamental principle of law, known by the Latin phrase *nulla crimem, nulla poena sine lege*, protects individuals against retroactive prosecution.

The third phase of historical development is post-contractual. After the formation of the social contract, society can begin a period of orderly existence under the rule of law. A society should govern itself through the promulgation of laws. Society determines how leaders shall be chosen and limits the extent of their authority, thus reconfiguring social relations. After choosing to participate in the social contract, people are obliged to obey the rules of the governing authorities. Past identities are wiped away, and the people under the contract adopt a new identity as a people under law. The forward-looking social contract offers its people many benefits: greater liberty, security, predictability, and prospects for individual development. It does so in part by erasing the past.

In particular since the American Revolution, the social contract metaphor has been used to describe constitutional moments in which a society establishes a new framework for the legal exercise of power. Constitutionalism, though sharing much with social contract theory, brings something new to the old concept. The constitution is a much stronger force in organizing society. It is a written document, to which legal and justiciable appeals can be made. The constitution establishes the possibility for the exercise of political power, but it simultaneously limits power—both by dividing the exercise of political power into three separate branches of government and by carving out an inviolable space of liberties for the individual.

We have now entered an age of peaceful transitions to liberal democracy—an era for which the American constitutional moment, rather than the more tumultuous and bloody French Revolution, offers the relevant paradigm. However, many of these transitions are taking place in countries with conditions more like history-worn France than boundlessly new America.[7] In recently democratizing countries, the past is a cauldron overflowing with injustices and inequities, which the *sans-culottes* might find a familiar stew. This context of past injustice and peaceful transitions begets the dilemma of transitional justice. No longer can the dialectical flow of history be relied upon to sweep away the nasty vestiges of the past. Or, as one observer notes, "The absence of a revolution interferes with a full thematization of the crimes of the past, and the assessment of full responsibility for them."[8] Instead, inspired by liberal ideology, the men and women involved in politics today must make decisions about how to deal with the past. They must craft a response to it.

The social contract's main contribution to liberal democracy is a model for peaceful political change. The social contract also structures the perception of political time. The state of nature is marked off with a thick line, and under the new contract, society will not concern itself with what came earlier. Again, social contract theory is essentially forward-looking.

This leniency has a key advantage: It promotes universal participation. If the state of nature's strongmen had to fear retribution once the contract was in place, then they would have an incentive to remain outside the contract and assail it with their considerable force. This certainly would not bode well for the emerging society. Instead, the strongmen are invited into full participation with the protection of law. As a result, the new society is less vulnerable to attack. Leniency toward the strongmen of yore makes the social contract more feasible, though arguably less just.

The social contract introduces the values of the rule of law and inclusivity, which merit separate discussion.

The Rule of Law

The rule of law is a crucial aspect of the liberal heritage. Anarchy and arbitrariness inspired liberal theorists to imagine a superior social order. Society's foremost task was the control of violence. This could be accomplished in several ways, of course. Hobbes ordered society under a leviathan ruler who had the right to use force according to his wishes. The Hobbesian solution to the horrors of anarchy creates yet another problem for liberal theorists—arbitrary rule. Though people had escaped the violence of the state of nature, they might sorrowfully find themselves victims of the arbitrary violence of a despotic ruler. For centuries, legal scholars weighed what might be done about the ruler's potential for violence. In the Middle Ages, they debated whether the king was bound to follow the laws he proclaimed.[9] While the moral superiority of rule according to law was consistently proclaimed, the medieval (and later the absolutist) conception of sovereignty did not permit limitations on the king's ability to set rules and exceptions. The courts had no jurisdiction over the sovereign monarch. By the seventeenth century, however, English scholars and practitioners were declaring the primacy of law. The monarch, parliament, and ordinary citizen alike were obliged to regulate their behavior according to the standards set forth in law. The rule of law implies that government will proceed by the crafting and proclamation of legal instruments.

The rule of law also signifies the equality of all people before the law. The courts must judge the actions of all people equally, regardless of their political or social position, under the existing laws. No one may be punished for actions that were legal at the time they were committed. Punishment can be meted out only after an individual's actions are examined by judicial authorities in light of the existing laws. Summary punishment is thereby excluded.

The rule of law imposes many limits on how a new democracy may come to terms with its past. It prohibits extralegal violence and bans the retroactive application of law. Furthermore, it insists that each person be judged individually, treated equally, and extended the full protection of due process. The rule of law thus curtails the use of trials to come to terms with the past.

History provides many examples of bloody retribution, especially after war and oppression: the French and Bolshevik Revolutions; the extrajudicial killings of suspected collaborators after the Second World War in France and Italy; the assassination of political leaders in Romania. Liberal democracy cannot condone these extralegal punishments, regardless of the victims' blameworthiness. The violent acts of well-intentioned avengers challenge the supremacy of law and the legally constituted powers, which is hardly conducive to the reestablishment of legitimate authority. Extralegal violence threatens a devolution into anarchy—always anathema to liberal democrats.

Any government, liberal or authoritarian, will quickly attempt to rein in private attempts to seek vengeance, since private justice usurps the state's sole prerogative of using force. However, a young democracy must condemn extralegal punishment more severely that its authoritarian counterpart. The legal procedures contravened are more than just procedural niceties; they are bedrock principles of liberal democracy.

In some cases, a break in legality may permit a short legal vacuum, where private justice can be sought without fear of the law's sting. Politicians negotiating a transition to democratic rule try to avoid legal gaps for precisely this reason. Legal continuity decreases the likelihood of extralegal violence with its attendant risks of anarchy, upheaval, and a return to the rule of the strongman. The rule of law in a liberal democracy, no matter how young, serves as a deterrent force, underlining the impermissibility of vendetta.

Because extralegal punishment of past offenders is proscribed, one might believe that trials of these individuals would take on great importance. Indeed some have argued that a political trial of the old regime will enhance the newcomers' legitimacy, satisfy the popular retributive passions, and remove the offenders permanently from public life.[10] Yet in liberal democracies, the rule of law limits the use of trials as a political tool.

An individual tried for abuses committed under the old regime must be judged according to the laws that were in effect at the time the crime was committed. Many liberal democratic constitutions expressly ban retroactive punishment, which protects citizens against arbitrary rule. A liberal democratic government cannot make laws that punish an individual for actions, which were not proclaimed and known to be illegal at the time they were committed. If it could retroactively criminalize an action, citizens could never state with certainty that they had not made themselves culpable; they would always fear the police officer's cuff.

The ban on retroactivity means that in prosecuting members of the old regime for their abuses, the courts of the new liberal democratic regime must apply the laws of the old regime. At the same time, they must not compromise the principles of liberal democracy—a daunting and confusing task.[11] All this is much easier if the old regime's legal system proscribed the actions that the new regime would like to punish. Sometimes this is the case. Many authoritarian regimes, including those of the Soviet type, had well-developed legal systems that formally protected citizens' basic rights.

Yet, the new democracy's courts must not only find the appropriate law; they must interpret and apply it. They have three options for interpreting the old law. First, they might follow the old law strictly, in accordance with the statutes, practices, and norms of the old regime. However, this might lead the new democracy's courts to act in an illiberal fashion. How could the new regime deny the defendant the right to a vigorous defense simply because that was the practice of the old regime? Furthermore, under the legal practices of the old regime, the defendant may be found not guilty of any crimes.[12] Second, the new regime might choose to prosecute representatives of the old regime using the letter of the old law, but ignoring past practices that are incompatible with the rule of law. Selectively recreating the old law is also problematic: Which practices should be maintained and which discarded? Do the old laws make any sense without the context of past practices? As a third alternative, the courts may try to infuse the old law's carcass with a new spirit. For example, they may try to interpret the old regime's law in light of the regime's decision to sign international human rights agreements. This new interpretation of the old law might be an unrecognizable hybrid—a product only of the judicial imagination. Furthermore, if the reinterpretation of past laws harms the defendant's position, this may be interpreted as a retroactive application of law.[13]

All these solutions beg legal questions. Though authoritarian constitutions guarantee certain rights, they usually contain clauses that limit those rights or set up competing values. For example, the Soviet-type constitutions gave the communist party a "leading role" in society. Should the judiciary of the new democracy give consideration to all the provisions of the old regime's legal order, or just the ones it finds suitable? Is it acceptable to ignore past judicial practices? Strictly applying the old laws certainly makes the trials of yesterday's offenders more difficult. However, a new *Rechtsstaat* values the dutiful application of law.

Other laws also complicate prosecutions. Most legal systems impose a statute of limitations, circumscribing the time period during which prosecutions may be initiated. Once the statute of limitations lapses, prosecutions are time-barred.[14] Also, the outgoing regime may have passed an amnesty law excluding certain people from prosecution. In both cases the alleged perpetrator of abuses enjoys a right to repose, which a law-based state cannot lightly sweep away.

A liberal democratic regime might choose to judge the old regime's criminals according to the letter of the criminal code, ignoring the contradictory clauses, statute of limitations, and amnesty laws, as well as the jurisprudence of the old courts. The defendants will then seize the mantle of liberal democracy and claim they are victims of retroactive justice. The conundrum is altogether vexing. In punishing members of the old regime for committing human rights abuses, the courts uphold the value liberal democracy places on the protection of the individual against the powers of the state. They demonstrate that henceforth all will be equal before the law. At the same time, they may uneasily suspect that they are violating hallowed principles of liberal democracy.

Some might argue that the dilemma is an edifying one for the judicial system and society, for it illustrates a typical conflict among the principles of liberal democracy. The judicial system (and society at large) are invited to debate which principle—nonretroactivity versus the punishment of known torturers—deserves primacy. The public should engage in reasoned deliberation to formulate an acceptable compromise. However, it is equally likely that such a debate will overburden the agenda of a society in transition and raise doubts about the strength of democratic institutions.

The ban on retroactivity is not the only limitation the rule of law places on the prosecution of the old regime's criminals. The rule of law also demands that the state prove individual culpability, treat everyone equally, and abide by the restrictions of due process.

Individual culpability means that past political associations cannot be taken into account in choosing to prosecute an individual or finding him guilty. All persons enjoy freedom of political association. Mere membership in a political association or possession of a certain job title is not punishable under liberal laws.[15] Individuals can be punished only for actions of which they were the author. That is, they cannot be punished collectively for acts committed by a group of which they were members.

Establishing a connection between a particular individual and a criminal act is often difficult in a modern era of bureaucratized government. Under the old regime, a few powerful leaders may have met secretly to plan a policy of terror or torture, which then trickled down through the state apparatus, often without written directives. The liberal courts may not have difficulty in ascertaining which foot soldier actually pulled the trigger: Records often show who was where at what time. However, showing who formulated the policy of terror and passed along instructions is a more formidable task.

Punishing only the low-level officials who directly participated in the crimes would be a skewed incidence of selective prosecution. While this is not illegal in a liberal democracy (as retroactivity is), it does conflict with the principle of equality before the law, which is at the center of discourse about the rule of law. This principle demands that the law treat people fairly, punishing only in proportion to the severity of the criminal act. The foot soldiers will certainly marshal this defense, and it might significantly mitigate their punishment. Even if the prosecutors find the political leaders and bureaucrats who ordered and administered the policy of terror, the courts must find a reasoned way to parcel out the burden of responsibility among them. Equality before the law therefore implies that the lowly executor of a brutal policy should not be punished more harshly than his supervisor.[16]

Of course, each of the defendants enjoys due process of the law in these trials. The liberal state carefully delineates the procedures necessary to guarantee an individual his freedom, and procedure is important. Liberal democracy's list of procedural guarantees is impressive, as evidenced by international human rights instruments such as the International Covenant on Civil and Political Rights. Most importantly, the accused is presumed innocent—a challenging and counterintuitive presumption in the case of political leaders who permitted and seemingly ordained heinous, inhumane policies. Even extraordinary criminals must be treated as ordinary men under the rule of law. They have the right to counsel, even at the public's expense. They cannot be compelled to testify against themselves or confess guilt. The state carries the burden of proving the defendant guilty. To the surprise of prosecutors, it may be very difficult to muster the necessary evidence. Though "everyone" may know that the former political leader ordered a policy of terror, documentary evidence of that fact may not be forthcoming. Perhaps the files went up in smoke as the democratic transition loomed. Or perhaps verbal orders were all that ever existed. Witnesses' testimony may be unreliable, contradictory, or concocted. Prosecutors may unexpectedly find themselves in a surreal world where they fail to prove what everyone knows to be real. This takes on the note of tragedy in those societies where a previous generation of political trials easily proved the guilt of those whom everyone knew to be innocent.

Criminal trials are certainly a preferable alternative to violent retribution in young democracies. However, the rule of law places constraints on the state's ability to conduct trials of the old regime's offenders: the ban on retroactivity, individual culpability, equality, and due process. These legal constraints (not to mention political and prudential constraints) complicate a new democracy's efforts to use trials as a political tool. Trials in a liberal democracy should not degenerate into political retaliation, as profound as the political consequences of dealing with past crimes might be.

A limited round of trials may serve valuable political and moral purposes. It may buttress a regime's legitimacy and satisfy the victims' call for retributive justice. It may cement commitment to the norms of human rights.[17] Timing is important.[18] Sometimes democratic leaders permit quick, legally messy trials. However, the longer these drag on, the greater the demand for a full extension of due process guarantees. A regime claiming to be a liberal democracy cannot long sustain a policy of trials that are legally flawed. Frequently, however, new democracies cannot ensure the swift and cathartic punishment they desire. The criminals escape their jurisdiction; the courts are slow; investigators lack evidence. They may then slide down the scale of options and choose a civil law remedy against the offenders.

The civil law remedy usually chosen is that of lustration, the purging of individuals from the public bureaucracy. If a new democracy cannot put the former torturers in prison because of the rule of law's constraints on criminal trials, it can at least dismiss them from the state's employment rolls. Lustration serves multiple purposes: the reorganization and revitalization of the state's administrative organs; the imposition of economic and social penalties on the old regime's functionaries; and the overall circulation of elites, which provides employment opportunities for the new regime's supporters.[19] It can serve the goals of both retributive and restorative justice. It punishes the old regime, though not with the loss of liberty. At the same time it creates opportunities for the opposition to rise to prominence in the new government.

Some argue that the rule of law imposes few constraints on the new democracy's abilities to carry out a thoroughgoing policy of lustration.[20] That is, the functionary does not enjoy the full protection of due process, the ban on retroactivity, and equality before the law. These observers believe that the legal hurdles in these civil cases are very low, and recommend lustration as the preferred means of coming to terms with past injustices. Legal minds are not however at one concerning the degree of protection a state functionary deserves during a regime transition, nor lustration's efficacy as a means of political restructuring in a country where suitable replacement elites may not be available.[21]

Granting that lustration should not be a lawless matter, policymakers must decide which laws should govern the civil servant's dismissal—the laws of the old regime, new civil service laws, or other transitional measures? Liberal democracies generally have civil service laws that protect the politically neutral status of the state's employment policies and shield the civil servant from politically motivated dismissal. In developing a policy of lustration, which of the civil servants' rights must be protected and which are dispensable given the extraordinary circumstances? Should an employee enjoy all the fruits of due process—presumption of innocence, the right to appeal, and access to information that might exculpate him? Must people of all political persuasions be treated equally? While the rule of law does not provide definitive answers to these questions when posed in the civil law context, the overall thrust of liberalism is the protection of individuals against the state's arbitrary incursions. Any derogations from the rule of law must be justified, in particular by demonstrating that other liberal democratic concerns outweigh the violations associated with lustration.[22] For example, advocates of lustration may point to liberal democracy's need for a neutral administrative apparatus or the deterrence value of lustration in preventing future human rights abuses. The deterrence argument applies most convincingly to those areas of the government apparatus directly involved in the use of force, especially the police or judiciary. So lustration is most likely to succeed in these areas.

The old bureaucrats are unlikely to leave quietly. In their rhetorical arsenal is the powerful liberal democratic language about the rule of law.

They can demand its full protections. The government could try to give each dismissed bureaucrat a fair trial, but the costs of this are enormous: Many judges, lawyers, and court officials would have to spend a great deal of time on thousands of cases. Each individual case of lustration would become just as difficult as the criminal trials described earlier. Retroactivity, selective punishment, due process, and the paucity of solid evidence can plague lustration. To be effective, the procedures for lustration must not evolve into trials conducted by the standards of a criminal court; however, any derogations from the full protection of individual rights must be fully justified in terms of liberal principles.

With trials and lustration proving so difficult, new democracies grasp for some uncontroversial strategy for coming to terms with the past. Rather than seeking retribution against those who committed crimes in the past, the state can offer a measure of restorative justice to the former victims. The state can rehabilitate the victims and offer them compensation for their suffering. At least these policies allow the state to provide some remedy for the old regime's wrongs. The rule of law does not constrain these efforts at restorative justice, at least in theory. However, in attempting to write and implement these laws, states may run up against the rule of law's limitations. Equal treatment under the law is the main challenge in devising a policy of restorative justice. The state must make every effort to treat people equally. Yet the complexity of defining which classes of victims are equally deserving may overwhelm the state's bureaucracy and the politicians' moral fortitude. In the former communist countries, one can argue that a large proportion of the population was victimized in one way or another. At the same time, many of these people also participated in the system's persecution of others. "The sheer scale of the injustices, their variety and multitudinous kinds of victims makes any effort at identifying the victims and quantifying their suffering impossible."[23] One can anticipate a flood of complaints that the state is not treating similar groups of victims equally. Deluged by the claims, a financially strapped new democracy may turn its attention away from the former victims.

Inclusivity

Since excluding particular individuals from the public bureaucracy on the basis of their past political involvement is problematic, some new democracies may decide to take the simpler step of banning certain political parties or associations. They may argue that only democrats—politicians committed to democratic political values—are welcome to participate in the new democracy. Anne Sa'adah refers to this as the "cultural strategy" of political reconciliation in which a society tries to "create a community of conviction" based on democratic norms as a precondition for building political democracy.[24] However, this step conflicts with the liberal democratic principle of inclusivity. As discussed earlier, the metaphor of the social contract stresses that all future political obligation depends on every individual's (and by extension every group's) agreement to participate in the social contract. In excluding certain individuals from political participation, society would relegate them to a state of nature, that is, outside of the purview of law and obligation. Ostracizing the old regime invites retaliation, which could disrupt a peaceful political transition. Inclusivity is a key to ensuring social peace and stability, preconditions for a liberal democractic order.

In a liberal democracy, individuals should be permitted to join the political association of their choice. All views are welcome in a democracy. As Arthur Stinchcombe notes, "Democracy means turning the interests and ideologies of the old regime into democratic parties that can be defeated (or can win without overwhelming) in democratic elections."[25] That is, the former rulers must be allowed to participate in the new democracy; they must have the freedom to form the political groups of their choice.

Of course, many democracies set limits on the freedom of political association. The German constitution bans national-socialist parties and justifies this breach of liberal inclusiveness and equality by arguing that a liberal democracy may limit some freedoms in order to protect the liberal order against destructive attacks.[26] This justification seems reasonable, especially in light of German political history. The Germans could accept the ban on national-socialism with relative ease after the loss of the war and under the Allied powers' tutelage. The remaining national-socialists were not in a position to defend themselves.

The communists in Eastern Europe can afford to be much bolder in mounting a defense of their right to participate in politics. In many cases, the communist parties themselves were important agents in the transition. They did not crack down on demonstrators, and they negotiated peacefully with the opposition. Arguably, such behavior indicates that the communist parties are not potential threats to democracy. The communists may marshal the principle of inclusivity in their favor. Those proposing a ban on the communist party must justify a derogation from this rule; the burden of proof is definitely on them.

Openness

Many countries have established parliamentary committees or independent groups to investigate the crimes of the past not with the purpose of organizing trials, but with the goal of establishing and acknowledging the facts about the past. These "truth commissions" investigate the evidence and put together an authoritative account of the past. While the ideology of liberal democracy does not value truth in any transcendental or metaphysical sense, it does uphold the importance of openness in human affairs. The freedoms of speech, press, and association are necessary for political decision-making since wise solutions emerge from the competition among competing viewpoints and interests. Openness in politics is analogous to market freedoms in that the best solutions proceed from healthy competition.

Knowledge about the events of history (and the recent past) is important insofar as it constitutes a factual basis for open deliberation about the protection of natural liberties and the responsibilities of the political community. Hannah Arendt recognized that shared agreement on the facts of a common history was a necessary condition for freedom. Totalitarian regimes, which strive to erase all freedoms, hold factual knowledge about social reality in "supreme contempt."[27] The totalitarian state forbids the public discussion of information about widespread injustices and thereby subverts any effort to carry out reasoned political deliberations about how to eliminate injustice. Factual truth can be reestablished only if people speak openly about it.[28] But this creates a Catch-22. Arendt believes that factual truth is a necessary precondition for freedom of opinion. At the same time, she believes that freedom of speech must precede the establishment of factual truth. Thus, it is unclear which must come first—freedom or truth. Though the causal relationships are uncertain, the correlation is clear: Factual truth, freedom of opinion, and the exercise of public reason all go together. Liberal democrats can cogently argue that allowing a free exchange of information about the past is relevant to their political project. In practice, this means that new democracies reveal the truth about their past in the hopes that they might learn from it and avoid repeating past errors. Truth-telling is thus a part of the optimistic Enlightenment era politics of human progress.

Countries in Eastern Europe have inherited the immense detritus of state socialism in the form of secret police files. In these files lies buried information that could convict criminals, exonerate the condemned, rehabilitate victims, and reshape the historical consciousness. The question is what to do with these files. A truth commission would obviously be interested in the files that would help to write history: political resolutions, internal documents of the leading institutions, and cases involving public figures. However, the victims and perpetrators have different interests.

The demand for openness seems relatively uncontroversial, but it must compete with other liberal principles to define the agenda for dealing with information about the past. Victims of the previous regime often prefer to define this as a question of their right to information. Many victims would like to have access to the information that the former police state gathered about them. They would like the right to read and dispose of the files collected through secret police surveillance. In modern bureaucratic states, and particularly in the former Soviet bloc, the state can intrude ruthlessly into citizens' personal lives and record these private details on paper, tape, computer disk, and photograph. The victims claim a right to read and use this information—to secure their rehabilitation, obtain compensation, procure incriminating evidence against perpetrators, or simply to better understand their lives. They may claim a right to destroy their own files. These goals do not always coincide with the aspirations of a truth commission, which pursues public openness. For example, a truth commission might oppose victims' desire to destroy their files.

Meanwhile the former perpetrators cling to other liberal principles, arguing that the files should be closed or even destroyed. They argue as follows: A liberal state may not intrude on individuals' private lives unless they are suspected of a crime and a court authorizes wiretaps and searches. Since the police-state did not follow these strictures, the information contained in police, state, and communist party archives is illicit. In the liberal state, illegally obtained information is not admissible in court, and it is not made available to the public at large. Perpetrators can muster the powerful rhetorical tools of procedural guarantees and the right to privacy in an effort to counteract the victims' demand for information. To further neutralize the argument in favor of a truth commission, the perpetrators might question the "truth-value" of the evidence under consideration, suggesting, for example, that the archives contain much false and exaggerated data.

There are basically three ways to deal with the problem of the files. The state can partially open the archives for use by a truth commission, throw wide the archive's doors so that victims may use the files, or seal (possibly even destroy) the archives. While liberal democratic ideology offers at least partial support for each option, the value of openness militates in favor of providing access to the files.

Justice and Political Responsibility

Our strong human desire to achieve justice has been described as a "drive to correct a perceived discrepancy between entitlements and benefits."[29] People's experience of communist rule made them acutely aware of the system's jarring discrepancies: between a wealthy, corrupt communist elite and the rest of the population; between the constitutional and international guarantees of human rights and the practices of repression; between the glowing reports of communism's economic progress and the empty shelves in stores. Under these circumstances, liberal democratic ideology is very attractive, for it is perceived as a superior means of correcting the discrepancies and achieving justice. This desire for justice inspired people in Central and Eastern Europe to take to the streets and call for the end to communist rule, and the hope for justice sustained their support of the new liberal democratic regimes.

Liberal democracy's reputation for excellence in the securing of justice rests on several of its institutional provisions. Liberal democracy protects individuals against arbitrary incursions of state power. The rule of law guarantees that all laws will be written and promulgated before they are enforced. All people are treated equally under law. Those accused of crimes enjoy the protections of due process. An independent judiciary will judge their guilt or innocence. All these liberal guarantees are the very image of justice in an authoritarian society, where the system of "justice" has turned into an instrument of grievance. Furthermore, democracy promises that citizens will be allowed to participate in making the rules that define justice and injustice. If citizens consider a particular act unacceptable, they may raise their voices in protest, elect new legislators, and change the laws.[30]

If the transition to democracy succeeds, the people's demand for justice in the future should be attainable. Members of the communist party will no longer have advantages in the legal system. Politicians will have to act within the framework of law. Those accused of crimes will enjoy numerous protections. Liberal democracy can assure this measure of justice. The question is whether this kind of justice satisfies popular demands. Can a liberal democracy—should it—provide redress for crimes committed under the preceding authoritarian regime? As discussed earlier, the ideology of liberal democracy places many constraints on the means available for seeking retributive justice for these crimes. The question is whether the ideology also contains positive recommendations for justice, factors that could balance against the legal constraints.

While liberal democratic ideology does not validate backward-looking justice as an end in itself, it does contain resources for arguing that a democratic regime ought to take political responsibility for the abuses committed in the past. The social contract metaphor offers a strong rationale for setting aside the past in the interests of building the future on an inclusive basis. However, the metaphor is only partially accurate in cases of new democracies. Their pasts were not the state of nature where men and women roamed in the wilderness carrying heavy clubs. For new democracies the ugly past is one where the state acted against the interests of its own people.

A general principle of democracy is that citizens bear responsibility for their state. They are the source of the government's legitimacy, and each must bear "his share (to be fixed on some equitable principle) of the labours and sacrifices incurred for defending the society or its members from injury or molestation."[31] Thus, if the state causes injury to an individual, citizens are responsible for making reparations to him. The question is whether citizens are responsible for acts taken by a government that did not rest on their consent. The authoritarian government committed the crimes; however, it did so by invoking the name of the state and pressing the levers of the state's institutions. The government used the state's bureaucracy, military, police, and judicial system to abuse citizens. After a transition, a new democratic regime takes control of the instruments of state.

If a constitutional moment marks an entirely new beginning, the democratic regime is not responsible for crimes committed in the past. However, in the course of a democratic transition, the state remains. This important continuity makes the metaphor of the social contract questionable. Democrats inherit a more or less intact state and derive certain benefits from it. They take over ready-made institutions for the police, military, economy, and social security, this institutional continuity facilitating the continued governance of the territory and security of persons. If the democratic regime derives benefits from its inheritance, then it should also bear the costs.

International law may provide a solution to the problem. Countries in transition may rely upon emerging international norms in trying to find justice for past human rights abuses. International law is so important because responsibilities under it remain fixed even when domestic laws are in flux; it is a focal point of legal stability. Though this area of law is still under development it may become a tool for assisting and maybe even requiring regimes to take political responsibility for the acts of their predecessors.

International law has developed a set of restrictions concerning governments' treatment of their own citizens.[32] The Convention on the Prevention and the Punishment of the Crime of Genocide and the Convention Against Torture explicitly require states to prosecute instances of genocide or torture. The provisions of the International Covenant on Civil and Political Rights (ICCPR) are less explicit regarding the duty of the state to prosecute any violations of the international agreement, but in requiring states to ensure and protect certain rights, the treaty creates an implicit obligation to punish violations of those rights. (An individual cannot truly claim possession of a right unless there is access to a remedy when this right is violated.) The Human Rights Committee, which assesses states' compliance with the ICCPR, has interpreted that states have a responsibility to "investigate summary executions, torture, and unresolved disappearances; bring to justice those who are responsible; and provide compensation to victims."[33]

If states have certain obligations to prosecute violations of human rights, then this obligation is inherited by successor regimes within that state. Like financial and treaty obligations, human rights obligations do not dissolve when a new regime comes to power. International law stipulates that regime changes and name changes do not alter a state's identity and responsibilities. These legal obligations establish the principle that a government must assume political responsibility for the actions—just or unjust—of its predecessor.[34]

The argument that international commitments require prosecution of human rights offenses draws on the legal concepts upheld in liberal ideology. States must abide by the written and promulgated laws of the international system, that is, international treaties and covenants. They must not make exceptions for reasons of political expediency.

When laws change, as in a regime transition, justice may prove elusive. As one East German dissident complained, "We wanted justice and got the rule of law."[35] This frustration with the limits of transitional justice is a challenge of the democratization process. "Disappointment is a cost of democratization; the thirst for authenticity and transparency is a cost of disappointment; and disappointment is, at the moment, a very widespread political sentiment."[36] International law can bridge these transitions, providing a stable set of rules covering both the old and new regimes. In the midst of upheavals in the domestic legal system, international law may be the only resource for defining the parameters of justice.

Conclusion

In reading the political debates surrounding transitional justice, one is struck by the omnipresence of the language of liberal democracy. Political opponents, victims, and perpetrators alike, find support for their positions in the principles of liberal democracy. This is not to say that every conceivable political position could cloak itself in liberal raiment; certain policies are proscribed outright, such as extralegal punishment and forgetting the past altogether. Yet, since liberalism is in large part a theory of political procedures, many perspectives can secure a place under its broad tent. In deciding to negotiate a transition to a liberal democratic state, political actors need not pledge themselves to any specific substantive outcomes. No one knows who will prevail in elections or which policies will be adopted a few years hence. Yet in choosing a liberal democratic framework for their negotiations, political actors do affect the kind of policies likely to emerge. They also structure the years of debates concerning transitional justice likely to ensue. Liberal democracy ensures that most debates about the past will be legal debates about how justice can be pursued within the rule of law.

Debates about transitional justice are contentious for many reasons. They pit against one another perpetrators and victims, whose identities were shaped by searing political experiences. The differences are irreducible and many times irreconcilable. No one can give back the victims their lost loved ones or years spent in prison. This human element gives the debates much of their moral drama. However, these debates also contain a second kind of drama—a political struggle about the limits of the liberal democratic state. The hope for justice rubs against hallowed due process. And liberal principles collide with one another. The goal is to find an approach to transitional justice consonant with liberal democracy, that is, one that satisfies, indeed buttresses, the principles of liberal democracy and provides society with a sense that justice has been done.

Critics would argue that in transitions to liberal democracy the cards are stacked against retributive justice. The social contract metaphor emphasizes that new democracies must make a fresh start, leaving behind the injustices of the past. The rule of law means that retroactive punishment is forbidden and that all people must be treated equally before the law, even if they benefited from inequality in the past. An effort to prosecute yesterday's tortures encounters irksome, seemingly trivial procedural difficulties—the guarantees of due process, the statute of limitations, amnesties, and the necessity of proving individual guilt. Democracy stresses inclusive rights to participate in the political process.

Meanwhile, liberal democratic ideology contains only fragmentary resources for advocating justice for the victims of past abuses. Some would argue that this means demands for justice must override the rule of law, and especially the procedural guarantees, during a limited revolutionary period. "[T]he insufficiencies of justice according to law make it imperative to look to justice beyond law, including political justice."[37] Underlying this argument is the assumption that retributive justice is necessary for the liberal democratic project to succeed.[38]

Other advocates of liberal democracy are less dismayed at the ideology's meager resources for pursuing policies of retributive justice.[39] Liberal democracy is no panacea for the multitude wrongs committed in the past, they admit, but no political system can rectify all of history's injustice. Instead, liberal democracy holds out hope for a future in which justice will prevail. The most important task in a democratic transition is to lay the constitutional, institutional and political groundwork for the future development of democracy. A secure liberal democracy is the best imaginable reward for all the people who suffered under the authoritarian regime. Transitional justice is a costly distraction from the paramount task of building democracy. These observers assume that liberal democracy can safely develop without justice.

Over the last 30 years, many democratizing countries have carried out liberal democratic debates about transitional justice. From the clash of principles in these many contexts, a liberal democratic model of transitional justice emerges. This model has three components. First, a new democracy should engage in retributive justice; however, the retribution may not become political justice. It must be constrained by the rule of law. International law is particularly helpful in providing depoliticized solutions to the knotty legal problems involved in trials and lustration. Second, a new democracy should commit itself to an agenda of restorative justice, carrying out policies of rehabilitation and compensation even if these policies are expensive and politically unhelpful. Finally, a new democracy should construct policies of truth-telling. In revealing the facts about the past, the state creates an open society, which can learn from the mistakes of the past. Moreover, truth-telling contributes to restorative justice by revealing the leaders' actions and the victims' suffering. These policies of truth and justice are the boundaries of political responsibility in a liberal democracy.

Chapter 3

Germany Comes to Terms with the Past, Again

The debate in East Germany about coming to terms with the past is intense. Unlike in neighboring Poland, political leaders and academics consider the topic of great importance to the country's future as a liberal democracy, and their debates have generated a voluminous literature.

Does this mean East Germany is a *Sonderfall*, a special case that does not meaningfully fit in a comparative framework? One can advance two arguments in favor of this perspective. First, East Germany is burdened with the legacy of a "double past," the weighty history of both fascism and communism.[1] After 1989, East Germans had to confront both histories. The second unique aspect of the East German case is the unification of the two Germanys in 1990, just a year after the East had toppled the ruling communists. This meant that the newly unified German state took over the task of dealing with the communist past, a context that influenced the dynamics of policy-making. West German participants brought a new set of concerns to the process. They recognized that their state had been insufficiently rigorous in condemning the Nazis' crimes and sought to atone for this mistake by adopting stricter policies with respect to the communists. The West Germans had ample experience in evaluating their past. They had already created patterns of discourse about the past, and postwar legislation on dealing with the legacy of Nazi rule was a body of useful precedents. Moreover, unlike the other post-communist countries, East Germany was subsumed into a wealthy state with an established administrative and legal apparatus. A vast cadre of scholars, bureaucrats, lawyers, and entrepreneurs was available to carry out the policies of coming to terms with the past.

Despite these factors, several reasons make East Germany a useful case for comparative analysis. East Germany was a part of the communist space for 40 years, and its legacy of abuses is comparable to those of other countries in the region. Furthermore, its legacy of the "double past" is not so unusual. In the 1990s, other countries in the region were still tidying up unfinished business from the Second World War. Hungary considered the restitution of property confiscated from Jews, and the Czech Republic contemplated an apology to the Sudeten Germans. Finally, though unification did alter the politics of transitional justice, the West did not swallow the East whole on the very eve of the transition. During the year that separated the crumbling of communist power and German unification, East Germany set its own agenda for transitional justice.

After unification, many East Germans began to believe that the West had taken over their indigenous process of coming to terms with the past.[2] Policies of transitional justice thus came to be seen as Western dictates, with some saying that the Federal Republic of Germany was playing the role of an occupying force. For these frustrated *Ossis*, it seemed like the process of coming to terms with the past had accelerated and taken on a more retributive tone after the unification with the West.

I see the dynamics of policy-making differently. While it is true that unification created new political opportunities, it did not cause a sharp change of course. From the very beginning of the transition to democracy in October 1989, East Germans took seriously their task of dismantling the communists' institutions of repression: They preserved secret police files and rehabilitated victims; they made provisions for lustration and initiated criminal investigations. Coming to terms with the past was prominent on the political agenda during the public demonstrations in fall 1989, the Round Table talks of the winter, and the six months in which the freely elected Volkskammer functioned. In those early days of the transition, the East Germans set a course for coming to terms with the past; their policies were relatively retributive.

While the Bundestag initially perpetuated this approach, in later years the policies grew more moderate. By the mid-1990s transitional justice in Germany no longer appeared so different from that in the Czech Republic, Hungary, or Poland. Ultimately, then, this is another significant reason for including East Germany in a comparative study of post-communist countries: Its approach to transitional justice is not anomalous.

Legacy of the Past

From its inception under the heel of the Soviet military, East Germany's communist state was very repressive. The state quickly put down the country's first outbreak of workers' protest in 1953 and successfully prevented further public unrest until 1989. The German Democratic Republic (GDR) had two major strategies for curtailing dissent. First, it established rigid control of its borders, culminating in the erection of the Berlin Wall in 1961. The Wall curtailed the free flow of information, tourists, and day-trippers across the inter-German border. East Germans could no longer as readily compare their poor economy and political restrictions to the wealth and freedom of the West. The workers and scientists whom the rapidly industrializing country so desperately needed could not get visas to travel abroad, while the country's socially disruptive dissidents were encouraged to head into Western exile. Second, the regime formed the Ministry for State Security, known as the Stasi, to carry out internal intelligence operations. The Stasi infiltrated the country's institutions, especially those such as universities, churches, and environmental associations that encouraged critical thought. It harassed dissidents and gathered information about potential unrest. Given the possibility of exile and the Stasi's exertions, dissident groups in East Germany never had an opportunity to thrive. The regime's sharpest opponents either left the country or spent their efforts in largely futile attempts to evade the Stasi.

East Germany's opposition was rudderless, lacking any organizational expression. The dissidents gathered in small environmental and cultural groups, often using meeting space provided by a local church. They could not develop a nationwide movement, as the Poles did, because the Stasi infiltrated and harassed them so thoroughly.[3] Given the opposition's weakness and the broad extent of the population's participation with the regime, one might expect that transitional justice would never emerge as a significant issue during the process of democratization. The opposition would be too feeble to raise it, and, not wanting to consider their own guilt, the mass of the population would want to avoid it altogether. This was not the case.

Transition to Democracy

The East German transition to democracy is usually categorized as a rupture: The communist regime collapsed rapidly and entirely, leaving few institutional traces. A freely elected parliament was soon in place, and then it ceded power to a new parliament for a unified Germany. East Germany traveled the path from communist rule to German unification in one eventful year.

Throughout the transition, one thing remained constant: the prominence of the Stasi question on the country's agenda. In no other country was the secret police such a central symbol of communist rule. In East Germany, the Stasi question catalyzed protest against the regime and figured prominently in the negotiations surrounding the transfer of power.

In summer 1989, all eyes throughout Central and Eastern Europe were on Poland. The communist party's striking loss in the June election and the formation of a Solidarity-led government emboldened reformers throughout the region and put reactionaries on warning. For Erich Honecker, general secretary of the communist party (SED), this meant that the long eastern border with Poland posed a potential danger. East Germany, proud of its status as the economic powerhouse of the Warsaw Pact, now compared unfavorably with its poor eastern neighbor in terms of political freedoms.

In September, East Germany's other borders became the source of new problems. Hungary quietly removed a barrier separating it from Austrian territory. East Germans on holiday in Hungary and the Black Sea region soon exploited the enormous potential of this seemingly minor alteration to the border regime. They poured into Austria and headed north to West Germany, where they could automatically claim citizenship.

Dissidents back at home also reacted to the region's developments. A group of people who had applied for exit visas to emigrate to the West began to hold weekly meetings in Leipzig's St. Nicholas Church. Monday after Monday others began to join their group, including many who were committed to staying in the GDR.

The dissidents began to form citizens' movements (*Bürgerbewegungen*), such as New Forum in September and Democratic Awakening in October.[4] A Social Democratic party also came into being in October. The citizens' movements were weak, grassroots organizations under local control. New Forum, for example, had an organizing committee in Berlin, but it developed independently and spontaneously in the country's cities and towns.[5] Though they lacked organizational capacity and broad membership, the movements created a focal point for political mobilization. Technically, the citizens' movements were illegal since the government had not allowed them to register. Protesters, even those not associated with the movements, made the legalization of the citizens' movements a central demand.[6] Besides creating a touchstone for evaluating the reality of political change, the citizens' movements also provided a context for recognizing leaders. The leaders who emerged in the citizens' movements represented but a small segment of the population. Nevertheless, they became the de facto leaders for a short, but crucial historical juncture.

In spite of the embarrassing flow of emigrants and the stirrings of a now hopeful opposition, Honecker was determined to maintain the steady rhythm of life in the socialist republic. The government attempted to deal with these extraordinary challenges by ordinary means: meeting with its allies, stepping up secret police activities, and imposing new travel restrictions.[7] These methods had always succeeded in shoring up socialism in the past.

The timing of these troubles was inconvenient for Honecker and the country's old guard. On October 7, the GDR would mark its fortieth anniversary, and the tottering members of the Politburo planned to look back on their lifetime's achievement with pride, pomp, and public celebration. As a matter of course the East Germans had invited the Soviet leader to speak at the celebration, but the planners must have felt queasy about the presence of Mikhail Gorbachev. His policy of *glasnost'* had not pleased the SED's leadership, and it had already banned some Soviet publications for being too liberal.[8]

The anniversary celebration got off to a difficult start. The public holiday and open-air gatherings gave the country's small opposition a chance to jab at the country's "achievements." Gorbachev then exacerbated matters for the East German government. In his speech, he told the people, "He who is late will be punished." This was a clear reference to the East German leader's slowness to initiate reforms. The external buttresses of East German legitimacy were in collapse. The Warsaw Pact allies had already turned their backs on Honecker, with Hungary and Poland moving toward democracy and even Czechoslovakia permitting the transit of East German emigrants. Now the almighty USSR had joined the chorus of criticism. East Germans understood the message that their government was weak.

After Gorbachev's speech, people protested on the streets of Berlin. The police used nonlethal force in breaking up the demonstrations and then jailed many people. Democratic Awakening, a citizens' movement founded just a week before these events, took the lead in obtaining justice for those imprisoned or injured during the anniversary protest. It worked with a Berlin church to put together a 100-page report describing the police's activity during the protest.[9] The work of this independent committee provided the first indication of how this new, unknown opposition would approach the problem of dealing with past injustices. The citizens' movements made inquiry and truth-telling—*glasnost'*, really—the focus of their efforts. East German society was starved for the kind of information that had already become available in neighboring countries.

Honecker's proud moment at the anniversary passed quickly, soon eclipsed by his ultimate humiliation. Less than two weeks after the anniversary, younger members of the SED overthrew him in an attempt to salvage the party's damaged legitimacy. Egon Krenz stepped into the role of general secretary and attempted to put a lid on the burgeoning protest. The number of participants in Leipzig's regular Monday demonstrations now exceeded 100,000, and their demands were escalating. Their rallying cry was to dissolve the Stasi and break the monopoly of power held by the SED.[10]

Just a few days after the decision was made to form a new government, Günter Schabowski, the government spokesman, held a press conference and made the surprise announcement that the GDR would open its borders with the West. At midnight, the border guards allowed East Berliners to walk past the Wall and into the West. The picture of East and West Germans celebrating atop the Wall captures for most outsiders the high point of the communist collapse; the rest of the transition appears as mere denouement. Within the GDR, however, perceptions were different. For the SED, opening the Wall was a strategic concession, after which it intended to consolidate its reduced, but still significant, power.[11] It formed a new government and began to reform the Stasi, changing its name, dismissing some personnel and, controversially, destroying some of the most incriminating files.[12]

Later in November the SED also responded favorably to Democracy Now's proposal to form a Round Table along the lines of the Polish model. As communist parties throughout the region retreated and pressure from below mounted, the SED recognized the need to limit its losses. It had more to fear than most other communist parties: Not only could it lose its monopoly of power, but it also faced a threat to the continued existence of the state's territorial integrity. Soon after East Germans first visited their Western counterparts, the possibility of reunification found its way into the country's political lexicon. To some, the suggestion was strange and unwelcome: Chancellor Kohl received a frosty response when he advocated reunification during a speech in East Berlin. Nevertheless, demonstrators in Leipzig increasingly voiced their support for the abolition of the East German state.

In the days before the inaugural session of the Round Table, East Germans were increasingly agitated about the activities of the Stasi. Though the command to destroy the files was a secret, even the Stasi had difficulty in concealing such a massive operation. Onlookers saw smoke mysteriously billowing from the regional Stasi offices, and trucks laden with old files made their way to overburdened paper-recycling factories. The new citizens' movements, especially New Forum, made it their business to watch over the Stasi.[13] Though New Forum was not a centralized movement, the various local groups that claimed the name shared a commitment to dismantling the Stasi. In fact, opposition to the Stasi and the SED's monopoly on power were the main issues drawing together individuals of vastly different political outlooks.

A group in Erfurt called "Women for Change" made the decisive move on December 4.[14] Several members of this group—ordinary East German citizens—walked into the local Stasi office and sat down. They demanded that the Stasi lock up the files until a court could decide their fate. And the mighty Stasi's response? In an effort to appease the women, the general-major in charge of the office offered to discuss the Stasi's activities with them. The women had brought a prosecutor with them, and he sealed the doors of the archives. The women's group set up a vigil and waited. Truly the emperor had no clothes.

The events in Erfurt established a powerful precedent; in the next days groups of citizens occupied Stasi offices throughout the GDR. The mini-coups followed a basic pattern. Several people, usually claiming some affiliation with a citizens' movement, marched into the Stasi office. After speaking with the officials, they asked a prosecutor to seal all the rooms where files were stored, so that no one—neither Stasi officers nor opposition activists—could have access to the files. Then they maintained a presence in the Stasi offices to prevent the renewal of activities, and set up a citizens' committee (*Bürgerkomitee*) to oversee the dismantling of the local Stasi office.

In East Germany, it was ordinary citizens who began the process of dismantling the communist state's repressive apparatus. They were to encounter many difficulties in this effort. They lacked information about the many-tentacled beast they were up against. East Germans expressed shock when they learned that the Stasi had nearly 86,000 salaried employees and 109,000 secret informants.[15] The individuals who made up the citizens' committees were volunteers, generally honest people with no experience in the twisted manipulations of an intricate domestic intelligence organization. Meanwhile, the Stasi officers and public prosecutors, who were of necessity their partners in the task of dismantling the Stasi, were extremely knowledgeable, and they had an interest in concealing as much as possible.[16]

At first blush, the citizens' occupation of the Stasi offices might seem to be a revolutionary act; however, even with their low level of organization, the citizens' movements tried as far as possible to hew their actions to fit in a legal framework. This is why their first tasks in taking over a Stasi office were to call in a state prosecutor to close off the files and then the police to monitor the building. Members of the citizens' committees did not just open the archives and start to read, nor did they force the Stasi officers out the door. Rather they carefully locked up the files and began negotiating with the officers about how the office should be dismantled. The presence of the prosecutors was "de-escalating": "They gave the whole proceedings a legal form, that was acceptable to both sides in this tense situation for which no social rules existed."[17] Following legal procedures meant that the takeovers involved the careful process of compromise, which frustrated some participants. "Legal methods used in dismantling an intelligence organization reach their limits too quickly," wrote one member of Frankfurt-on-Oder's citizens' committee.[18]

The question of what to do about the secret police files quickly became a critical issue for the overwhelmed citizens' committees. The citizens' movements were to be plagued by diverging opinions on this topic. In Leipzig, New Forum was adamant that the files remain in their city and be opened, at least selectively. They managed to save 6,000 meters of files, and they called on citizens to use the files to work through their personal histories.[19] Other groups objected to this, saying that opening the files would open old wounds and violate people's privacy.

On December 7, the opposition groups represented at the newly convened Round Table outlined their approach for coming to terms with the past. One of their priorities was to call on the government to take measures to stop the destruction of documents and to bring the Stasi under civilian control.[20] In fact, the Round Table would later bring to light much of the GDR's untold history, including the scandals of corruption, ecological disasters, financial mismanagement, and the surprising size and reach of the Stasi.

While the Stasi offices in the provincial cities and towns slipped out of the government's control, the SED still commanded the Stasi's headquarters in East Berlin, a jewel it desperately wanted to keep in its treasure chest. A week after the Round Table's first session, Prime Minister Hans Modrow abolished the renamed Stasi and gave orders for the formation of a new agency called "Constitutional Protection." It was the second time in as many months that the SED had abolished the old Stasi simply by renaming it. The party needed to retain something along the lines of the Stasi, since it believed that an intelligence service was a hallmark of a sovereign state. Without a Stasi, there would be no East Germany.

The SED's tinkering with the Stasi's name did not placate the opposition, which initiated a strike in the Round Table, refusing to participate in further sessions until the government had answered questions about the dismantling of the Stasi. The government was chastened by the Round Table's demands. On January 12, Modrow announced to the Volkskammer that the GDR would have no security service until after the first free elections.

Though this was the news that the Round Table and the citizens' movements had been waiting for, they were not altogether pacified. In the GDR's provinces, citizens' committees could assist and observe the abolition of the Stasi's network of offices; however, at the headquarters in East Berlin, a state committee, and a discredited one at that, was in sole control. Meeting at a nationwide conference, the citizens' committees decided to protest the lack of public participation and oversight in razing the organization's headquarters. New Forum called for a demonstration to be held at the Stasi office on Normannenstrasse on January 15.

The week of January 15 was the true *Wende* (turning point) in East Germany's revolution. Early that day Hans Modrow appeared before the Round Table ready to make last-minute concessions to permit the Round Table to play a significant role in overseeing the process of dismantling the Stasi headquarters.[21] In light of the demonstrations planned for later that afternoon, he also made a plea that the revolution remain a peaceful one—"*keine Gewalt.*"[22]

New Forum certainly took appropriate steps to organize a peaceful demonstration. It established contacts with the police and asked the Stasi to send its employees home early to avoid provocation. The citizens' movement planned to erect a brick wall on the square outside the Stasi offices, symbolically sealing the hated security institution shut. The plans were thrown off, however, when someone opened the doors of a central building. Many eyewitnesses testified that the doors were opened from the inside, and not by the demonstrators outside.[23] The demonstrators rushed into the building and destroyed Stasi property, including many files.[24] The relatively minor acts of vandalism were upsetting to all factions at the Round Table. The Round Table as a whole passed a resolution condemning the violence, and New Forum expressed regrets: "Forty years of constitutional violations, psychological and physical violence against the citizens of the GDR by the State Security compared to one hour of vandalism. But this was one hour too many."

The main result of the *Wende* was exactly what the citizens' movements intended: The government no longer had a monopoly on the task of dismantling the Stasi's central structures. The demonstrators at Normannenstrasse formed a citizens' committee that established a physical presence at the behemoth headquarters. The committee set up several subcommittees to monitor the dismantling of Stasi headquarters, and like the other citizens' committees, it sent representatives to consult with the Round Table's new working group on security.[25] While the citizens' committees in the provinces had initiated and controlled the dissolution process until mid-January, the Round Table and its working group on security, with their semiofficial status, soon took leadership of the process. The citizens' committees began a slow decline into irrelevance. Until free elections were held in March, a mixed state-societal commission was to oversee the dismantling of the Stasi. This committee had an apparatus of 176 employees who reported not just to the government, but also to the Round Table's working group on security.[26]

The guiding principle in dismantling the Stasi was to reveal the truth about its activities. The task of the committees was not merely to physically dismantle the offices and discharge the personnel, but, as one of the Round Table's representatives wrote, to "discover the structures of this apparatus and to make it public."[27] The Round Table resolved, "A peaceful and democratic future for our country is unthinkable without a full and truthful opening of the past and the present."[28] It instructed the committees to unravel the Stasi's structures and its links with the SED; to examine the chain of command; to open the SED's archives; to investigate the destruction of the Stasi's files; and to audit its finances. The Round Table's emphasis on truth-telling is also evident in its resolution that the Stasi complex at Magdalenenstraße in East Berlin be turned into a research institute, which would study the history of Stalinism in the GDR.[29]

While truth-telling was the most important principle organizing the work of the committees charged with dismantling the Stasi, the Round Table also emphasized democratic inclusivity and due process. Former Stasi employees were to be included in the new democratic project. In the early months of 1990, many people feared that East Germans would take revenge on their neighbors and erstwhile spies.[30] As early as January 15, the Round Table warned that a failure to include former Stasi employees in society could lead "to their radicalization, which has unforeseeable consequences for society."[31] Werner Fischer, a member of the state committee for the dissolution of the Stasi, believed that this issue was crucial. His final report for the committee included a section called "An Important Dimension of the Dismantling," which concerned how society should treat former Stasi employees. He warned against the dangers of revenge and emphasized the importance of adhering to the rule of law. "If we want the rule of law, then this also applies to former Stasi employees. They are only guilty if it is proven in their individual cases." He added that if the country failed to guarantee the rule of law as applied to them, it would lose its claim to be a democracy. The task of the Round Table was not only to dismantle the Stasi, but to "guarantee the human rights and dignity of all the people in this society."[32]

While these principles were helpful in guiding the work of the committees, they did not yield a clear solution to the question of what should be done with the Stasi's files. The debates about the Stasi's files began within the complex context of institutions involved in dismantling the security agency. The asymmetry of information between the Stasi's old friends and the citizens' committees affected the formation of opinions during this period. The Stasi and its erstwhile supporters in the SED had an obvious interest in destroying the files, which contained much incriminating information. In the "Dissolution Reports" that they filed with Stasi's headquarters in early January 1990, Stasi's district offices commented on the climate of opinion in the citizens' committees regarding the files. Some reported that the citizens' committees were willing to support the destruction of files; however, most said that the committees rejected the destruction of files.[33] The Dresden district office regretfully reported that the citizens' committee was unanimous in opposing the destruction of files, but, it added, "We are working with experts from the State Archive, the Prosecutor's Office and other state organs to achieve a destruction of the documents."[34]

Even after the takeover of Stasi's headquarters, opinion ranged widely about what should be the ultimate fate of the files. The files were essentially closed, so the citizens' committees and the Round Table could not actually view the files about which they vociferously debated. The democratic opposition could not find a single voice on the issue. On the one hand, the impulse toward truth-telling led many people to advocate opening the files. The Greens seemed to take this position when they recommended that people be able to go to the proposed research institute at Magdalenenstraße to read their personal files.[35] Democratic Awakening made the straightforward recommendation: "Every citizen must be handed 'his' file at his wish."[36] On the other hand, the Initiative for Peace and Human Rights and some citizens' committees believed that opening the files would violate privacy rights and lead to greater civic unrest.[37]

Though the institutions that existed prior to East Germany's free elections could not legitimately pass a law concerning the Stasi files, they turned over the reins of governance with several recommendations concerning the future of the files. In its final report, the Round Table encouraged the new Volkskammer to deal with the question of the files expeditiously and surprisingly recommended the destruction of Stasi files containing personal data.[38] This would ensure the revolution's peacefulness and political inclusivity. The report said that opening the files would lead to a climate of suspicion and possibly revenge. It called on East German citizens to offer former Stasi employees an opportunity to personally rehabilitate themselves, and it encouraged the employees to speak openly about their experiences with psychologists and pastors. The report seemed to envision coming to terms with the past through a kind of talking therapy, an approach it contrasted with retribution. "Truly coming to terms with the past can occur only with the participation of perpetrators and victims . . . This approach to the past can take place only in a societal atmosphere where the individual is given a chance for a new beginning."[39]

Meanwhile, the state committee on dismantling the Stasi contradicted this call for forbearance, recommending that the new Volkskammer carry out background checks on the candidates for the country's first democratic elections to see who had collaborated with the Stasi. In early March, rumors began to circulate that several leading members of the citizens' movements had collaborated with the Stasi. Just in time for the parliamentary elections, it came out that Wolfgang Schnur, founder of Democratic Awakening, was an unofficial worker or "*inoffizieller Mitarbeiter*" (IM) for the Stasi.[40] As other accusations were leveled in the heat of the electoral contest, the citizens' committees began to call for lustration of the deputies newly elected to the Volkskammer. They suggested that the catalogue of IMs (the electronic version of which they had voted to destroy a month earlier) be checked to see which of the new deputies had spied on their neighbors.[41]

The support for lustration contradicted the Round Table's proposal of a few weeks earlier that all files with personal data be destroyed. Indeed, the whole question of the files was bound up in knots of contradiction. The democratic opposition could not decide which principles should guide them in deciding the fate of the files. Opening the files would serve the goal of telling the truth about the past, a principle that had guided the revolution. However, destroying them would protect the peacefulness of the revolution and the privacy rights of individuals. It would also prevent the West German intelligence service from using information gathered by the Stasi. While in the early months of 1990, influential members of the opposition advocated the destruction of the files, the issue of vetting members of parliament quickly complicated that position. If the files were destroyed, there would be no way of telling whether former Stasi employees and IMs were in the Volkskammer.

The Volkskammer and Transitional Justice

Lustration of the Volkskammer Deputies

After East Germany's first (and only) free elections on March 19, 1990, rumors about a Stasi presence in the new Volkskammer continued to circulate, poisoning the political climate. Tens of thousands of people participated in demonstrations calling for lustration.[42] The Volkskammer responded quickly, agreeing to form a "verification committee" to examine whether deputies had collaborated with the Stasi. Their purpose was to ensure that citizens could trust the representatives they had just elected and that the deputies would not be vulnerable to blackmail.[43] The lustration procedures were as follows. First, deputies were asked to sign a release authorizing the commission to verify whether or not they cooperated with the Stasi. Each deputy also appointed a member of his party to be present when the commission reviewed his files. Second, the parties and factions carried out preliminary lustration by checking the names of their deputies in the central card catalogue of the Stasi archives. They forwarded the names they found in the catalogue to the Volkskammer's vetting commission, which then read the deputies' files. Third, the commission evaluated the contents of the files to determine whether deputies had actually worked for the Stasi and whether that cooperation had harmed a citizen of the GDR. If so, it recommended to the deputies and to the leader of their faction that the deputies resign. According to the law, deputies had the right to read their own files and dispute the commission's finding.

The commission found itself incapable of implementing the elaborate procedures as foreseen. Despite their unanimous agreement that lustration was necessary, the parties in the Volkskammer did not make serious efforts to actually carry out lustration, perhaps because they feared the destabilizing results. Members of the commission failed to show up for meetings, and the factions were slow in carrying out the preliminary lustration. The commission also got bogged down in the legal discussions about how to protect privacy rights. As a result, the commission did not begin to examine files until September 5, just a month before German unification.[44]

During the Volkskammer's very last session before unification, the vetting commission gave its final report. It had read the files of 69 deputies and 7 ministers, and in 15 cases, it recommended that the individuals resign because of their past links with the Stasi. The fact that unification was only days away did not mean that the information was totally irrelevant. Later in that session the Volkskammer chose 144 deputies to represent the East German *Länder* in the Bundestag, and those with Stasi links could not be among the selected representatives. After the report was given, the Volkskammer, already running out of time to finish up its legislative agenda, became embroiled in a debate about whether the vetting commission should name the names of the deputies and ministers who had been asked to resign. The commission recommended that the names remain secret, as the law envisioned. Deputies from the citizens' movements (united in a coalition party of former dissidents and environmentalists called *Bündnis 90/Die Grünen*) and the Christian Democratic party, not normally political allies, pushed a bill to reveal the names. They argued that the new democracy should confront its past in a spirit of total honesty.[45] Truth-telling remained the watchword of the East German transition.

After the commission revealed the names of the Stasi collaborators in a closed session, many of the accused chose to explain their activities, this time in an open session. Each man and woman denied the charges, and their explanations illustrate the many difficulties of labeling someone an *inoffizieller Mitarbeiter*.[46] The label attached to individuals carrying out a broad array of activities. Some informed on their colleagues' political views, while others filed reports about economic production and technical problems at the workplace. People signed agreements to act as IMs under various circumstances. Many people did so in order to have the opportunity to travel abroad or to advance in their careers. The deputies described the extenuating circumstances and swore that their connections with the Stasi never caused harm to anyone. Of course, without a thorough analysis of their files, it is impossible to decide whether these were self-serving justifications or truthful descriptions of difficult decisions made in a situation of moral ambiguity. Since the commission soon ceased to exist, the full truth would never be known.[47]

Lustration of Civil Servants

The Volkskammer made rather greater progress in establishing a legislative basis for the lustration of the judiciary. The Volkskammer passed a law on judicial reform, the *Richtergesetz*, on July 5, 1990. It established the following procedures for lustration. The law called on the Volkskammer and the district assemblies to form "judicial appointment committees" consisting of six deputies and four representatives of the judiciary. The committees had to decide within six months whether to reappoint judges who were already serving. The law did not specify which criteria the committees should use in evaluating whether an individual was fit to continue in service as a judge; the law refers only to "professional and personal requirements."[48] However, the parliamentary debates give us a clearer idea of what was meant: "loyalty to the free, democratic, federal, social and ecologically-oriented state under the rule of law" and "moral and political integrity."[49] The law also provided an additional mechanism for removing compromised judges: It extended the statute of limitations for disciplinary proceedings from six months to two years.[50]

The judicial appointment committees were barely in place on October 3 when unification occurred; however, the unification treaty did not alter the basic outlines of the *Richtergesetz*. Although the treaty called on other state organs to dismiss individuals who had violated human rights or had collaborated with the secret police, it did not apply these standards to the judiciary.[51] The new Bundesländer could establish their own criteria for the lustration of judges. Some committees handed applicants a lengthy questionnaire with detailed questions about their past political activities and contacts with the Stasi. Brandenburg's long questionnaire weeded out 46.5 percent of applicants. Other provinces were more lenient. Mecklenburg-Vorpommern and Sachsen removed only a third of their judges. Altogether, the committees reappointed 699 of the 1,300 judges who applied.[52]

While the Volkskammer felt that lustration of the judiciary was crucially important and made some progress toward reforming that institution, it did not get far in reforming the rest of the government's administrative apparatus. The parliament did not pass legislation to exclude former Stasi agents from public employment. The Round Table had expressed its concern that excluding Stasi agents would lead to dire social consequences, such as violent retribution and a divided society. Until mid-summer, the citizens' movements generally supported the recommendation that Stasi agents be given a soft-landing in the new democracy. Inclusivity took precedence over retribution.

In summer 1990, attitudes in the citizens' movements, now coalesced in an electoral bloc called Bündnis 90, began to shift, and they began to demand that all Stasi agents be banned from public employment. As time passed, the fear that East Germans would take revenge on the former spies evaporated. Months had passed, and despite the many rumors and leaks revealing the identity of agents, no violence had occurred. Lustration did not seem likely to disrupt the peaceful revolution.

The citizens' movements also became extremely frustrated with the government's handling of the Stasi problem. From December 1989 until March 1990, the citizens' movements had exerted a great deal of control over the dissolution of the Stasi. When the new government took over the task, many activists felt it adopted a half-hearted approach. They accused the Interior Ministry of hiring former Stasi agents and blocking efforts to remove agents who were permanently employed in other institutions.[53] A gentle approach to the Stasi no longer seemed like an enlightened policy of reconciliation, but more like a cover-up.

In late August, the Volkskammer called on the Council of Ministers to establish procedures to remove former Stasi agents from all areas of the civil service.[54] Deputies raised the issue of trust, saying that the public would not have confidence in the civil service if leading Stasi officials found well-paid positions there. The parliament itself did not have the time to work out the complex legal issues involved in such a law: the criteria for defining unacceptable levels of collaboration; the lustration procedures and appeals; and the range of positions to which lustration should apply. The Council of Ministers was to work out these details by September 1, presumably for inclusion in the unification treaty.[55] This was not enough time. As a result, the East Germans did not outline their own procedures for the lustration of the civil service. They made clear, however, that they believed lustration was desirable.

The unification treaty included only very general provisions concerning lustration of the civil service. It said that the "extraordinary dismissal" of tenured civil servants was permissible under several circumstances, including when the employee had violated "human rights or the principle of the rule of law" as defined in the International Covenant on Civil and Political Rights (ICCPR) or the Universal Declaration of Human Rights, or when he "worked for the former Ministry of State Security/Bureau of National Security."[56] Note that the treaty did not require ministries to dismiss these employees; dismissal was simply permissible. The treaty did not define what range of activities was included in "working for" the Stasi; thus, the ministries and Länder had a great deal of discretion in determining their own procedures and criteria for lustration. Notably, people with a Stasi past fared much worse than former SED members in the united Germany. West

Germany insisted that the unification treaty not place any restrictions on the employment of former communists in the civil service.[57]

The Stasi Files

By mid-June 1990, when the Volkskammer's new institutions for dismantling the Stasi were in place, there was broad support for following the Round Table's recommendation to destroy the files that contained personal information. Interior Minister Peter-Michael Diestel, who was in charge of the Stasi's archive, opposed any opening of the files. He said that the files contained many falsehoods, so they were not a useful basis for public debates. Furthermore, any revelation of the files' contents would violate the right to privacy. He also noted that opening the files would entail very difficult administrative tasks and could even disrupt the democratic transition. "To give certain groups or individuals the right to see their files may seem humane and understandable given their personal fate; however, it is not suitable for ensuring peace under the rule of law. It will create new conflict and new injustice."[58] The citizens' committees also advocated the destruction of the files on the grounds that the files were created by unconstitutional means and that they invaded citizens' privacy rights. The committees also grew more concerned about the possibility of Western intelligence agencies gaining access to the files. "The security of these material against inappropriate access, especially by secret services, cannot be guaranteed. Therefore we hold it necessary to reduce the information stocks of the former Ministry of State Security."[59]

Over the course of summer 1990, however, relations between the new institutions charged with dismantling the Stasi grew fractious, and opinions about the files began to shift. The citizens' committees were angry about their marginalization.

The Volkskammer committee, headed by Joachim Gauck, criticized the state committee, and especially Minister Diestel, on several other points as well. The parliament's access to Stasi files was uneven. Often deputies did not get access to files they needed for verification purposes, or they got them only after substantial delays. The Volkskammer was incensed when it learned Diestel had misled them about the continued employment of so-called officers in special operation (*Offiziere in besonderem Einsatz*, or OibEs). These were individuals whom the Stasi placed in ordinary jobs where they could spy on their coworkers regularly. Diestel insisted that he had removed the OibEs, but the Volkskammer committee then compiled a list of OibEs who continued to hold their positions.[60] In general, the Volkskammer committee charged that

Diestel was not diligently pursuing the task of dismantling the Stasi, and in mid-September, the Volkskammer as a whole voted no-confidence in the minister of the interior.[61] Like the members of the citizens' committees, the Volkskammer was frustrated with its lack of control over the dismantling of the Stasi; deputies realized that with the approach of unification, GDR citizens would never have adequate oversight over the process. In the Volkskammer, consensus grew that the solution should be to compensate for the lack of public oversight with total openness—broad access to the files the Stasi had left behind.

West Germany was not initially keen to open the files. Its Interior Minister Wolfgang Schäuble believed "access to the Stasi files should be as restrictive as possible."[62] The idea was to store files in a central location under the control of the Federal Archives where the commissioner for data protection would oversee access to the files.

On July 22, the Volkskammer debated a draft law on the files that the government commission had prepared. For the first time the official position represented in the bill was that the files should not be destroyed. The West German government was unhappy with the draft legislation, noting that "[D]ifferentiated regulations for destroying the files are viewed as necessary."[63]

The law adopted by the Volkskammer just two days later disappointed West German expectations. The Volkskammer law provided for the files to be stored in the new *Bundesländer*, not in a central location. A commissioner elected by the Volkskammer, not the head of the Federal Archives, would oversee the files. Regarding access to the files, the law put forth a compromise. People could have access to the files for the purposes of prosecuting offenses, dismantling the Stasi, carrying out legally defined lustration procedures, or rehabilitation. In addition, researchers could read personal files if the invasion of privacy rights was of minimal significance compared to the scientific value of the research. Finally, though victims did not have direct access to their files, they could receive information about the contents of their files. Victims could also add amendments to their files, make corrections, and request that some of their personal data be destroyed. Beyond this, the law did not provide for the destruction of any of the files.[64]

In the debates on this law, the deputies stressed that people had the right to know the truth about the GDR's history.[65] The dissenters from the former communist party, the Party of Democratic Socialism (PDS), took issue with the law by saying that it violated the rule of law, in particular the FRG's laws on data protection.[66] Others countered that data protection laws and privacy rights should not prevent East Germans from understanding their own history. While formal laws work well in a secure, functioning society, "in our situation, we have rules that do not fix laws, but instead minimize justice."[67] Many remained convinced that the files could reveal truths that would aid the new German democracy in rendering justice and understanding its history. The pain involved in this process was an unavoidable aspect of the democratic transition.

At this late stage, however, any law the Volkskammer passed had only symbolic importance if the West Germans would not agree to incorporate the new law into its legal system. The West Germans were not enthusiastic about the Volkskammer's law on the Stasi files, and Interior Minister Schäuble rejected the idea of incorporating the Volkskammer law via the unification treaty. The Volkskammer then demanded that the unification treaty be amended to include the law, even threatening to abort the unification process if the West did not comply.[68]

The citizens' movements dramatically reengaged with the issue. On September 4, 21 people occupied one of the buildings at East Berlin's Stasi headquarters and demanded that the West Germans implement the Volkskammer law. They were concerned that Western intelligence agencies would use the files and that the government would move the Stasi files to Koblenz, where the federal government housed its archives. The demands of the standard-bearers of the East German revolution went even further than the Volkskammer law. They called on the government to guarantee each individual access to his own file, sidelining once and for all the fear that the files could cause violent retribution. The citizens' movements further argued that the state should ban all former Stasi employees from the civil service and prosecute former officials for violations of human rights.[69] To press for these demands, the demonstrators began a hunger strike that lasted for 16 days.

This demonstration was a stark reminder that the files were an incredibly sensitive issue. The files had sparked the *Wende* and given the citizens' committees, the revolution's engine, their *raison d'être*. The files had become an emblem of the East German revolution; East Germans (especially the citizens' committees) took justifiable pride in their role in capsizing the Stasi. The idea that the West Germans would come into the Stasi buildings, box up the files, and ship them to Koblenz was an unbearable attack on East Germans' greatest achievement: the dismantling of their own corrupt security apparatus.

While the West Germans were not prepared to incorporate wholesale the Volkskammer law on the files, they signed an agreement that met many of the demonstrators demands. They agreed that the West German intelligence agencies would not have access to the files until a new law was passed. In the meantime, the Volkskammer would appoint a commissioner to oversee the files during a transitional period; for this time the files would be closed in central and regional storage locations on the territory of the former GDR. While the personal files were accessible only for purposes of rehabilitation, lustration, and criminal prosecutions, the agreement said that victims would be given the right to information about the contents of their files as soon as possible. In a useful summary of the conflicting legal principles at stake, the agreement called for a "suitable compromise between: political, historical and juridical studies; the guarantee of the victims' individual rights; and the protection of the individual from the unauthorized use of his personal data."[70] The unification treaty also called on the federal legislature to "consider the principles" reflected in the Volkskammer law as it prepared a new law to govern use of the files.[71] Thus, while it was left to the all-German Bundestag to regulate the matter of the files, the Volkskammer and the citizens' committees had defined a course of broad access.

Rehabilitation

Rehabilitating those who had suffered from the Stasi's depredations had long been a goal of the democratic revolution. The citizens' committees began accepting applications for rehabilitation soon after they took over the Stasi offices; however, they did not have access to the files or the authority to rehabilitate the victims. Instead they held on to the sheaf of applications and waited for a legislative resolution.

No one opposed rehabilitation. The former communists saw rehabilitation as a way to put the uglier aspects of its past behind it. The new political parties, along with the West German government, agreed that rehabilitation was a way to "extinguish the injustice committed by the previous system within the limits of possibility."[72] Of course, the West German government, which would eventually pay all the compensation claims associated with rehabilitation, was concerned with where the "limits of possibility" lay.

Having little interest in the financial impact of its legislation, the Volkskammer did not carefully calculate costs. Its encompassing rehabilitation law, passed on September 6, 1990, covered three types of injustices that occurred under communist rule: the use of criminal law, administrative law, or state employment rules to punish dissidents.[73] People who had been imprisoned for their political activities could apply for rehabilitation and receive compensation for the time they were falsely imprisoned. The amount of compensation was to be determined in accordance with the FRG's "prisoner's assistance law." Rehabilitation under administrative law applied to cases where the state had expropriated property, stripped a person of his citizenship, exiled a citizen to a foreign state, or forcibly committed him to a psychiatric clinic. These people could also claim social welfare benefits, though the Volkskammer did not specify the amount. Finally, if a state agency dismissed or demoted individuals because of their political or religious beliefs, the law specified that the agency should give those individuals special consideration if they reapplied for their positions. The law vaguely stipulated that those entitled to "employment rehabilitation" deserved social welfare benefits.

Since the Volkskammer passed the rehabilitation law after the two Germanys had already signed the unification treaty, the rehabilitation law was in a package of Volkskammer legislation the negotiators were considering for inclusion in a supplement to the treaty. The West German negotiators were disturbed by the vague language in the law, and they worried that compensation claims would create an unpredictably large drain on a budget already sapped by the financial burdens of unification. To West Germany, rehabilitating those who had suffered under the administrative and employment laws seemed like secondary priorities compared with the other pressing tasks. "Against this background I have always warned that given the range of [economic, social and ecological] problems and the short time period for solving them, we should concentrate on the present and the future, not on overcoming the past," said Wolfgang Schäuble.[74] West Germany refused to implement the entire rehabilitation law passed by the Volkskammer. Instead the unification treaty retained only those parts of the Volkskammer law that pertained to people who had been imprisoned for their political activities.[75]

Transitional Justice in a United Germany

From mid-1991 until early 1993, the Bundestag of the newly united Germany worked out a body of laws for dealing with the communist past. Setting an agenda for transitional justice is no easy task given the competing values inherent in liberal democratic ideology. Debates over a troubled past are contentious in any context. However, compared to the Polish Sejm, the German Bundestag was a less fractured and acrimonious setting. The former communists of the PDS were a needling presence, but never a real force in shaping the outcome of these laws. The electoral bloc Bündnis 90/The Greens, which drew together many former East German dissidents, the citizens' committees and environmentalists, vigorously supported the victims of the previous regime, but they too lacked the votes to affect outcomes. Their contribution was persuasive rhetoric and a perceived legitimacy as the carriers of East Germany's peaceful revolution. The traditional West German political parties—the Christian Democrats (CDU) in the majority and Social Democrats (SPD) in the minority—had the real responsibility for making decisions. These parties were essentially outsiders who, since they had not been enmeshed in the communist system, could debate the past relatively dispassionately. The CDU as the governing party was particularly concerned with the financial consequences of policies, as government spending was ballooning with the costs of unification. The SPD often picked minor differences with the CDU over the laws, but did not have any overarching difference of opinion. Both agreed that the principles of liberal democracy should guide them in their decisions. In contrast to Poland, Germany had only one government throughout the most active period of legislative activity surrounding transitional justice.

The Law on the Stasi Files (Stasi-Unterlagen-Gesetz)

Soon after unification, Joachim Gauck, whom the Volkskammer had chosen to be the Federal Commissioner on the Stasi files, began to build up an agency to oversee the vast archive. Employers and individual citizens started contacting the agency to request information from the files. In the first two weeks, the agency's 11 employees received 12,000 such requests.[76] The agency's tasks were immense: to build an agency that could organize and secure the Stasi archives and to establish temporary rules concerning access to the files.

Lawmakers recognized that the agency required a firmer legal basis for its activities, and in the months after the elections, they began a complex legal and political debate about the past. The citizens' committees opened the debate by demanding that the Bundestag permit victims of the Stasi's intrusions to see their own files. They also insisted that intelligence agencies should have no access to the files. In February 1991, the citizens' committees presented their version of a draft law on the files, which served as a catalyst for the major parties to work out their positions.[77]

Even though six months earlier the Kohl government had expressed its hopes that the files would be destroyed, the major parties readily agreed that victims should have a right to read their files. Two factors explain this shift. First, the West German lawmakers did not want to appear totally insensitive to the wishes of East Germans in this matter.

The citizens' committees responsible for bringing about the revolution insisted that the files be opened, and opinion polls showed that over 80 percent of East Germans supported this position.[78] Second, though one could debate the question of the files from many perspectives—moral, political, or legal—the legal discourse attained hegemony. In particular, the right to "informational self-determination" became the chief argument for opening the files. As Hansjörg Geiger, a director of the commission for the Stasi files, said:

> The federal constitutional court has made this formulation: Only when one knows who has gathered what information about him can he express his human dignity and develop himself freely, as the Basic Law guarantees. From this we derive the right to see the files. That is how the argumentation about the law is supported in constitutional law. The others are political, moral and social arguments, that have a real weight. But in many things one must argue in purely juristic terms.[79]

The first debates on the Stasi files were held in spring 1991. By this time there was general consensus on the broad outlines of the law. The Stasi's former victims would have a right to read their files, and the intelligence agencies would have limited access to the Stasi's information warehouse. Only the former communists in the PDS opposed the law's emerging framework, and instead of providing legal grounds for their opposition, they attempted to relativize the harm their party caused in the past.

The details of the law remained a matter of dispute. Legislators called the law one of the most complex pieces of legislation before them. It was born out of unusual circumstances—East Germany's legal revolution. As the minister of the interior said:

> Coming to terms with this inheritance is more difficult . . . because in the former GDR we have to deal with a very unusual revolution, a revolution that in its early stages was directed in legal lines. This had incalculable advantages . . . but it has remained a very unusual, incomplete revolution.[80]

The law had no precedents, and it involved an uneasy balance between conflicting rights. The rights of various individuals collided: The victim's right to "informational self-determination" potentially harmed third parties' right to privacy, since an individual's file contained information about other people as well. How could the law protect these innocent third parties while giving victims a right to know about their own past? Furthermore, the files contained the names of the people who gathered information for the Stasi. Should their right to privacy override the victims' right to know who had spied on them? Individual rights also conflicted with broader state and societal concerns. The state wanted to use the files to investigate crimes, but many victims wanted to restrict the state's access to their files. Finally, the state wanted to ensure that the opening of the files did not cause breaches of the peace. The law would be undermined if victims took violent revenge on their former denouncers. As much as possible, the legislators relied on legal principles to resolve these conundrums.

The debates on the Stasi files reflect a central theme: Truth about the past is salutary for individuals and for societies. First, many deputies argued that a person must know the truth about her personal history—"making clear why personal histories of life and pain took this course and not another"—in order to derive a meaning from her life's story.[81] The right to personally develop oneself is constitutionally protected.[82] Second, knowing the truth about the past is healthy for societies as a whole because it helps to prevent the repetition of dangerous mistakes.[83] With their history of dictatorship, Germans need to understand their past in order to fully reject all forms of nondemocratic government. Furthermore, truth about the past is the only way of achieving justice for the victims. The files could reveal information about the commission of crimes, and these crimes must be prosecuted. As one deputy argued:

> Everything must be tried to punish those who were most responsible. Not because we should exercise vengeance on a few old men. It goes much more to the trust in our law-based state. Politics and justice can earn this trust only if the citizens in the new federal states can also experience justice.[84]

Justice would build trust in the rule of law and Germany's democratic institutions.

The preface of the law on the Stasi files, passed on December 20, 1991, reflected the balance between the competing legal goods. The main goals of the law were:

> 1. To facilitate access by the individual to the information stored about him by the State Security Service, so that he can clarify the influence of the State Security Service on his personal fate,
> 2. To protect the individual from being impaired in his right of personality by the use of the information stored about him by the State Security Service,
> 3. To guarantee and further the historical, political and legal study of the activity of the State Security Service.[85]

The law achieves these goals by authorizing the commission on the Stasi files to prepare files for use by victims. The commission blackens out the names of third parties and spies mentioned in an individual's file. Individuals may request, however, that the identity of the persons who spied on them be revealed. Prosecutors and judges may use the files to prosecute serious crimes, but intelligence agencies may not have access to personal information regarding victims and third parties. They may use only the Stasi's general directives and personnel files.

The law requires that the commission execute labor-intensive procedures. A citizen's request to read his file initiates a 13-step administrative process. Even when a file consists of several thousand pages, the staff of the commission must read through the entire file and blacken all the names of third parties and spies, so as to protect their privacy.[86] As of 1995, over 950,000 individuals had asked to read their personal files. The commission had approximately 3,000 employees, and its annual budget between 1993 and 1995 was on average 256 mn. DM.[87] Knowledge of the truth does not come inexpensively. At a time of great financial strains, even the wealthy West German government chafed at the high expenditures; however, given Germany's difficult history, it was willing to bear the economic burden of revealing the truth about the past.

Despite the fact that the law on the Stasi files was so complex, and many thought it only provisional, the law worked more or less as intended. People read their own files and came to an understanding of their history. A poll of those who had read their files showed that 95 percent were convinced they had made the right decision in reading their files, and 80 percent of people said knowledge of the file's contents had made their personal history less burdensome. Only 27 percent of citizens felt hateful toward those who had spied on them.[88] Contrary to expectations, the opening of the files did not unleash retributive energy. The former victims were not inclined to take violent revenge on the spies. The media printed numerous articles about the files of public figures, and academic research into the role of the Stasi began in earnest. Over a thousand researchers had received access to the files as of 1995.[89] Five years after the law was passed, legislators were generally satisfied: One deputy referred to the law as the "gem" of German unification, the "heritage of the citizens' movement and the peaceful democratic revolution."[90]

While certainly not everyone was so enamored of the law, the work of the commission did not give them a very good opening for criticism. The commission's work proceeded in a business-like fashion, and public interest in the files waned. If anything, a spirit of boredom concerning the Stasi set in. The open question is whether this boredom with the past is healthy for German society. Arguably, it is. The secrets of the past are not locked in a dusty safe, but organized in an accessible public archive. Twenty years from now it will be difficult for a youth culture to allege that their parents covered up their collaboration with dictatorship.

Lustration

The law on the Stasi files said that the new commission on the files would give files or information from the files to certain categories of employers for lustration purposes. It stipulated that several groups of employees could be verified without their consent: members of the government, local representatives, civil servants and church employees, notaries and lawyers, and corporate directors. Other employees could also be verified if they gave their permission.[91] The law thus regulated who could obtain information from the files to use for lustration purposes, but it did not set forth procedures or criteria for lustration. The Länder, ministries, businesses, and churches would have to create their own mechanisms for lustration.

Though the interior ministry developed some general guidelines for using the Stasi files, these did not amount to universal criteria for lustration. Members of Bündnis 90/The Greens began to question whether the decentralized approach to lustration was appropriate. Lustration was proceeding at a different pace in various contexts, which some claimed violated the rule of law. It created legal uncertainty, since a person could conceivably be dismissed from a civil service position in one *Land* because of a Stasi connection, yet hired in another one with lax regulations. This created an impression of arbitrariness that was incompatible with justice. Furthermore, Bündnis 90 held that the entire lustration procedure lacked a legal foundation; it was carried out entirely on the basis of internal ministerial regulations or regional government laws.[92] Some of their fellow representatives reacted in astonishment to their position. "This may be in the only revolution in history in which the children of the revolution care about the people that they deprived of power through a societal upheaval," said one.[93]

The West German political parties also switched positions on this issue. They were satisfied to let the ministries and *Länder* handle the difficult problems of lustration. They argued that decentralization allowed agencies and *Länder* greater flexibility to purge personnel in accordance with their particular needs and with attention to individual cases. Universal criteria and procedures would be a coarse measure of the psychological subtleties entailed in a person's contacts with the secret police. They claimed that justice required *Einzelfallprüfung*, or verification in individual cases. The major parties were also concerned that any new lustration law would undermine the legality of all the dismissals that had taken place already. The whole process of lustration might have to start afresh, contributing further to unification's legal morass.[94]

One explanation for these seemingly inconsistent positions lies in the power of legal precedent. Faced with many complex tasks at once, West Germany's parties tried to apply familiar laws and solutions. This economized on the time and effort involved in resolving difficult questions. In the case of the Stasi files, lawmakers relied on the federal law on archives, which demanded central administration of the files. In the matter of lustration, they turned to employment law, which is a matter of local control and contractual obligations in Germany's federal system.

The lustration process in Germany was extensive. As of May 1995, employers had requested background checks from the commission on the files regarding over 1.6 mn. individuals. The commission consulted the Stasi's catalogue of employees and secret informants to see whether it had information on each individual. If it found information indicating employment or collaboration with the Stasi, it compiled a report evaluating the intensity and effectiveness of that involvement.[95] The employer then studied the report and rendered a decision about whether the individual was eligible for employment.

The commission found that approximately 7 percent of individuals verified for employment in the civil service had some connection to the Stasi; however, the incidence of collaboration varied widely among different categories of employees. Among Berlin's teachers, only 4.5 percent had Stasi connections, while nearly 22 percent of the East Germans verified for new positions with Deutscher Telekom were found to be "Stasi-positive."[96] Of course, employers did not dismiss all the individuals who were found "guilty." Because lustration was a decentralized process, no central body collected data on precisely how many individuals were dismissed because of their Stasi connections. At best one can piece together evidence from various institutions. For example, only 0.9 percent of Berlin's teachers lost their jobs because of their Stasi connections, representing just 20 percent of those whom the commission found to be Stasi collaborators. The regional commission in Sachsen-Anhalt found that 30 percent of those it found to be collaborators were actually dismissed. The commissioner on the files estimated that the majority of people who worked for the Stasi were able to continue working in the civil service.[97]

The lustration of representatives in the Bundestag was more controversial than the verification of civil servants. The law of the Stasi files provided for verification of members of the federal and *Länder* governments, as well as elected representatives at the local level; however, it did not address the lustration of federal representatives. The president of the Bundestag asked deputies to undergo lustration voluntarily, and 325 of the body's 662 members agreed. The commission submitted two reports about the Stasi involvement of deputies.[98]

Again, Bündnis 90/The Greens were dissatisfied. They called for the mandatory verification of all the Bundestag's deputies. Their position rested on a demand for equal treatment: If civil service employees and local representatives had to undergo lustration, then members of the Bundestag should as well.[99]

The major Western parties did not agree with the argument that civil servants and elected officials should be treated in the same way. Again, existing laws pointed the way. According to federal law, no one can be hindered in taking up office in the Bundestag. Compulsory lustration would violate the "freedom of the mandate," that is, the results of the citizens' choice in democratic elections. Though the majority voted against compulsory lustration, deputies from several parties encouraged their colleagues to consent to the procedure. Otherwise, they warned, the Bundestag would face a "crisis of trust." Citizens would not be able to trust deputies who functioned under the shadow of suspicion, and deputies would have difficulty trusting one another. "The Stasi-ghost stands between us. The Stasi-ghost makes us unsure in our encounters with one another."[100] After the debates, though, most deputies apparently decided that lustration was not so crucial to a climate of trust. After the 1994 elections, only 177 of the 672 deputies underwent lustration, and this number included some deputies who had been verified before.[101] The commission on the files found only one instance of limited cooperation with the Stasi.[102]

Trials

After German reunification in October 1990, the German courts slowly began to process the legacy of injustices committed during the period of communist rule in the East. The government had to decide how vigorously to pursue the investigation and prosecution of crimes that occurred under the previous regime. In truth, though, the federal government had only minimal control over these prosecutions. Germany's federal system assigns the task of organizing the prosecutors' offices and the judiciary to the *Länder*, so they were ultimately responsible for overseeing the prosecution of past human rights abuses. During the political transition, the *Länder* in the East faced the formidable task of building up these institutions so that they conformed to Western norms. In the midst of this work, they did make efforts to prosecute the abuses of the past by establishing working groups to focus on "government crimes." However, the prosecution of these crimes proceeded slowly and haphazardly. The flux in personnel hampered progress, since prosecutors had to master unfamiliar issues in putting together these cases.[103]

The federal government did, however, establish a central investigative organ to gather information about these crimes. The state interior ministers combined to form the "Central Investigative Organ for Government and Unification Crimes" in February 1992. With its 300 employees, the organ prepared extensive materials for the states' prosecutors, carrying out (as of 1994) 2,668 investigations concerning murder and attempted murder on the inter-German border, 362 concerning perversion of justice, and 550 concerning kidnapping.[104] Later, Berlin's justice department reported that it had investigated a total of 19,979 cases involving crimes committed in the GDR.[105] These categories of crimes—deaths and injuries at the border, judicial crimes, and crimes committed by the Stasi—comprised the bulk of the investigators' and prosecutors' work.

The results of the numerous investigations were relatively meager. As of August 1994, 45 indictments regarding deaths on the inner-German border had resulted in 20 verdicts. Sixty-one indictments for perversion of justice led to just nine verdicts, while 13 indictments against Stasi agents for various crimes had resulted in six verdicts.[106] By 1996, Berlin's justice ministry reported that it had brought charges in just 367 cases.[107] Of course, even in ordinary cases, the ratio of investigations to verdicts is high. It is safe to say, however, that the results were less than expected. Even the well-financed and relatively well-organized German criminal justice system faced extraordinary difficulties in putting together these cases. Witnesses were old and their memories unreliable. The files containing information about the crimes were widely dispersed among various institutions and regions. Finally, the prosecution of high-ranking officials required the review of an immense amount of materials, such as the stenographic protocols of weekly Politburo meetings over a period of many years. Preparing these materials was incredibly time and labor intensive.

Beyond the practical difficulties inherent in putting together these cases, prosecutors had to contend with numerous abstruse legal debates. The central issue was retroactivity. The German government could not punish individuals for acts that were not forbidden by the criminal law at the time they were committed.[108] Since only those crimes punishable under GDR law could be prosecuted, the West German legal community became embroiled in a debate about how to interpret and apply GDR law. Legal positivists argued that East German law in place at the time should be read literally. The German authorities could prosecute an action only if it was clearly proscribed at the time. This straightforward mode of interpretation was not so simple. East German law was a jumble of competing values. On the one hand, East Germany, like all the socialist states, made a pretense of being a law-based state. Its constitution protected individual rights and freedoms, offered legal certainty, and uplifted the "socialist" rule of law. How should the West German courts interpret this modifier? On the other hand, the constitution established the leading role of the SED.[109] Positivists reached various conclusions about the rules for interpreting GDR law.[110] Other legal scholars cited the precedents stemming from the postwar period and argued that the state should prosecute individuals for any act they knew to be violations of basic human rights, regardless of whether the act was technically legal.[111]

The trials of border guards played a crucial role in public debate and legal developments regarding transitional justice. The first of these trials involved four border guards charged with manslaughter for shooting and killing Chris Gueffroy, who attempted to flee across the Berlin Wall in 1989. Two of the four were found guilty, but their sentences were mild: One received a two-year suspended sentence, while the guard whose bullets actually killed Gueffroy received a three-and-a-half year sentence.[112] Many trials of other border guards ensued; Berlin indicted and tried over fifty guards.[113] The precedent of mild punishments held in subsequent cases. Judges acquitted many defendants and handed down suspended sentences for most others.[114] In sum, more than eighty individuals—including border guards and their superiors—were convicted of participation in the killings at the intra-German border.[115]

In legal terms, it made a good deal of sense to begin the process of holding trials with the border guards. Prosecutors could prove with relative ease which guards had shot and killed people at the border. The decision to prosecute the border guards first was, however, very unpopular. The public perceived that the prosecutors were only interested in the "little fish," while they let the "big fish" flit away. In fact, though, the decision to prosecute the border guards first had more to do with practicalities. Putting together a case against the border guards' superiors required a very large amount of documentary evidence, and the prosecutors combed through stenographic records of the National Defense Council and the Politburo looking in vain for a written order telling the border guards to shoot to kill.

Eighteen months after the first border guard trial, six members of the National Defense Council were indicted on charges of ordering the killings at the border. The most significant of the defendants was Erich Honecker, former leader of the SED. When the ailing Erich Honecker finally came before a German court after his exile in Moscow, he was supposed to face charges for illegally giving the order to shoot at people trying to escape East Germany at the Berlin Wall. The desired outcome was clear: to hold the former general secretary responsible for the deaths that his party ordered in a crude attempt to maintain political control. In theory, such a trial could explore important themes such as accountability, the limits of state power, the decision-making processes in the GDR, and the role of international human rights law. A German public reading the daily press about this trial would learn about the depravities of nondemocratic regimes and the basic principles of liberal democracy. The year of reports about the Nuremberg trials two generations earlier had had that effect.

The case against Honecker did not turn on such broad and edifying themes. In its brief course it took up three key questions: the jurisdiction of Berlin's Constitutional Court; the neutrality of one of the judges; and whether the defendant's ill health precluded a trial.[116] The German public came to view Honecker not as the former leader of an abusive political system, but as a cancer patient. Ultimately, the courts freed him, and he died four years later in Chilean exile.

The trial of the former Stasi chief Erich Mielke was no more successful. Mielke, another ill and elderly member of the National Defense Council, was also charged with ordering the border killings. At the same time, he was facing charges for murdering two Prussian police officers in 1931. The court decided that Mielke was too ill to participate in two trials simultaneously, so the charges relating to the border killings were dropped. Prosecutors focused on the prewar murders. After the young communist Mielke had assassinated the police officers, he fled to the Soviet Union and lived abroad until after the Second World War. Mielke then served as chief of the Ministry of State Security from 1953 until 1989. After his return to Germany and rise to prominence, Mielke gathered the documents about his involvement in the 1931 shooting and stored them in a large safe behind his desk at Stasi headquarters. With the discovery of the neatly compiled files, German prosecutors could move relatively quickly toward a trial of Mielke for the two murders. Of course, to have public value, the trial of Mielke should have investigated his actions as chief of the Stasi—his role in ordering kidnappings and staging political trials, in placing listening devices, and creating networks of internal spies. None of these important historical facts could come to the fore in a trial about the politics of the 1930s. Issues such as the statute of limitations and the reliability of Nazi era documents dominated the trial. In this context, Mielke could emerge as a relatively sympathetic figure.[117]

Three other members of the National Defense Council—Heinz Kessler, Fritz Streletz, and Heinz Albrecht—were found guilty of manslaughter for ordering border guards to shoot to kill. They were sentenced to between four and seven years in prison. All were released early, in part because of their age and ill health.[118] Later prosecutors also brought charges of manslaughter against three members of the Politburo. They received sentences of between three and six-and-a-half years.[119] In sum, then, six government leaders were found guilty of ordering border guards to shoot-to-kill.

The prosecutors' strategy of handling cases relating to former human rights abuses was to start with the easiest cases, like those of the border guards and the 1931 murders by Mielke. In the "easy" cases, the prosecutors had no difficulty in assembling the documents and summarizing the evidence. However, the easiest cases did not provide the desired political catharsis. Society did not join together in condemning the GDR's policy of shooting desperate people who were fleeing across the Berlin Wall. Instead, the public (and judges, as well) began to feel sorry for the border guards who had to make horrible choices in a very tense situation. In the context of his trial, Mielke emerged as an opponent of Hitler, rather than the organizer of the intrusive and abusive Stasi.

Political leaders could have only a minimal role in making decisions about trials. They could provide a budget for a federal investigative organ, which they did. Beyond that, matters took their deliberate legal course, leading one noted scholar to remark on the "juridification of the political process in Germany."[120] Prosecutors put together cases, and courts on the various levels pieced together a jurisprudence for dealing with the challenging cases. In one area, however, the politicians seized the initiative—the statute of limitations.

Representatives within the German Bundestag broadly agreed that the statute of limitations should be tolled for the period during which the communist party had controlled the GDR, approximately from when the GDR was formed in 1949 until German reunification in 1990. The explanation for this consensus along the political spectrum has to do with the fact that the German Parliament had dealt extensively with the issue of tolling the statute of limitations after the Second World War. Since the Federal Constitutional Court had ruled that the statute of limitations was a procedural rather than a substantive guarantee, extending the statute of limitations for any crime not already time-barred did not violate the Basic Law.[121] In order to facilitate the prosecution of Nazi era crimes, the Bundestag first tolled the statute of limitations, then extended it, and finally in 1979 abolished the statute of limitations altogether for both genocide and murder.[122]

These precedents emboldened the Bundestag to recommend a tolling provision for crimes committed during the period of communist rule in East Germany. The law made clear that the tolling provision should apply to all crimes not prosecuted for political reasons in the GDR, including those that were already time-barred.[123]

By changing the law on the statute of limitations, the Bundestag clearly stated its hope that trials of former East German functionaries would proceed. Former communist leaders should not be able to crouch behind liberal democracy's legal technicalities. The laws used for dealing with Nazi era crimes provided a useful precedent, which facilitated compromise.

Rehabilitation

Despite the fact that Article 17 of the unification treaty obligated the parliament to pass a rehabilitation law and arrange for appropriate compensation, the Bundestag was very slow in adopting further legislation on the rehabilitation and compensation of individuals who suffered injustices under communist rule. Until November 1992, when a comprehensive new law finally came into effect, people sought rehabilitation in two ways: by rehabilitation proceedings or cassation proceedings. The Volkskammer had set forth these procedures, which the unification treaty retained in part. In this way, 45,000 people were rehabilitated, and 13,000 cassation proceedings were carried out before the Bundestag adopted revised legislation.[124]

The unification treaty's provisions had numerous flaws. Depending on whether an individual went through a rehabilitation or a cassation proceeding, he was eligible for very different levels of compensation. The procedures were complex and slow. Each case had to be considered individually, and the person seeking rehabilitation bore the burden of proof. The rehabilitation law provided for only measly levels of compensation—approximately 80 DM for each month the individual spent in prison. Finally, the treaty did not address two types of injustices that the Volkskammer had deemed important: unjust administrative decisions and disadvantages in employment based on an individual's political or religious beliefs.

In its initial debates on a new rehabilitation law in May 1991, the Bundestag opted not to discuss the controversial issues of administrative and employment decisions. The focus was entirely on the rehabilitation of individuals who had received unjust and politically motivated guilty verdicts under the communist era criminal law. The tenor of the debates was dry and legalistic. The guiding theme was how to apply West German legal precedents to the novel circumstance of rehabilitating victims of East German injustices. The legislators had no sense of zeal for the moral purpose of the law, and no one described it as an important step in coming to terms with the past. This stands in odd contrast to Germany's experience after the Second World War, when compensation to the victim's of Nazism was considered a way for the country to take moral and political responsibility for its past. The majority in the Bundestag apparently felt they had a legal duty to pass a rehabilitation law, perhaps because the unification treaty explicitly committed them to do so.[125]

The victims' marginalization in German society explains, in part, the Bundestag's lack of enthusiasm for rehabilitation. In unified Germany, the victims of the GDR's injustice were a small and politically powerless group. They did not have strong contacts with any of the major political parties or elites, though, predictably, Bündnis 90 took up their cause. Like victims' organizations in other former communist countries, East German organizations fractured into numerous small groups, none of which could legitimately claim to represent the victims as a whole.[126] In addition, the media, while fascinated with stories about Stasi spies, did not display an interest in rehabilitation.[127]

The government's draft law did not provide for mass rehabilitation of entire classes of individuals who had been found guilty of political crimes. Such a procedure (e.g., used in Czechoslovakia) would be quicker and automatic because it would not require that the individual victim or prosecutor file a request for rehabilitation. However, West German law did not have any precedents for mass rehabilitation. In its legal system, rehabilitation requires consideration of individual cases. According to the draft law, a three-judge panel would evaluate each application for rehabilitation. (No more than one of the judges could come from the former GDR.) To speed matters, the draft law established a list of the GDR's political crimes. A person convicted under these statutes would be presumed eligible for rehabilitation, unless the state proved otherwise.[128]

The political parties disagreed on the amount of compensation. In a typical constellation of preferences, the SPD called for higher social spending, while the CDU, who had spent rather profligately over the course of unification, reclaimed the territory of fiscal restraint. Significantly, though, the parties did not argue for their proposed levels of compensation in terms of what the victims needed or what the budget could afford. Instead they focused on which legal precedent should be applied. The CDU said that the GDR's victims should receive a level of compensation comparable to the victims of Nazism. Since the Holocaust victims received 150 DM for each month they were imprisoned, the CDU suggested that the GDR's victims should receive 300 DM for each month they were imprisoned. The amount was doubled to account for inflation.[129] The CDU also proposed giving a supplement of 150 DM per month to those victims who had remained in the GDR until the travel restrictions were lifted in November 1989. This would compensate for the discrimination in work, study, and travel opportunities that they suffered after their release from prison.

Meanwhile, the SPD said that victims should receive 600 DM for each month in prison because this is the amount disbursed under the *Strafverfolgungsentschädigungsgesetz*, which regulates compensation for individuals who are held in jail and later released because they are innocent.[130] Bündnis 90 proposed an even higher level—900 DM per month—based on the fact that the 600 DM was intended to compensate only for immaterial losses. Former victims should receive an additional amount to cover their material losses, such as lost income.[131]

The compromise adopted allowed people who lived in the GDR until November 1989 to receive a supplement of 250 DM per month, rather than 150 DM.[132] The federal budget for the law was not huge—1.55 bn. DM.[133] The government expected to rehabilitate 100,000 people. As of May 1996, the state had processed 130,000 rehabilitation claims out of 140,000 requests, and it had paid out only 625 mn. DM.[134]

The difficulty in estimating financial consequences was a factor in delaying passage of the law on administrative and employment rehabilitation. The government feared that providing compensation to everyone who suffered from political or religious discrimination would prove procedurally complex and financially draining. When it finally proposed its draft law in May 1993, it made clear that it wanted to strictly limit the law's scope. Full compensation for these injustices was impossible, the government stated, so the law must encompass only the most serious cases.

The law provided for rehabilitation and compensation when an administrative or employment decision "plainly contradicted the rule of law" and when that decision resulted in consequences which "continued to have a direct, hard and unreasonable effect."[135] In particular, the law offered compensation when an individual lost property or a job or when he suffered ill-health as a result of an unjust administrative decision. Furthermore, people who had lost their job or educational opportunities as a result of their political or religious beliefs were given the opportunity for retraining, and their pensions were recalculated to make up for months when their contributions were reduced or nonexistent. They did not receive the right to return to their previous positions, nor did the government confer on the former victims any advantages when they applied for civil service jobs. Victims of unjust decisions could obtain additional transfer payments only if they had special economic needs.

The government estimated that the total budget for the second rehabilitation law would be 183 mn. DM.[136] As of late 1995, victims had filed only 29,000 claims, many fewer than the 70,000 the government had estimated.[137] In retrospect none of the parties were particularly satisfied with the law. Each party put forth recommendations for amending the two rehabilitation laws; even the CDU wanted to increase the amount of compensation.[138] However, the laws were already in place and functioning, and the parties were loath to make changes that would require a review of all the cases. Bündnis 90 complained, "the legitimate expectations of the victims and their organizations have remained unfulfilled."[139]

Given the extensive compensation programs devised after the Second World War and its affluence in comparison with other former communist countries, one might have expected that Germany would be more generous to the victims of the communist regime's injustices. However, many deputies from the West felt that they were already doing enough to make up for the evils of the East German past. They said, "We should remember that we have more to do financially than just come to terms with the past; we must build the future" and that "[t]he most important act of compensation is reunification and the rebuilding of the destroyed country."[140]

In a united Germany, compensation and rehabilitation slipped off the political agenda for several reasons. First, the vast majority of decision-makers had not personally experienced the communist regime's injustices. Debates about the past were thus more dispassionate; they were more like schoolchildren reciting a lesson than engaged politicians rendering a decision. Second, the victims' organizations were feeble, and they did not develop influence with the German political parties. Third, while the postwar experience provided a precedent for offering compensation to victims of unjust imprisonment, it did not establish a template for dealing with administrative and employment rehabilitation. The lack of guidelines made the task of lawmaking more difficult. Parties had very different expectations about what was feasible. Finally, most West German deputies felt that in absorbing the enormous costs of unification, the German state had done enough for their eastern neighbors. Unification was to be their ultimate rehabilitation and compensation.

Truth Commission

By autumn 1991, many East Germans were becoming frustrated with the way the united Germany was coming to terms with the GDR's past. They cited many of the drawbacks of using legal mechanisms to resolve past injustices. First, the law could not work rapidly. Formulating a legal basis for rehabilitation and lustration took time, and then administering these laws involved even greater delays. Second, the rule of law appeared to be a coarse instrument: A defendant in a trial must be found guilty or not guilty, so the state could not affix any intermediate label to political behavior. Politicians could not be found to be "morally responsible" for their offenses. Lawmakers found it exceedingly difficult to craft legal definitions that promoted justice. Any definition of who was a victim of communist rule inevitably excluded some worthy individuals. The legislature avoided the necessity of defining who was a Stasi collaborator because any set definition seemed inadequate. The trials of former communist leaders were filled with complex, technical arguments about the statute of limitations, the applicability of GDR law, and the leaders' legal responsibilities. Finally, a liberal democracy's legal system focuses intensely on the individual: his or her guilt or innocence, qualification for certain benefits, and eligibility to hold certain positions. Collective responsibility is conceptually anomalous. As a result, the legal system cannot address broad questions about the nature of a political system.

The solution proposed by several East German public figures was to form a tribunal to investigate the past. They agreed that a tribunal should make judgments about individuals' moral and political guilt, as well as analyze the nature of the GDR's political system. These judgments would not be legally binding, but they would express society's disapproval of certain behavior. An important aspect of the tribunal would be its origin in society rather than the state. Many East Germans believed that the state of the unified Germany had no right to judge the behavior of former East German officials. Instead, East German society should take over this responsibility. In particular the activists of 1989 had the moral authority to render judgments about the past.[141]

While many political leaders agreed that the legal mechanisms for coming to terms with the past were inadequate, the suggestion to form a tribunal fell under heavy attack. Many felt that there was no one with the moral authority to sit on such a tribunal. The concept of moral guilt was also troublesome. Karl Jaspers had defined it after the Second World War as an element of the war guilt and recommended penance as the means of overcoming this guilt.[142] No one knew exactly what penance would mean in practical terms. Would a person found "morally guilty" suffer any consequences? If not, was moral guilt simply a category of unpunishable guilt? Furthermore, the relationship between a tribunal and the judicial system was unclear. Could a tribunal subpoena witnesses and compel testimony? Would it be at all effective without these powers?

The advocates of a tribunal could not offer convincing, answers to these pressing questions. A former GDR activist and SPD deputy in the Bundestag, Markus Meckel, offered an alternative—a parliamentary commission to investigate the abuses of the past.[143] In March 1992, all the parties in the Bundestag agreed to form an "Enquete-Commission for Coming to Terms with the History and Consequences of the SED's Dictatorship."

Three purposes animated the call for the commission. First, the commission could make up for the inadequacies of the legal mechanisms for dealing with the past. It would offer moral rehabilitation, and ultimately a sense of justice, to the victims. It would place the stain of moral condemnation on the GDR's leaders, even when criminal charges would not stick.[144] Second, publicizing the truth about the GDR's political system was seen as a way of preventing the recurrence of dictatorship in Germany. Knowledge of the truth would contribute to the society's "anti-totalitarian consensus," as the deputies phrased it.[145] Many felt that this reinforcement was very important. With their amazing creative faculties, people are able to manufacture nostalgia around even the ugliest epochs of history. The Germans were witnessing such efforts with the gradual rise of so-called *Ostalgie*, or nostalgia for the east. A legitimate account of the past's troubles would be a splash of icy water in the face of warm, sentimental memories of the cradle-to-grave security in the GDR. Finally, the legislators believed that a better understanding of the past would promote social trust in Germany's divided society. The cleavages between East and West, SED and opposition, as well as Left and Right, had created a suspicious and inhospitable environment for democratic politics. "The report of the Enquete-Commission wants to bring people in Germany into conversation with each other. When people speak with one another and tell each other about themselves, when they work and celebrate together, they will learn to know each other better. They will grow together and be better prepared for our future," said Rainer Eppelmann, the head of the commission.[146]

Germany's Enquete-Commission worked for 27 months, during which time it held 44 day-long hearings and listened to the testimony of 327 witnesses and scholars. The commission studied the power structures of the GDR—the role of ideology, law, the police, the church, the opposition, and the West German government in the political development of the East German state. In addition to a 300-page report submitted to the Bundestag, the commission offered a 15,000-page compilation of its findings and the research submitted to the commission.[147] In general, the commission's work was well received. The Bundestag then established a second Enquete-Commission to continue the work of telling the truth about the past. Germany began to develop an official account of its history.

Conclusion

In East Germany, the democratic transition took place by rupture. Negotiations between the regime and opposition did take place, especially at the Round Table, but the SED was not in a position to impose many conditions on the transition. Its control seeped away to be claimed, not by the democratic opposition as in other countries in the region, but by a powerful West German state.

A transition by rupture leads us to expect a high degree of retribution. In reality, though, the approach to transitional justice during the year 1989–90 was quite mixed. Violent retribution was absent altogether. Trials did not get underway, but this may not indicate the lack of a retributive spirit as much as it shows how the East German judicial system held its breath in confused anticipation of what German unification would bring. The freely elected Volkskammer passed laws facilitating the lustration of its own deputies, members of the government and judges, but it did not have time to carry out these procedures properly. Lustration of the civil service was on the agenda. The Volkskammer's rehabilitation plans were extensive, setting the goal of providing moral satisfaction and compensation to many who suffered under the communist regime. The opposition's approach to truth-telling wavered. During winter 1989–90, members of the citizens' committees agitated in favor of opening the Stasi files, but in the spring, the movement's leadership publicly opposed that step. After the Volkskammer elections, fears of violent retribution subsided, and concern about the integrity of elected officials grew. Opposition figures came out in support of opening the secret police files. In general, East Germany's opposition set a moderate course for transitional justice, navigating between the extremes of violent retribution and passive forgetfulness.

With the unification of Germany, the dynamics of East Germany's transition no longer provide a helpful explanation for the country's approach to transitional justice. Neither is party politics a useful approach. The main West German political parties were not seriously divided about how to come to terms with East Germany's communist past, and they were able to reach a compromise on most of the related issues.

Instead, liberal democratic ideology was important in shaping the debates on transitional justice. Since most of the lawmakers in the German Bundestag were not personally implicated in or affected by the East German regime, they were inclined to view transitional justice as a set of technical problems that demanded legal solutions. Their debates on transitional justice were highly legalistic, leading some to complain about the "juridification" of the issue. German legislators found it easier than their neighbors to find consensus on these issues because they did not always have to go back to the broad foundational principles of liberal democracy. Instead they could turn to precedents from the postwar era. While there was often debate about how to apply legal precedents, these provided a focal point where discussions could begin. The unified Germany came to terms with the legacy of East German communism by applying legal solutions that had already been worked out within the liberal democratic framework of the postwar West German state.

The Bundestag adopted a series of policies of truth and justice:

Trials The Bundestag did what it could to facilitate trials: passing a law to toll the statute of limitations and setting up a central organ to investigate communist era crimes. Nevertheless, the legal barriers to prosecution were high, and there were relatively few trials.

Lustration The united Germany continued the process of vetting judges, and, eventually (on a voluntary basis) members of the Bundestag. It also established a legal basis for the lustration of members of the government and civil service.

Rehabilitation The Bundestag continued the process begun by the Volkskammer. It passed two laws to facilitate rehabilitation of those who suffered imprisonment and/or discrimination by the communist regime.

Compensation Individuals who had been rehabilitated were eligible for compensation.

Truth-Telling The Bundestag opened the Stasi files broadly to both former victims and researchers. It also established a parliamentary commission to analyze the East German political system and its repressive practices.

In the twentieth century Germany devised a useful set of legal tools for dealing with the legacy of repressive regimes. It emphasized that a new democratic regime must take political responsibility for the crimes committed in the name of the state by adopting policies of truth and justice. Now as a united, liberal democratic state, Germany hopes it will never have to use these tools again.

Chapter 4
Poland's Long Search for Justice

Poland took nearly a decade to put in place a series of policies for dealing with its legacy of communist era crimes. The country's negotiated transition to democracy in 1989 is key to understanding why the government chose not to pursue transitional justice in the months after the first elections. When the regime and opposition negotiate the conditions for holding free elections, the regime demands velvet treatment. The opposition, eager for the opportunity to measure its popularity in the electoral process, is willing to accommodate. The result is a democracy where members of the old regime and its collaborators retain the right to hold public office and comfortable civil service jobs.[1] However, the issue of past crimes did not evaporate after Poland's first free elections. In fact, the issue proved to have a remarkable ability to endure.

Polish scholars and politicians have pointed to power politics—a rather crude, jumbled business—as the best explanation for the country's belated adoption of policies of truth and justice.[2] It is true that compared to Germany, where unification largely depoliticized the issue of transitional justice, Poland's debates about how to come to terms with past injustices were messy. Politicians eagerly seized on the issue to advance themselves in the hurly-burly of the post-communist political scene. The former communists attempted to hinder transitional justice, which only served to remind voters of their predecessors' shady dealings. The former opposition had every reason to press the issue, which burnished their fading moral sheen. There is some truth to these generalizations. Poland's first (botched) attempt at lustration was undertaken by the rightist government of Jan Olszewski in 1992. When the former communist Union of Leftist Democrats (SLD) came to power in 1993, they buried the issue in ineffective parliamentary committees.

Power politics is not a sufficient explanation, however. It does not explain two anomalies. Most puzzling is the position of Poland's liberals, heirs to the Solidarity movement who, rather than promoting policies of truth and justice, opposed them strongly for several years after the transition. Furthermore, power politics does not explain why a former communist president would eventually approve both lustration and opening the secret police files.

Ideology, not just power politics, has shaped Poland's approach to resolving the dilemmas of transitional justice. Polish politicians used the conceptual framework of liberal democratic ideology in debating transitional justice. The key question in the debates was: Are policies of truth and justice compatible with the principles of liberal democracy? This framing had important consequences. It meant that the debates tended to focus on the acceptable procedures for implementing various legal remedies. Politicians were constantly measuring proposed legislation against the procedural protections required by the rule of law.

The debates about transitional justice in Poland are largely debates about legal procedures, not historical justice and truth. While procedural debates do not generate intense public deliberation about the moral responsibilities of citizens in a repressive regime, they do create a foundation for broad agreement. Procedure is a tedious topic, but also an inclusive one.[3] The focus on procedure allowed the former communists to enter the debates with confidence. While they were naturally disposed to oppose transitional justice, liberal democratic ideology gave them the opportunity to offer good public reasons for doing so. The former communists' embrace of liberal democratic reasons helped to forge an unexpected alliance between former communists and the committed liberals from the Solidarity camp—an alliance that prevented lustration in Poland during the early years of its transition.

Unlike in Germany, however, Polish politicians could not rely on precedents to solve the knotty legal issues of transitional justice, and they did not immediately grasp all of the ideology's implications for transitional justice. Over time they came to appreciate the subtleties of the relationship between transitional justice and liberal democracy, and their debates grew more nuanced. Their learning occurred in two ways. First, they learned from their own experiences, especially the failed attempt at lustration in 1992. Second, they learned from international experience, both the examples of neighboring countries and the explicit guidelines of international organizations.

Legacy of the Past

A common explanation for Poland's less retributive policies is that its experience of communism was less harsh than that of its neighbors: Easygoing communism evoked minimal retribution. Compared to Czechoslovakia and East Germany, the natural reference points, Poland had a less repressive political system. Instead of the old Stalinist guard of Husak and Honecker, General Wojciech Jaruzelski was Poland's more flexible leader. Unlike Husak, he did not force intellectuals to work at menial labor, and unlike Honecker, he did not muster an all-pervasive secret police. Poland, alone in the Soviet bloc, did not collectivize its agricultural production, so many people sampled the nectar of economic freedom in the countryside. The Catholic Church also provided dissident activity a sanctuary, which was unavailable in more secular communist countries. In its evaluation of political rights and civil rights in Poland for 12 years between 1972 and 1987, Freedom House labeled the country as "partially free" for 8 years. During the same 12 years, Czechoslovakia and East Germany consistently earned the label "not free."[4]

Though Polish communism was in general less repressive than in neighboring countries, the burden of the past is nonetheless weighty. In Czechoslovakia and East Germany, the term "communist past" evokes accumulated, everyday injustices—strict restrictions on career advancement, the meddling of the secret police, and other such smoldering resentments. In Poland, the "communist past" is a series of dates marking occasions when the militia opened fire on striking workers, such as at Gdańsk in December 1970, the Wujek mine in December 1981, and Lubin in August 1982. Whereas Czechs, Slovaks, and Germans talk about their individual experiences with the communist regime, Poles draw on a reservoir of shared communal experiences, and dramatic ones at that. When protesters were shot down on the city streets, the news spread throughout the country. The workers' protests forced the state to engage in open acts of repression. It no longer had a veil of secrecy behind which it could apply its force selectively to troublesome individuals the way its neighbors could. Even Poles who did not personally suffer during these crackdowns share in the recollection that people like themselves did suffer, and they continued to mark the anniversaries of repression with solemn rituals and public conversation.[5] This qualitative difference in the nature of repression means that Polish political leaders have ready opportunities to debate the past: Anniversary dates and public rituals bring large numbers of people together on an annual basis.

Poland's Negotiated Transition—the Round Table

The decision to negotiate with Solidarity was a tortuous one for Poland's communist party, the Polish United Workers Party (PZPR). After the imposition of martial law in 1981, the PZPR had attempted to normalize economic and political developments in the country, but then Solidarity members and other frustrated workers retaliated with a series of strikes in 1988 as economic conditions soured. The PZPR was agonizingly split over the prospect of negotiations. A hard core of party hacks from the lower and middling ranks opposed negotiations, while the party elite favored a more moderate approach in accordance with Gorbachev's reforming spirit.

Solidarity had extended an offer of negotiations to the PZPR in 1987. After its experience with martial law, Solidarity's leadership became convinced that compromise, not radical demands, was the only way to achieve progress toward its political and economic goals. The first Round Table talks between the PZPR, Solidarity, and various other government and opposition groups began on February 6, 1989.

The PZPR's main goal in holding the talks was to acquire the opposition's support and thus the popular legitimacy necessary to carry out desperately needed economic reforms; however, the central issues raised at the Round Table discussions were fundamental political reforms, as Solidarity demanded.[6] The main debates surrounded the rules for carrying out parliamentary elections that were scheduled for 1989. The PZPR wanted to retain control of the parliament and establish a strong presidency, which would act as a guarantor of the PZPR's hegemony. Solidarity wanted to secure the right to participate in the electoral process and to circumscribe the power of the presidency. The compromise allowed for 35 percent of the seats in the Sejm (lower house) to be filled in free elections, while the remaining 65 percent of seats were reserved for the PZPR and its affiliated bloc parties; the entire Senate was to be freely elected. In addition, the PZPR would retain control of the government, the presidency, and the "power ministries" (i.e., the ministries of foreign affairs, interior, and defense), while Solidarity would gain the opportunity to function as a legal organization, contest for parliamentary seats, and share in some of the tasks of governing.

This compromise led to the groundbreaking elections of June 4, 1989, in which the PZPR won only one of the Senate seats and absolutely none of the contested seats in the Sejm. Neither Solidarity nor the PZPR had expected that the electorate would deal the communists such a catastrophic defeat. The months after the elections were filled with cautious hedging. The PZPR could not legitimately retain all the powers granted them in the Round Table agreements, and the bloc parties (mainly the agrarians and small Catholic parties), now unmistakably aware of the PZPR's deficit of authority, shifted their loyalty to the Solidarity camp. Solidarity, however, was loath to see the Round Table agreements unravel; they were the only guidelines for managing a very uncertain political situation. The aftermath of the elections thus led to a new compromise. Solidarity helped in electing General Wojciech Jaruzelski to the presidency, as outlined in the original agreements, and permitted the PZPR to dominate the power ministries. But the opposition claimed the office of prime minister for one of its own, Tadeusz Mazowiecki, who became the first noncommunist prime minister in the Soviet bloc.

As we might expect, Poland's negotiated transition involved many guarantees to the old guard and a conscious decision not to politicize the past. At the beginning of the Round Table talks, both sides made it clear that they understood they could not become embroiled in a discussion of the past, in particular about the imposition of martial law. At an early meeting of the political reform committee of the Round Table, Janusz Reykowski, a PZPR Politburo member, suggested that the two sides would be able to negotiate effectively only if they "would not open conflicts about the past."[7] In earlier talks, Lech Wałęsa had acknowledged, "We should speak about the future. We have different evaluations of the past—of the last 48 years, but we think that it is necessary to save the country."[8] In addition, both sides used the metaphor of the social contract to describe what they wanted to achieve in the Round Table agreements. "Reykowski suggested that the roundtable agreement take the form of 'a social contract' and create a new institution called 'a Council of National Understanding,' which would serve as a forum 'for the creation of the new rules of politics in Poland.' "[9] Meanwhile, Bronislaw Geremek, his Solidarity counterpart on the political reform committee, called for a "social contract for a transitory period."[10] Their shared use of the social contract metaphor outlines an area of agreement: A written declaration based on consensus would usher in new social arrangements, and the past would be set aside.

While the leaders of Solidarity recognized that a negotiated transition would allow the PZPR to retain significant political controls, they viewed gradual reform as the only acceptable option. The PZPR had a monopoly on force and had proven willing to use force in the past; thus, any attempt at revolution would entail bloodshed. Jacek Kuron candidly acknowledged that a negotiated transition would preclude efforts at decommunization: "If the liquidation of the nomenklatura meant that its people would lose everything, then there would be no chance that democratic changes could be accomplished in a peaceful manner."[11] Peaceful reform was Solidarity's main goal.

The "Thick Line"

In summer 1989, the PZPR could not muster support to stabilize its government, and the opposition and the former bloc parties rallied behind the idea of a Solidarity-led government. This turn of events was certainly not foreseen in the Round Table agreements, and Solidarity activists were split about the extent to which the opposition should include the PZPR's reformers in the government. On August 24, the Sejm charged Tadeusz Mazowiecki, one of Solidarity's chief negotiators at the Round Table discussions, with forming a government in which key ministries, including defense and the interior, would remain in PZPR hands.

The appointment of a noncommunist prime minister seemed very revolutionary in August 1989: The rest of Central Europe was under firm communist rule, Poland was a member of the Warsaw Pact, and the USSR still appeared as a threat.[12] Furthermore, Mazowiecki was almost embarrassingly popular. During the autumn months of 1989, more than 80 percent of Poles expressed satisfaction with his leadership as prime minister.[13] It was in this context that Mazowiecki made his famous "thick line" speech before the Sejm on August 24, 1989.

This speech is remembered for setting the tone for how Poland would come to terms with its past. In reading the whole speech, one realizes that Mazowiecki's main goal was to address the country's economic problems and the development of the rule of law.[14] Regarding the latter point, Mazowiecki stressed that the law would protect all people, and he emphasized that any personnel changes would be carried out only in compliance with legal mechanisms. Mazowiecki also spoke of Poland's rightful place in Europe, saying "Europe is a unit which comprises not only the West but also the East." Finally came the most famous line of the speech: "We mark off the past with a thick line. We will be responsible only for what we have done to rescue Poland from the current state of collapse."

One of the intentions of the thick line speech was certainly to reassure Moscow that Solidarity was not about to start anticommunist witch-hunts, which might have inspired the feared Soviets to take action. In being the first Soviet bloc country to elect a noncommunist political leadership, Poland tread very cautiously.[15]

The speech also had a domestic purpose. It sent the message that the new Solidarity leadership, though flush with its unexpected electoral sweep, would not spoil the spirit of the negotiations with the communists.

By permitting negotiations, the communists had earned the right to participate in the politics of democratic Poland.[16] Those Solidarity leaders who had participated in the Round Table discussions with the communists were particularly adamant that there be no lustration.[17]

The "thick line" rhetoric indicated to the PZPR that Solidarity would maintain the cooperative spirit of the Round Table despite the unexpected electoral results. This was not merely a tactical concession to the PZPR. If that were the case, Mazowiecki could have spoken privately with the PZPR to offer them guarantees rather than make a public speech. At the very least, his rhetoric could have been less stark. And if a fear of communist uprising, violent retribution, or Soviet invasion were on his mind, then Mazowiecki and his colleagues could have abandoned the policies of the thick line after the political context changed.

For Mazowiecki and his supporters in Solidarity, the "thick line" was an ideological statement, building on fundamental concepts inherent in liberal democratic theory. The "thick line" involved a principled forgetting in service to a new beginning. Like a social contract, it emphasized a fundamental break with the past and an inclusive new start, which would allow everyone, regardless of their past, to participate in the new political arrangements.[18]

The idea of making a fundamental break with the past is a cornerstone of liberal democratic theory, but the prescribed way of accomplishing the new social contract is to write and ratify a constitution. Poland did not take this route. The "thick line" did not have the symbolic weight of adopting a new constitution. In fact, the transitional year of 1989 involved no symbolic acts with broad social participation to mark the end of the old regime and the inauguration of a new one. Only one speech—a few sentences really—was supposed to serve as a new beginning. Unsurprisingly, this later appeared as an inauthentic break to many Poles, and given the lack of social participation in drawing the "thick line," it was easy for others to portray the policy as the preference of a single party or a single man. The term "thick line" is a catchy phrase, which explains its popularity as a tool for interpreting Poland and its past, but the concept is obscure. No one is sure exactly when the line was drawn or who drew it. And Mazowiecki never went on to elaborate why this approach to dealing with the past was superior.

It is hard to account for the durability of Solidarity's position on the thick line. Why did it not shift its position after the elections and the collapse of communist governments throughout the region? The power politics model suggests that a shift would be advantageous. Pursuing lustration would not be costly: The Soviets were not going to invade the country, and the communists were everywhere under immense pressure. Why not remove them from politics entirely? What constrained Solidarity from banishing the communist party from politics?

During 1989–90, the key political parties developed their positions on the question of transitional justice. To some extent, these positions correspond with the expectations of power politics. The former communists, now called the Union of Leftist Democrats (SLD), and their agrarian counterparts, opposed transitional justice. They obviously had no interest in reminding Poles of the abuses of the past. The more the public remembered the difficulties of life in the People's Republic, the more likely they would be patient with the opposition despite the current economic problems. Interestingly though, the former communists framed their objections in liberal democratic terms. They argued that lustration was legally incompatible with democracy since it violated the principles of inclusivity and due process, as well as the bans on retroactivity and collective punishment.

The extraordinary speed with which the communists adapted to the norms of liberal democracy shows how very attractive the ideology can be. Liberal democracy is essentially an ideology about procedures, which compared to substantive issues provides a more inclusive basis for agreement.[19] The communists pledged allegiance to the procedures, which promised them a fair chance in future political competitions, as well as a guarantee against retribution for past injustices. The ideology contained resources that served the communists' strategic interests.

Poland's nationalist parties, such as Confederation for an Independent Poland (KPN), favored policies of truth and justice, which were vehicles for their political advancement. The nationalists had built their identities around criticizing the communists, and this strategy had rallied supporters successfully in the past. Tarring the communists was a method for reinvigorating a waning sense of solidarity and shifting attention from the problems of the present. Transitional justice also fit in with the nationalists' political philosophy, which stressed moral purity and national sovereignty. The priority was to cleanse the country from foreign influence, and particularly to condemn those who had collaborated with the Soviet-inspired secret police.

Some of the Solidarity movement's heirs on the Center–Right, such as the Center Alliance (PC), joined the nationalists in advocating for policies of truth and justice. Given the weakness of the communists, this portion of the political spectrum saw the liberals—particularly, in the person of Prime Minister Mazowiecki—as their primary source of political competition. They criticized the "thick line," rallying around Lech Wałęsa given his stronger anticommunist position during the presidential campaign of autumn 1990.

Finally, the liberals' position was somewhat puzzling. While power politics would predict that as heirs to the opposition, the liberals would promote transitional justice, Poland's liberal parties, grouped in Democratic Union (UD) and later Freedom Union (UW), opposed it. They argued that transitional justice violated liberal democratic principles and posed a dangerous distraction from the important tasks facing the country. Unlike the other groupings, however, the liberals seemed to have few ulterior motives in adopting this position, which did not seem to enhance their electoral prospects: A dash of anticommunism could have reminded the electorate of the extraordinary leadership many liberals had exhibited during their years in opposition.

Their strong commitment to liberalism helped to differentiate UD from the Center–Right. The liberals had created for themselves a political identity linked to liberal democratic ideology, and they were willing to stick with it even if it did not always yield the most popular results. Liberal democratic ideology thus helped to cement a strange alliance between liberals and former communists, who in agreeing that transitional justice was a violation of the new democracy's fundamental principles, worked together to prevent the passage of laws on lustration and the opening of the secret police archives.

The Contractual Sejm and Transitional Justice

The "thick line" speech and the continued geopolitical uncertainty inhibited transitional justice during fall 1989. Proposed reforms of the Ministry of Internal Affairs and the Security Service (SB) did not envision the dismissal of individuals who had violated human rights during their tenure. Similarly, a bill for reforming the judiciary stopped short of introducing procedures for removing judges who had cooperated closely with the communists and the secret police.[20] The government announced that it would make no efforts to retrieve the PZPR's assets or seize its property.

With the dismantling of communist regimes across Central and Eastern Europe, the precarious balance between the PZPR and the opposition in Poland also begin to shift. Not fearing the Soviet Union's or the Warsaw Pact's disapproval, some subgroups within Solidarity—though not the Mazowiecki government—began to push the issue of transitional justice more forcefully.

Unsurprisingly, the freely elected Senate took the lead in this issue, making it the subject of its first legislative initiative. In December 1989, it proposed legislation to rehabilitate people who were found guilty of political crimes during the communist period. In the ensuing debates, senators emphasized that rehabilitation would make the truth known about the terrible crimes that happened in the past. On a related point, various senators called on the Ministry of Internal Affairs to halt the destruction of its files.[21]

The Senate also called for lustration of the judiciary, even though Solidarity's blueprint for judicial reform had purposely omitted this.[22] Solidarity's defenders claimed that it was impossible to carry out lustration without violating the judges' civil rights. As one senator noted, "We wanted the rule of law, but now we are considering the introduction of a provision which is not based on the rule of law."[23] Adam Strzembosz, the author of the legislation, warned that lustration would create new injustices, rather than remedying old ones.[24] The Senate accepted Solidarity's arguments, and lustration of the judiciary slipped from the political agenda for several years.

Secret Police Files

The year 1990 began with a series of protests against the PZPR. Members of the Independent Students' Union and other youth organizations occupied several PZPR buildings throughout the country and demanded that the buildings be turned over to the state for use by social or educational institutions.[25] The takeover of party buildings also raised the question of what should be done about the party's, and by extension the Interior Ministry's, archives. As they occupied buildings, the students in some cases came across the party's equipment for destroying incriminating files. Outraged by the sacks of shredded documents, they demanded that the state take over and preserve both the party's and Interior Ministry's archives.[26]

The government responded by condemning the students' unlawful occupation of PZPR buildings.[27] However, it also began to take seriously the question of the archives. Sejm deputies from the Citizen's Parliamentary Club (OKP), a faction including many Solidarity supporters, asked the government to guarantee the security of the Interior Ministry's archive. In response, on January 31, Interior Minister Czesław Kiszczak issued an order to halt the destruction of files. This order was praised as a sign of the ministry's goodwill, and neither the government nor the parliament set up an external monitor to ensure compliance with the order.[28] The ministry did form a commission "concerning the archival resources of the Ministry of the Interior," which included individuals from outside the ministry, such as the historian Jerzy Holzer and Solidarity intellectual Adam Michnik. The commission had access to the ministry's archives for a few months, and it compiled a short report on their contents.[29]

At this point, no political group suggested the possibility of opening the files and making them accessible to historians and the broader public. The paucity of debate at this stage in the transition is very different from the experience in Germany where a transition by rupture along with significant social mobilization had placed the issue of secret police files squarely in the center of political debate. In Poland's negotiated transition, the Interior Ministry, still under the leadership of a PZPR functionary, did not want to open the files, which could damage numerous political careers and expose its network of informers. Solidarity did not disagree. Even Poland's Helsinki committee concurred, saying that opening the ministry's archives would create insecurity in the country.[30] Poland's liberals, like their German counterparts, were intent on preventing violence; thus, the files had to remain closed.

It is difficult to be absolutely sure how many of the files were destroyed or when the destruction stopped. In May 1990, the Deputy Prosecutor-General Aleksander Herzog asked the head of the Department of Protection of the State (UOP), the SB's successor institution, to investigate the destruction of documents in a particular district. The UOP responded with a report on the destruction of archives. The report stated that from late August 1989 till early February 1990, a significant proportion of the security service's documents were destroyed, including the operational materials on 1,200 secret informers and materials regarding infiltration of the church and opposition circles.[31] A few years later, the minister of the Interior estimated that 50 percent of the SB's operational materials and 50–60 percent of its documents on informants were destroyed.[32] Some district offices managed to obliterate even more documents—it is estimated that 90 percent of the security service's documents in Gdańsk, birthplace of the Solidarity movement, were destroyed.[33]

The UOP acknowledged that high-ranking SB officers had given the orders to destroy documents in violation of standard protocol. Prosecutors attempted to bring charges against some of the individuals responsible for ordering the destruction of documents. The district court in Łódź heard a case against three state officials who were alleged to have ordered the destruction of files regarding the clergy and the Solidarity movement. Later though, the court halted the investigation on the basis of an amnesty law.[34] A military court did find six military intelligence officers guilty of destroying documents, indeed as much as 30–50 percent of the military intelligence service's archival stores.[35]

Lustration

During the first half of 1990, the Sejm considered several pieces of legislation to overhaul the state's central institutions, including the Ministry of Internal Affairs and the procuracy. The issue of lustration, usually referred to as "verification," arose in the debates concerning both of these legislative packages. It was a particularly controversial topic within the Solidarity camp.

In 1990 it became clear that Solidarity could not remain a united front, and it soon split into various groups, which for simplicity's sake we can divide into conservative and liberal wings. While lustration was not the major issue in determining the split, it did highlight sharp differences between the groups. The conservatives began to advocate a firmly anticommunist agenda, including lustration, while the liberals insisted on strict adherence to the rule of law, which in their view prohibited all but the mildest forms of lustration. Since the ruling faction of Solidarity tended toward the liberal side of the spectrum, the efforts toward lustration were moderate and included ample legal guarantees.

Despite general reservations about lustration, most lawmakers agreed that they needed to design a lustration policy for the Ministry of Internal Affairs, which had exercised repressive policies vis-à-vis the Polish people. In February 1990, the Sejm began consideration of two bills for reforming the ministry. The authors of both bills acknowledged that at least some SB officers could not be reappointed to serve, but they differed sharply in the procedures they recommended for dismissing certain personnel. The government's bill recommended that the Ministry of Internal Affairs verify its own employees.[36] The other bill was sponsored by the OKP, which usually supported the government, but in this case called for more comprehensive reforms than the government was proposing, including an external review of every former Security Service functionary's eligibility for future employment.

Interior Minister Kiszczak's opposition to lustration is instructive. Instead of basing his argument against lustration on what would be good for the ministry under his supervision, he claimed that lustration violated the principle of equality before the law and that it introduced retroactive and collective punishment. That is, lustration would contravene the rule of law.[37] Furthermore, "During the Round Table we together adopted the principle that Polish reforms will be carried out in a peaceful and evolutionary manner."[38] Lustration, he believed, contradicted this principle. Kiszczak praised the Interior Ministry for supporting him as he reached out to Solidarity for the delicate political negotiations of 1989. He went on to emphasize that the ministry, a thoroughly trustworthy and democratic institution, should decide for itself which personnel changes were appropriate.

Ultimately, liberals and conservatives agreed on an arrangement that served as a template for the reform of other bureaucratic institutions. The law abolished the SB and formed an entirely new organization, the UOP. The destruction of the old institution had both symbolic and practical importance. Symbolically, it clearly demarcated the past and the future. Practically speaking, in destroying the institution, the Sejm also abolished the existing regulations on employment. While documents and property were transferred directly from the old to the new institution, the personnel of the old institution were not automatically rehired.[39] The new institution could rehire employees only after they passed through a lustration procedure.

The procedures for lustration were as follows. Each district formed a "qualification commission," which reviewed applications from candidates who had served in the SB and wished to be appointed to the UOP. A central commission in Warsaw heard appeals. The commissions considered whether the candidate had the "moral qualifications" for service, and in particular whether he fulfilled three requirements: He had not violated the law in his previous service; he had not violated the rights or dignity of other persons; and he had not used his position for private gain.[40]

Given the broad wording of these requirements and the diverse composition of qualification commissions in different districts, lustration of the officers was uneven from one district to the next. This led to charges of gross unfairness. Leftist members of the Sejm complained that lustration was an act of revenge, while the liberal ombudsman for civil rights said that the lustration procedures were a form of "procedural nihilism."[41] Of the 14,500 individuals who applied to the qualification commissions for appointment, around 8,000 were approved for further employment in the Interior Ministry's forces.[42] More than two-thirds of those who were rejected appealed to the central commission for a review of their cases, and the ombudsman for civil rights received complaints from 589 people regarding the lustration procedures.[43] Despite the many complaints about the justice of the system of lustration, it was not substantially revised.

The lustration of public prosecutors involved slightly different procedures. The government's bill created a period of exception during which the normal rules for hiring and firing did not apply. Prosecutors signed a declaration describing their professional qualifications and activities. If the Ministry of Justice determined that the declaration was false, the prosecutor would not be reappointed. The Minister of Justice Aleksander Bentkowski, defended this proposal by emphasizing the value of its relative simplicity. The ministry would not have to carry out lengthy, costly, and disruptive disciplinary proceedings for each case. The former communists used liberal democratic ideology to criticize the policy, saying that it violated the rule of law: Prosecutors should not be punished for carrying out the law, even if the law was bad. After the passage of the law, 359 of Poland's 3,278 prosecutors were not reappointed. Later some of these complained to the ombudsman of civil rights that they did not have a means of appeal, and the ministry of justice established a commission to review appeals. It overturned 48 cases.[44] In the end, around 10 percent of the country's prosecutors were dismissed as a result of the lustration procedures.

Trials

As lustration began in the secret police and procuracy, the justice system, under the leadership of Aleksander Bentkowski, began to investigate past human rights abuses. In September 1990, Bentkowski urged military prosecutors to begin investigations into the military's use of force in pacifying the strikes in Gdańsk in 1970.[45] Prosecutors opened cases concerning 23 of the alleged murders at the hands of the SB, and Warsaw prosecutors brought charges against two SB generals for allegedly ordering the murder of the priest Fr. Jerzy Popiełuszko.[46] Despite the justice ministry's evident interest in pursuing cases concerning past human rights abuses, the statute of limitations imposed a serious legal barrier. Furthermore, political leaders were not encouraging these prosecutions, which were perceived as a distraction from the more pressing tasks of judicial reform.

In April 1991, the Sejm rapidly discussed and passed a law to give the existing Central Commission for the Research of Hitler's Crimes additional responsibility for investigating Stalinist era crimes. The stated purpose of the law was to "create real legal and institutional instruments for the . . . search for truth about various actions."[47] The law aimed to facilitate criminal trials of individuals responsible for human rights abuses during the Stalinist period by establishing a group of investigators to examine these cases and by abolishing the statute of limitations for these crimes. However, the Constitutional Tribunal overturned this law in September 1991, arguing that by defining "Stalinist crimes" so broadly, the law retroactively lifted the statute of limitations.[48] This conflicted with Article 1 of the constitution, which says that Poland is a democratic state under the rule of law.

Rehabilitation and Compensation

Hampered in prosecuting crimes, the Ministry of Justice took up the question of rehabilitation. At a press conference on Stalinist crimes, Bentkowski said that a team in the ministry of justice had been working on rehabilitations since October 1989. As of September 1990, he said that the ministry had completed a review of 800 out of the 5,000 rehabilitation cases under consideration.[49] In 1990, the Supreme Court carried out 271 "extraordinary revisions" of cases that involved rehabilitation, mostly of individuals who received unjust sentences during the period 1944–56.[50]

The Supreme Court could not handle all the potential rehabilitation cases by means of extraordinary revision without creating an undesirable logjam in the justice system. The Sejm began to consider legislation to simplify and expedite the rehabilitation procedures, as well as to offer compensation.

The Sejm decided to deal with the question of compensation for past abuses by amending the law on "combatants." The existing system of veterans' benefits along with its administrative apparatus thus came to frame Poland's approach to compensation. As in Germany, relying on precedents was a useful way of simplifying the legislative debates on a complex issue. However, the choice of this particular precedent proved unfortunate. In suggesting that compensation for past abuses by the state should take place within the existing scheme of veterans' benefits, the Sejm put itself in the difficult position of discussing several contentious aspects of coming to terms with the past simultaneously. First, it had to decide which of the existing veterans should continue to receive the benefits of that honor. Some of these individuals had earned their laurels by spying on internal "enemies" for the SB and passing down harsh sentences in the military courts. Should they continue to receive special privileges for this service to the state? Which groups should be excluded? Second, the Sejm had to decide which additional groups of people should be eligible for the benefits.

Both of these questions came up for heated debate in the parliament and later in the courts. The problem of deciding whom to deprive of veterans' benefits was particularly difficult. The bill proposed to deny veterans' benefits to the following groups: Those who collaborated with the Nazi occupiers, individuals who voluntarily served in the German army or the NKVD, and people who were employed in the security apparatus or military intelligence. It also singled out individuals:

> who during the years 1944–1956 were employed or carried out functions in units or in positions associated with the execution of repression of people suspected or found guilty of activities favoring the sovereignty and independence of the Polish Republic, including those in the organs of the prosecutor and the military prosecutor, in the ordinary or military judiciary, and in the prison system.[51]

The post-Solidarity factions in the Sejm were split over this provision. Several deputies raised questions about its legality, asking, for example, how it would be possible to judge people after 45 years and who was really in a position to judge. Liberal members of the OKP called for a full verification of each individual's actions during the war period in order to decide whether that person should retain his or her benefits, perhaps not appreciating the complexity of evaluating the credentials of hundreds of thousands of individuals.[52] Meanwhile, the Left criticized the bill for introducing collective punishment of individuals who served in certain state organs during the Second World War, and it echoed the liberals' insistence that a liberal democracy must establish individual guilt. Others responded that the law would not punish individuals, only deprive them of certain benefits; therefore, the usual guarantees of criminal procedure did not apply. They complained bitterly about the lengthy debate over "whether we will harm one just person from the former Security Department."[53] In its final form, the law did deprive several groups of their veterans' benefits, but court challenges and organizational inertia delayed implementation of the law.

The law also extended veterans' benefits to several groups of people: individuals who fought in Polish underground military groups or in independence organizations; those who fulfilled civil functions in the underground government during the war and in other independence organizations during 1945–56; teachers who secretly taught children during the war; participants in the Poznań uprising of June 1956; and former prisoners of German concentration camps and the Soviet gulag.[54] The combatant law was used to offer compensation to those who suffered during the Second World War and the immediate postwar or Stalinist period. It did not offer compensation to people who suffered repression under Polish communist rule. (The decision to include participants of the Poznań uprising passed narrowly.) The Sejm resisted efforts to include groups like those injured during the 1970 crackdown on demonstrators in Gdańsk in the combatant category.[55]

Instead, the Senate proposed to offer compensation to the victims of post-Stalinist injustices (between 1946 and 1989) on the basis of judicial rehabilitation. The Sejm made two logically interconnected objections to the Senate's proposal. First, several deputies in the Sejm—both former communists and liberals—opposed the fact that the bill covered sentences handed down well past the Stalinist period. Former dissidents like Jacek Kuron and Adam Michnik felt uncomfortable voting on a law that would give them the right to material compensation for their past imprisonment. Michnik scrupulously called on all Sejm deputies who had been repressed in the past to abstain from the vote.[56] The Sejm's second major concern regarding the bill was financial. The Ministry of Justice could not estimate how many people would apply for rehabilitation or how much compensation would be paid out, so the financial impact of the bill was uncertain. At a time of economic difficulties, this potentially heavy burden on the state treasury seemed unjustifiable to many deputies.

Of course, a failure to pass legislation to deal with the problem of rehabilitation would also have costs. The Supreme Court's docket would be clogged with extraordinary revisions for rehabilitation cases, and people who succeeded in these cases could receive compensation for unjust imprisonment under the existing statutes. Furthermore, it was a matter of some embarrassment that Poland's neighbors, Czechoslovakia and Hungary, had passed rehabilitation laws in 1990, while Poland, which had led the march away from communist rule, lagged behind. The Sejm forged a compromise that would limit the potential costs and avoid the sticky debates about when judicial repression ended—a rehabilitation law that encompassed only the years 1944–56.[57] Table 4.1 shows the number of cases and the amount of compensation paid out on the basis of this law.[58]

Table 4.1 Rehabilitation of persons who were repressed during 1944–56

Year	*Applications*	*Cases reviewed*	*Individuals receiving compensation*	*Compensation paid (new złoty)*
1991 (May–Dec.)	8,332	5,369	n/a	4,570,396
1992	10,940	8,670	3,923	43,951,878
1993	8,519	9,020	6,614	88,195,609
1994	5,439	5,586	7,538	88,481,588
1995	7,873	9,363	7,546	87,039,191

Truth-Telling and the October 1991 Election

As early as August 1989, the Sejm established a parliamentary commission to investigate allegations that the Security Service—which was still under PZPR control—had been involved in political murders during the 1980s.[59] The commission, later known as the Rokita commission after its leader Jan Rokita, compiled a list of 93 persons who had died under suspicious circumstances in the Interior Ministry's custody from 1981 to 1989 and began investigating the cases one by one. Even though leading intellectuals favored the thick line and inclusivity, they also saw that truth-telling was a valued goal. Thus, the commission had the support of the opposition members of the Sejm, such as Adam Michnik, who spoke of the need for "historic truth" in the midst of the country's changes.[60]

The Rokita commission encountered numerous difficulties in trying to carry out its tasks. First, the commission included several members from the PZPR who failed to do their share of the investigatory work, thus burdening other members of the committee.[61] Second, the commission did not have the power to subpoena witnesses. While it did question some witnesses and visit the location of a few alleged murders, it could not compel the testimony of the most prominent witnesses.[62] Third, though the Ministry of Internal Affairs was supposed to provide the commission with the necessary documentation, the ministry, still under Kiszczak's leadership, had little reason to be forthcoming. Even as the commission began its work, the ministry was destroying many of its files, including those that were deemed relevant to the commission's cases.[63] Given the dearth of witnesses and documents, the commission had recourse mainly to the files of the Ministry of Justice, which was headed by an individual more sympathetic than Kiszczak to the commission's goals.[64]

The commission made its final report to the Sejm just before the October 1991 parliamentary elections. The report included recommendations concerning specific cases, as well as general comments about the policies and practices which led to the suspicious deaths. The commission had investigated 122 suspicious deaths of persons in SB custody, recommending in 88 cases that prosecutors begin (or renew) criminal proceedings against Interior Ministry officials and/or other individuals, especially prosecutors, who may have been involved in covering up the cause of the death. The commission named nearly one hundred Interior Ministry officials and 70 prosecutors whom it considered unsuitable for further employment in the state organs.[65]

Given the limitations on the commission's investigatory powers, the commission made use of the available evidence, namely the record of the initial investigations in these cases. As a result, they were in a position to comment extensively on how Poland's communist regime had made a legal reckoning with these suspicious deaths. Their main conclusions were: (1) that cooperation between the interior ministry and the prosecutors was extensive, and (2) that the Interior Ministry acted in an atmosphere of almost total impunity. Under communist rule, top–state officials made it clear that Interior Ministry employees should not be brought to justice for their crimes. As a result, prosecutors did not bother to request documents from the Security Service, and the courts routinely dropped charges against Interior Ministry employees. In the rare cases where an Interior Ministry employee was tried and found guilty, the courts applied the mildest possible sentence.

The Interior Ministry cooperated closely with procurators to protect themselves against judicial inquiries. The cooperation took several forms. The commission found the handwritten comments of Interior Ministry officials (including the minister himself) in the margins of prosecutors' files.[66] The Interior Ministry gave prosecutors express instructions on how to investigate a case, and sometimes it carried out the necessary investigations itself. In some cases, the Interior Ministry actually prepared documents for the prosecutor's signature. The report stresses that these practices were not unusual; they were not merely the product of close personal relations or the operation of an "old boys' " network. "This model had a systemic character. It had a range of unwritten, but universally observed principles."[67] As a result, the Interior Ministry did not eschew illegal acts. "Interior Ministry officials knew that they would enjoy immunity, regardless of the results of their activities."[68]

In the Sejm, reactions to the Rokita commission's report varied. Conservatives generally approved of the report. OKP deputies called for further lustration of prosecutors and the Interior Ministry based on the report's information. The former communists did not exactly repudiate the report, but they tried to minimize its importance. They warned that the report should not be used for electoral purposes, and they called for a "Spanish model" of reconciliation between different social groups. They argued that the Interior Ministry should not have to take collective responsibility for the crimes of the past; rather, individuals who committed criminal acts should be brought to justice. Finally, the former communists also reminded the deputies that their party had been ready to take the path toward democratic reforms; therefore, not everything about the old system could be condemned.[69] Jacek Kuron, representing Solidarity's intelligentsia, offered support for the report, but with significant reservations. He argued that the country should not blame any one group or institution for all the problems of the last 40 years, calling collective responsibility unacceptable in a state under the rule of law. He agreed with the former communists that Poland should adopt the Spanish model of setting the past aside for the sake of building a strong future.[70]

Unlike truth commission reports elsewhere, including in neighboring Germany, the Rokita commission report was never broadly circulated. This is probably because the report names Interior Ministry officials, prosecutors, and judges suspected of committing crimes, even though the privacy of suspects in criminal proceedings is protected by law. While the report is available to the public in the parliamentary library, it is not to be found elsewhere. In the midst of Poland's last-minute preparations for important parliamentary elections, the report received very little attention from the media.

In the run-up to the elections, the splits in the Solidarity camp grew sharper. The conservative PC resisted cooperation with liberals, who now coalesced in groups like the Congress of Liberal Democrats (KLD) and the UD. While the main differences between the PC and the liberals had to do with personality conflicts and the methods of economic reform, the groups' diverse evaluations of Poland's transition to democracy also crept into their public statements. The liberals, whose leaders had participated in the Round Table and the Mazowiecki government, held that Poland was on the right course; it needed to stick with the painful economic reforms and the gradual legal and political transformations for a few more years before all the benefits of this path would manifest themselves. The liberals' party documents did not directly address the question of de-communization, but they made the point that the entire transition should take place in accordance with the rule of law: "Limiting or suspending the democratic rules of the game or civil and employee rights may not in any case be a means for . . . solving social problems and conflicts."[71]

Meanwhile, the PC offered a critical evaluation of Poland's gradual transition. "Authority cannot be returned to the Republic without an express break with the fatal principle of the continuation of communist structures and institutions. Only special parliamentary laws can once and for all separate us from the *nomenklatura*, unjust laws, bureaucratic centralization and undemocratic social relations."[72] Though the parties disagreed fundamentally about the necessity and proper means of coming to terms with Poland's communist past, the issue of economic reform eclipsed lustration as a campaign issue. The 1991 elections were not about the past, but about Poland's economic future.

The Olszewski Government's Botched Lustration Attempt

After the country's first totally free election in October 1991 gave Solidarity forces the opportunity to form a government, the process of putting together a coalition moved very slowly. The PC insisted on Jan Olszewski as the candidate for prime minister because they believed only he would guarantee a thorough process of de-communization. Meanwhile, Wałęsa attacked de-communization, saying that the conservatives' anti-communist "witch hunts" had mobilized the former communists and contributed to their strong showing in the election. Finally the Center–Right formed a government under Jan Olszewski. As a model of power politics would predict, Olszewski's government took a strong interest in the issue of lustration. At his first press conference, the new Minister of Internal Affairs Antoni Macierewicz announced that he was prepared to release the names of all people who collaborated with the SB if the Sejm adopted the appropriate legislation, and he called for the lustration of all high government officials.[73] Macierewicz continually toyed with the lustration issue. He leveled numerous accusations at his predecessors, suggesting that they had allowed certain politicians to see their personal files and that they had carried out secret lustration before the 1989 and 1991 elections. The predecessors denied these charges. The Ministry of Internal Affairs began preparing a lustration bill, using the German and Czech laws as models.[74]

Olszewski's government was chronically weak. Throughout the first several months of 1992, members of his government carried out negotiations with potential coalition partners, but he could not draw all the non-leftists into a solid base of support. The liberals (UD, KLD) and conservatives (PC, KPN) were too far apart. Olszewski's uncommitted, sparse supporters had little sway in the Sejm. By late April, the attempt at forming a grand coalition had collapsed, and factions of both sides heaped blame on one another. On May 26, President Wałęsa wrote a letter to the speaker of the Sejm stating that he had lost confidence in the Olszewski government.

On May 28, Olszewski and the lustration-hungry interior minister were handed a strange opportunity. A small, conservative party called the Union of Real Politics proposed a draft resolution giving the Interior Ministry one week to turn over full information about state officials' collaboration with the SB. After some discussion about procedural issues, the Sejm decided not to hold a debate on this extraordinary document. It voted against sending the resolution to committee and then adopted it in its first reading.[75] The SLD refused to participate in the voting. Liberals were also upset. After the resolution passed, Jerzy Ciemniewski, a UD deputy, walked out of the Sejm saying, "In this situation I feel an obligation to inform you that I cannot participate in the further work of the Sejm." He complained that the law violated basic human rights and the rule of law.[76]

The resolution was fundamentally flawed, as the Helsinki Committee and the ombudsman for civil rights were quick to point out.[77] It did not specify to whom the Interior Ministry should release the information about collaborators, and it did not envision any process for individuals to appeal their designation as collaborators. The deadline for releasing this information was very short—only about a week away—making errors extremely likely.[78] To complicate matters, just three days after the resolution passed, President Wałęsa publicly withdrew his support from the Olszewski government. A weak government trying to cling to power was handed a flawed law that invited abuse. Political disaster ensued.

On June 4, Interior Minister Macierewicz sent the parliamentary factions a list of elected officials who were designated as SB informers in the ministry's archive. The list included not only the opposition activist Leszek Moczulski (KPN), but also President Lech Wałęsa. While Wałęsa admitted that he signed certain papers with the Security Service in the 1970s, he certainly did not act as an informer. The presence of Wałęsa's name on the list made the entire lustration effort incredible. Later that night the Olszewski government lost a vote of confidence in the Sejm.

Soon after Olszewski left office, the Sejm charged a committee with investigating the execution of the May 28 resolution. Interestingly, the committee was headed by Ciemniewski, the liberal who had walked out of the Sejm after the resolution passed. The parties differed greatly in their evaluation of what had happened during the tumultuous days of early June, and they could not agree on how a democracy should approach lustration. In general, the debates surrounding the committee's report were of very poor quality, largely consisting of *ad hominem* attacks.

Despite the highly emotional tone, it is possible to make the following generalizations about the parties' strategies. While the SLD was eager to discredit the whole idea of lustration for political reasons, its deputies employed liberal democratic arguments to make this point. They maintained that both the resolution itself and its execution were legally flawed. Lustration could not be carried out in a fair way. Individuals in the Interior Ministry had falsified many documents, making any attempt at discerning who was a collaborator impossible. The SLD criticized the conservatives for advocating an illiberal project such as lustration.[79] Employing a similar ideological language, the liberal UD insisted that individuals named on Macierewicz's list be presumed innocent of the charges of collaboration. Given the poor state of the archives, they argued that no one could determine who had collaborated. Lustration was impossible.[80] Meanwhile, the more conservative factions did not condemn the lustration effort so wholeheartedly. They acknowledged that the Interior Ministry had made mistakes in its execution of the resolution, but they wanted to salvage the resolution, or at least some form of lustration. They argued, "Society should learn the truth, in accordance with the principles of democratic openness."[81] The debates pitted the leftists' and liberals' commitment to due process against the conservatives' call for truth-telling.

The UD Government and Transitional Justice

After the collapse of the Olszewski government, the post-Solidarity forces managed to cobble together another coalition, this time led by the liberal UD's Hanna Suchocka. No one could make the issue of lustration magically disappear from the country's agenda, but the liberals wanted to minimize the issue's explosive political impact and prevent any disruption of their fragile coalition. By early September, the Sejm was considering six proposals on how to carry out lustration.

With a new government in place and greater distance from a summer of mutual recriminations, the parliamentary debate in the autumn took on a more measured tone. It indicated that a certain amount of learning had taken place since the last attempt at lustration. The main lesson was that lustration procedures must respect the principles of due process. Without protections for the accused, lustration could damage the political reputation of innocent persons, as well as the good name of the new democracy. The debate was lengthy, detailed, and focused, unlike the cursory discussions that preceded the hasty passage of the May 28 resolution. The individuals presenting their parties' lustration proposals emphasized the provision of legal protections for the accused and appeals processes to guard the innocent.

The debate of September 5, 1992, was a fruitful ideological deliberation on the relationship between democracy and lustration. The liberal UD and leftist SLD believed that lustration was incompatible with democracy. The UD argued that lustration could not be done in a way that respected all the principles of liberal democracy. The files were too unreliable; people could be removed from their jobs only on the basis of costly legal proceedings; the idea of lustration stemmed from a "totalitarian" way of thinking.[82] The leftists took a similar tack. They argued that lustration involved an unconstitutional violation of due process and an illiberal concept of collective guilt. In fact, Józef Oleksy called lustration "a direct legacy of the practices of bolshevism and authoritarianism," and his colleague warned that lustration was leading the country "to the brink of a new totalitarianism."[83] Both the UD and the SLD charged that lustration violated the principle of democratic inclusiveness. They defended the decision made at the Round Table to embark on a gradual course of reform, saying that compromise was a core value of democracy. The SLD lauded the Spanish model of reform, where a gradual, negotiated transition paved the way for inclusive politics.[84]

Another liberal party, the KLD, did not reject lustration outright, since they thought it could be useful in preventing blackmail and political instability. However, they recognized that lustration posed many procedural difficulties in a democracy. They attempted to write a lustration bill that would meet the procedural requirements of a liberal democracy—ample guarantees for the accused and a very limited definition of who would be screened in a lustration procedure. Nevertheless, they pointed to unavoidable practical difficulties. Any lustration procedure would have to rely on the documents of the Security Service, which have a questionable level of accuracy.[85]

Meanwhile, the more conservative parties were no longer so emotional or abrupt in voicing their support for lustration. Instead, they were increasingly careful to hew their arguments to fit in a liberal democratic framework, emphasizing the importance of certain rights. Their core argument was that lustration was necessary for the building of a stable young democracy. This was explained in two ways. First, they maintained that in a democracy, people had the right to know the truth about the past. If a candidate for public office previously collaborated with the secret police, then his electorate should be able to factor this piece of information into their calculations of democratic choice.[86] Second, they contended that former secret police agents might sabotage the process of democratic reform.[87] Democracy has a right to defend itself against subversive anti-democratic forces.

The conservatives were adamant in arguing that a lustration law could be crafted carefully so as to respect the principles of liberal democracy. A lustration law must afford the accused a right to defend themselves and an opportunity to appeal; it must clearly define the criteria for finding someone guilty of collaboration.[88]

Following the debates, all six lustration bills were sent to committee for further discussion. Several months later, the Sejm decided to establish a special subcommittee to continue work on two of the bills—the KPN's and KLD's. Citing its opposition to lustration, the UD refused to participate in this committee.[89]

Though the liberals and former communists wanted to keep lustration off the political agenda, the issue continued to nose its way to the surface of public life. The absence of lustration was creating the opportunity for wild allegations that were difficult to refute. The breaking story in early 1993 was the publication of a book *Lewy Czerwcowy* in which Jarosław Kaczyński, formerly one of Lech Wałęsa's supporters, accused the president's aide Mieczysław Wachowski of collaboration with the Security Service.[90] This accusation was only one of the many criticisms leveled against Wałęsa by Kaczyński and other conservative politicians who had stomped out of the Wałęsa camp. Kaczyński indicted the entire transition process in Poland, arguing that Solidarity had made many tactical errors at the Round Table because certain (named) members of Solidarity's negotiating team were very eager to please the communists. Wałęsa tried to clear Wachowski's name and threatened a libel lawsuit against Kaczyński. After Prime Minister Suchocka ordered an investigation of the case, the Justice Minister appointed a prosecutor to be in charge; however, it came out that the prosecutor had participated in political trials in the 1980s. Suchocka then dismissed the Justice Minister.[91] Wałęsa asked the Ministry of Internal Affairs to publicize all its files about him to refute Kaczyński's allegation that he had collaborated with the Security Service in the early 1970s. The ministry refused, since the president did not have legal authority to order the release of secret documents.

Besides this messy affair, numerous libel cases stemming from Macierewicz's release of the names of alleged secret agents were winding their way through the courts. The lingering conflict and potential for further destabilizing, if untrue, revelations might have encouraged the Solidarity-led parliament to pass a lustration law; however, the UD remained opposed to lustration on principle. The liberals' ideological commitment determined their anti-lustration stance.

Contrary to the predictions of power politics, the Solidarity coalition in the Sejm did very little to come to terms with the past during its ten months in power. At the same time, slander and scandal became a distressingly common aspect of Polish political life. Even the opponents of lustration were frustrated with this outcome. One noted, "The issue has been resolved in the worst way one can imagine. It remains in the center of attention, yet in practice nothing has been done."[92]

Trials

The liberal regime did not change laws or build an institutional apparatus to facilitate the prosecution of past human rights abuses. Criminal trials against individuals who had committed crimes under the old regime continued at a slow pace. The Central Commission for the Research of Hitler's Crimes made little progress in studying Stalinist era crimes and preparing cases for prosecution, in part because the legal situation was confused. The Constitutional Tribunal had overturned part of the original legislation, and it was not clear how the statute of limitations would apply to crimes committed in the 1940s and 1950s.

Other problems plagued the commission. Despite its new responsibilities, it did not have the money to hire additional personnel.[93] Many of the researchers were reluctant to investigate the communists' crimes, since they feared that the communists might return to power. The Central Commission's slow progress in bringing charges derived in part from the division of labor between the commission and the prosecutors. The commission prepared evidence against a particular individual and then forwarded its file to the appropriate prosecutor's office. The prosecutor then decided how to pursue the case. Sometimes prosecutors perceived the need to refer the case back to the commission for supplementary materials. During these delays, more witnesses died or lost the ability to testify. Furthermore, district prosecutors did not always have the deep historical understanding necessary for handling these cases.[94]

By August 1992, the commission had investigated 293 crimes of the Stalinist era; however, these investigations did not lead to a single arrest until Adam Humer, former director of the Investigation Department of the Ministry of Public Security, was detained on charges of murdering an opposition activist and beating and torturing prisoners.[95]

Meanwhile, the judicial system was processing several cases involving crimes committed during the later period of communist rule. The District Court in Katowice heard charges against 24 people, including General Czesław Kiszczak, for the shootings at Wujek. The District Court in Warsaw indicted three people from the Citizens' Militia for the alleged beating and death of Grzegorz Przemyk, the teenaged son of the opposition poet Barbara Sądowska. In Legnica, the District Court began hearing arguments against three Citizens' Militia officers for shootings that occurred during the suppression of a 1981 strike in Lubin. Meanwhile, in Gdańsk, the military and civilian procurators disputed which office had jurisdiction over the shootings that took place during the 1970 strikes.

Rehabilitation

While the rehabilitation of individuals sentenced during the Stalinist period continued apace, the parliament had not adopted legislation to facilitate the rehabilitation of people who had been sentenced for their political activities in the later communist period, especially during martial law. Under a relatively stable post-Solidarity government, the Ministry of Justice took this matter into its own hands. In December 1992, the first deputy prosecutor-general requested that district prosecutors review all cases that had to do with the decree on martial law or any opposition activity during the period 1981–89. The prosecutors had various tools at their hands to effect a rehabilitation of those who had received unjust sentences. In some cases they carried out an extraordinary revision of the case, while in others they annuled the sentence. Throughout 1993 the district prosecutors went through the cases with the assistance of three prosecutors in the Ministry of Justice assigned specifically to this task. As of February 1994, the district prosecutors recommended rehabilitation in 1,081 cases affecting at least 2,016 people.[96]

On May 28, 1993, just a year after the disastrous lustration resolution, the Sejm again took action that led to an unexpected political transition. It voted no-confidence in Hanna Suchocka's government. President Wałęsa responded by disbanding the parliament and calling for new elections. Thus, Poland marked the collapse of the Olszewski government in 1992 with yet another failed government in 1993.

The Left Returns to Power

The splits in the post-Solidarity groups gave the Left an opportunity to consolidate forces. The SLD and Agrarians (PSL) put together an electoral platform that appealed to Poles who were frustrated with the meager rewards of the country's economic reforms. After the elections, the two parties formed a government headed by PSL leader Waldemar Pawlak, which enjoyed a 66 percent majority in the Sejm. The former communists' electoral success led the losers to introspection. Throughout Central Europe, the Left was proving surprisingly adept at reinventing itself.

The former communists in Poland used this moment—four years after the transition—to reassure the country that they had made a decisive break with the past. Once in power, they could afford to make a gesture of repentance. In November, Aleksander Kwaśniewski, the leader of the SLD, gave a speech to the Sejm in which he apologized on behalf of the SLD for the abuses of the past. He also stressed that his party wanted to "finish the process of coming to terms with the past" and to undertake cooperation with all political parties, regardless of their history. Members of UD, along with President Wałęsa, responded very favorably to the apology.[97]

With the Left's ascendance to power, one might expect a dramatic change in the country's policies of coming to terms with the past; however, the shift was subtle, largely because the post-Solidarity governments had adopted very modest policies of truth and justice during the years 1989–93: lustration of the prosecutors and secret police; rehabilitation of political prisoners from the Stalinist era; investigation into mysterious deaths from 1981 to 1989. The Left had a rather ambivalent attitude toward transitional justice. On the one hand, Poland's political Left did not favor extensive efforts to come to terms with the past. The more the Polish public discussed the past, the more likely they were to think about the abuses and injustices committed by the PZPR, the SLD's immediate forebear. The SLD wanted to keep attention focused squarely on the present and the future. On the other hand, the Solidarity forces' efforts at coming to terms with the past had not been particularly harmful to the SLD; in fact, one could argue that they were rather beneficial. The Solidarity forces used the issue of decommunization to attack one another, rather than to rally against the Left. By 1993, both the SLD and the post-Solidarity forces considered the past a political quagmire.

The Left's return to power resulted in only slight changes to the legislative agenda. The new Sejm did not resurrect the lustration subcommittee. The Sejm ceased its investigation into the destruction of Politburo files.[98]

Compensation

In February 1994, the Constitutional Tribunal overturned the provisions for depriving veterans of their benefits on the basis of their previous employment in the security apparatus. The ombudsman for civil rights had complained that Article 21.2 of the law "on combatants" violated the principle of equality before the law in that it deprived all persons "who were employed in the apparatus of public security" of their veterans' benefits, regardless of what a specific individual did while working for the security apparatus. The Constitutional Court agreed with the ombudsman's assessment that the law was not tailored narrowly enough. It should have excluded only individuals who worked in those parts of the state security apparatus that were engaged in repression. The Constitutional Tribunal defined the repressive apparatus as including only the Security Department (UB), Security Service (SB), and Military Intelligence (IW), but not the entire police and judiciary.[99]

The SLD-controlled Sejm used the occasion of the court's decision to press the issue even further. It proposed an amendment to the law on combatants to narrow the categories of persons who would be excluded from veterans' benefits. According to the bill, only people employed in those divisions of the UB and the IW that were known to commit acts of repression would lose their benefits *en masse*. In all other cases, such as those involving the military courts or the SB, the state would have to show that a particular individual had violated the existing law or basic human rights before depriving him of his veterans' benefits. This test was much stricter than the Constitutional Tribunal required.

In parliamentary debate, some SLD deputies complained that the bill still contained an element of collective responsibility. They sponsored an amendment saying that individuals could lose their benefits only if the state proved that they personally carried out repressive acts. Perhaps this appeal to the rule of law would have carried more weight if the SLD's representative, Marek Dyduch, had not gone on to give a very controversial account of Polish postwar history:

> In the years 1944–1956 a kind of ideological war and a real armed struggle occurred. . . . These reprehensible methods were applied by both sides, maybe not to the same extent, but a crime . . . is always a crime and should be condemned.[100]

He was constructing the argument that since all sides had committed crimes, mutual forgiveness was the only way to facilitate a national reconciliation, similar to that which occurred in Spain.

Dyduch's speech raised the ire and consolidated the opposition of the post-Solidarity forces. Despite its deep concerns about the rule of law, the UW, the successor to the UD, criticized the SLD's amendment and rejected the idea that Poland had experienced a civil war with comparable atrocities on each side. Other former opposition groups emphasized the fact that the state was not planning to punish individuals who worked in the repressive apparatus, but only wanted to deny them certain privileges. The procedural requirements for the latter were considerably less stringent than for the former. The agrarians, who had opposed the Soviets' imposition of a communist regime, also could not accept this revisionist view of history.

Parties of the Right kept silent as the UW made a spirited defense of its bill. In this debate one senses the onset of the liberals' frustration with the Left. Though the Left was carrying out many of the economic reforms that the liberals had inaugurated, the Left insisted on its own version of Poland's history. Its unwillingness to acknowledge the truth about the past greatly upset the liberals' usual equanimity. As one UW member exclaimed, "I tell you, one could think that soon we will confirm that in those years nothing evil at all happened, that some strange red dwarves made all the trouble."[101] Ultimately, in light of President Wałęsa's veto, the Sejm had to abandon its efforts to revise the law on combatants.

Lustration and the Secret Police Files

The Left-dominated Sejm held its first debates on lustration in the middle of 1994. Before it were no less than eight bills containing proposals for some form of lustration. Despite the great variation in the bills before the parliament, the debate was muted. The SLD put forth bills that had little in common with lustration: Their idea of lustration was for the government to run a general background check on high officials to make sure they were not felons. They also wanted to give the Ministry of Internal Affairs the power to declassify documents and to lift the oath of secrecy at its discretion. The Minister of Internal Affairs lauded these bills, saying that they were similar to laws in the West—a high form of praise.[102]

Meanwhile, the liberals' attitude toward the secret police files gradually began to change. In 1994, UW, the new alliance of liberals, put forward a bill recommending that the secret police open its files to the public. For nearly five years they had said that the files could not be opened without unacceptably violating due process and civil rights. These concerns still weighed heavily on the liberals' minds, and the change in policy was reluctant. Introducing his party's bill, Janusz Niemcewicz first outlined all the pitfalls of opening the files and then said, "We are putting forth our project without enthusiasm, but with the hopes that we can close this chapter of our history."[103]

The liberals' new focus on the fate of the secret police files can be explained in two ways. First, the liberals had refined their ideological position on the basis of experience. Leaks from the secret police archives spurred the circulation of damaging rumors, forcing victims of these allegations to undertake expensive and lengthy libel suits to clear their names. The closure of the files was imposing heavy costs on innocent people. Liberals began to call for "civilized lustration" to order the chaos caused by accusations that could not be decisively refuted.[104] Second, the former communists' victory in the Sejm elections of 1993 gave rise to sobering reflection among the heirs of the Solidarity movement. As in East Germany, liberals became more concerned about the fate of the files once they were no longer in control of them. Some liberals suspected that their acceptance of the former communists' right to participate fully and unreservedly in the new democracy had made it easier for the public to cast a vote to return them to power. The "thick line" was supposed to include the communists in the new democracy, but not to facilitate their full political rehabilitation.[105]

The liberals' proposal came at the wrong time, however. The leftists controlled the Sejm, and they sent only their watered-down bills to committee. The Sejm abandoned the topics of lustration and the files for another two years.

Trials

Despite the ongoing efforts of the Central Commission to facilitate the prosecution of crimes committed during the Stalinist era, and in particular the long-running trial of Adam Humer and his 15 associates, the question of whether the statute of limitations applied to these cases was still unclear. With controversial cases in the pipeline and the statute set to lapse for several cases stemming from the martial law era, UW brought forward a proposal to amend the criminal code to say that:

> The statute of limitations for deliberate crimes against life, health, freedom or the administration of justice, which are punishable by the deprivation of liberty for a period of more than three years and were committed by public officials in the period 1 January 1944 until 31 December 1989 during or in connection with their official duties, begins to run as of 1 January 1990.[106]

The SLD responded by saying that the bill was completely unnecessary. "How long will we continue to carry out exorcisms of the past?" asked one deputy.[107] The SLD held that any trial should be carried out under the existing guidelines of international law. If a crime was a war crime or crime against humanity, then no statute of limitations applied. If the crime did not fit this definition, then the domestic laws regarding the statute applied.

UW, the party of the "thick line," was moving toward a new appraisal of the ongoing political relevance of the past. "Responsibility for the past is such a puzzle that it returns like a boomerang in long historical periods."[108] It introduced a new comparative reference into the debate about Poland's past by describing France's half-century of efforts to come to terms with its relatively brief period of Vichy rule. After expressing his shock that many younger SLD deputies seemed oblivious of the harm caused by their party in the past, Jan Rokita mused, "Did we really do the right thing by eliminating collective responsibility from Polish public life in the last five years?"[109]

Ultimately, the SLD-controlled Sejm approved UW's language on tolling the statute of limitations as a part of a large package of reforms to the criminal code.[110] As a result of the law, the statute of limitations would not lapse for several important cases from the martial law era, such as those concerning the shootings at Wujek in 1981 and Gdańsk in 1970.

On March 7, 1996, the Warsaw Regional Court found Adam Humer guilty on nine of the twelve charges of torture. He was sentenced to nine years in prison; ten of his subordinates received sentences ranging from three to eight years. The judge described the case's significance by saying, "Despite everything, the case captured a history that was an open wound in the hearts of many Polish families. It exposed the mechanisms, which were unprecedented in acts of terror and lawlessness."[111]

Neither the Ministry of Justice nor the Central Commission for the Investigation of Hitler's Crimes collects data on the number of trials of state officials from the communist era, so it is difficult to state with any certainty how many have occurred. A review of government documents and press reports has turned up at least thirty trials of former state officials, stemming from both the Stalinist and martial law eras.[112] Though Poland has the reputation for having eschewed trials of former communist and police leaders, in reality the number of trials is not much lower than in Germany. Even without much institutional and legal support, Polish procurators took this work seriously.

The Oleksy Affair

The presidential election of November 1995 led to the next eruption of bitter allegations about the past. After his defeat by the leftist Aleksander Kwaśniewski, Lech Walesa accused the Prime Minister Józef Oleksy of spying for the Russian intelligence service. In the waning hours of his presidency, Lech Wałęsa called together a group of the country's highest-ranking political leaders to inform them of the charges and to ask them to authorize emergency action. Instead, they withdrew to give the matter further consideration. The news of the allegations spread quickly. Two days later the Interior Ministry openly informed the Sejm that Oleksy had passed secret documents along to a Russian agent. The Sejm responded cautiously. Leaving the task of investigating Oleksy's actions to the prosecutor, it formed a commission to study whether the UOP had acted legally in passing along this information.

The charges against Oleksy were too serious and shocking to be treated dispassionately. The political Right, chagrined at their electoral losses, called for Oleksy's resignation. The Left launched an attack on the Ministry of Internal Affairs and the UOP. The press filled with allegations and counter-allegations, and the public grew confused about whether a leftist or a rightist conspiracy was responsible for the country's instability.

On January 19, 1996, Alexander Kwaśniewski, the country's newly elected leftist president, put his first legislative initiative before the Sejm—a bill on lustration and the secret police archives. He proposed creating a Commission of Public Trust to oversee the secret police archives. The commission would use the files to check whether political candidates and other high-ranking state employees had collaborated with the secret police. Individuals would have access to the files pertaining to themselves.[113] This presidential draft was added to four other lustration bills under consideration by the Sejm. Though the Sejm did not take prompt action on lustration, the president's bill marked a fundamental shift in the political dynamics of lustration. The Left's opposition to lustration had melted—at least temporarily. And ironically it was the Left that brought renewed energy to the issue.

Until the Oleksy affair, the issue of collaboration and lustration had divided the Solidarity camp. The liberal and conservative successors to a unified Solidarity had wrangled with one another, which could only benefit the Left. Indeed one of the paradoxes of lustration is that it generally causes more harm to the former political opposition than to the former ruling party. The secret police had no need to riddle the ruling party with spies, so few former PZPR activists were collaborators. The secret police did infiltrate the opposition, which raised suspicions and damaged trust in these circles. Furthermore, the media and the public tended to accept the fact that a communist had worked with the security organs as a matter of course. The revelation that a member of Solidarity had acted as a stool pigeon was newsworthy—a scandal that revealed base hypocrisy.[114]

The Oleksy affair changed the Left's perception of matters. The issue of collaboration had now brought down a leftist government, in addition to a rightist one. The Left had learned that the lack of lustration imposed costs on parties from both sides of the political spectrum, and it burdened the political system as a whole. In 1996, political leaders began to believe that some form of lustration was necessary and inevitable, even though some still expressed regret at this necessity.

By and large, the Polish people concurred. In February 1993, only 27 percent of Poles agreed with the statement "Today lustration is one of the most important problems which needs to be solved in Poland." By February 1996, 44 percent agreed with the statement. This indicated that the public was also drawing the lesson that lustration was necessary. At that time, a poll found that 67 percent of people believed that individuals who worked with the SB should not be allowed to work in high government positions.[115] This data reveals an interesting gap. While 67 percent of people thought lustration is necessary, only 44 percent thought it is one of the country's most important problems. Poll-takers also asked the following question:

> There is a proposal to create a Commission of Public Trust, which would take over the archives of the UB and the SB. The Commission would verify the past of individuals running for leading state offices, as well as individuals wrongly accused of secret collaboration with the Security Service. Do you believe that the creation of this commission is currently: 1) indispensable and urgent; 2) necessary, but other issues are more important; 3) unnecessary.

While 29 percent chose the first option, nearly twice as many (57 percent) agreed with the second one.[116] In general, Poles approved of lustration as a necessary evil. They harbored no illusions that lustration would make the country a better place, but they believed it might help prevent political instability.

The Sejm began to consider the question of lustration afresh, forming an extraordinary commission to focus on the issue. By the time the commission held its first session in late August, the atmosphere of crisis stemming from the Oleksy affair had evaporated, and the SLD was no longer so sure that lustration was a good idea. The SLD deputies in the subcommittee did not support the president's bill, instead shifted their muted support to the PSL bill, which permitted individuals access to their personal files, but defined collaboration very narrowly.[117] The SLD could not back off the lustration issue entirely, so it cloaked its aversion to lustration in a concern for procedural guarantees.

Meanwhile, the PSL distanced itself from its own bill to join a coalition with the liberals around a compromise bill, which the committee later chose to use as a basis for negotiations. This bill required political candidates and the holders of certain high government positions to write a declaration saying whether or not they had collaborated with the communist era secret police. A special lustration court would examine the declarations to determine their veracity, and anyone who made a false declaration would lose the right to hold certain public offices for a period of ten years.[118] That is, lying about past collaboration, and not the fact of collaboration, was grounds for removal from office.

The negotiations were long and arduous. The commission held 17 sessions, with the SLD continually raising procedural obstacles—the bread-and-butter of liberal democracy—to the discussions. The SLD maintained that it was impossible to guarantee individuals their civil rights in executing lustration. The party's deputies said that the files did not contain sufficient evidence to prove decisively whether an individual had consciously collaborated with the secret police and whether that collaboration had caused demonstrable harm.[119]

While the liberals had previously expressed similar concerns, they now supported a bill that weighed other considerations against the civil rights of the accused. The UW emphasized the importance of truth, saying that constituents deserved to know the facts about a political candidate's character.[120] The liberals had come to favor lustration with little reserve. The lesson from Poland's experience was clear: The absence of lustration had created opportunities to incite political instability. Spy scandals had already brought down two governments, and Polish prime ministers seemed to circle through a revolving door every 12 months or so. The country needed clear procedures to assess the validity of such accusations.

The liberals were also drawing new ideological lessons from international experience. Since 1989, Polish legislators had been comparing their experience of democratization to the Spanish transition of the 1970s, and they had downplayed comparisons with their closer neighbors of Germany and Czechoslovakia. They had been particularly critical of Germans' lustration and opening of the Stasi files; however, by 1994, Germany's solution no longer looked so problematic. Lustration had occurred peacefully, without the predicted attacks of revenge and resulting social unrest. East Germans were able to learn from the files about how the Stasi had affected their lives. The Germans had succeeded in clearing the Stasi legacy off the political agenda. During fall 1996, Polish legislators listened carefully as Germans presented their country's experiences.[121] In 1996, the Council of Europe also adopted a resolution outlining how lustration procedures should be designed in order to respect the principles of the rule of law.[122] In sum, the liberals saw that lustration might be necessary, and they had begun to believe that lustration could be compatible with liberal democracy. This realization allowed them to reaffirm their ideological commitment and to expose the communists' strategic appropriation of liberal democratic principles.

President Kwaśniewski was dissatisfied with the coalition's lustration bill. The bill did not define collaboration as narrowly as he preferred, and it did not offer all citizens the right to see their own files.[123] Despite his misgivings, President Kwaśniewski signed the lustration bill into law on June 18, 1997. With parliamentary elections quickly approaching, he did not want his party to appear to be concealing or justifying the errors of the past. Many members of his party disagreed with this electoral strategy, thinking that lustration would focus attention on the past to the party's detriment.

Though the absence of a lustration law had created numerous political scandals, the presence of the law registered barely a murmur in the 1999 elections, after which Solidarity was again able to form a government. A few candidates admitted that they had collaborated, and the SLD permitted such individuals to remain on their party lists as candidates.[124]

Poland's lustration law began to function in earnest in 1999, ten years after the country's transition to democracy. Nearly 23,000 government officials, judges, and members of parliament filed statements saying whether or not they had collaborated with the SB. Around 130 admitted to collaborating, and their names were published in the government journal *Monitor Polski*.[125] The Appellate Court in Warsaw began to consider the truthfulness of the other statements. During autumn 1999, allegations of collaboration led to three resignations in the government, even before the court had an opportunity to decide the officials' cases. Later the court handed down several decisions, finding a lawyer, two senators (from Solidarity and the SLD respectively), a former deputy prime minister, and a former vice-director of the Ministry of Defense guilty of lying in their statements.[126]

As the presidential election campaign began in summer 2000, each of the candidates had to make an official statement about whether he had collaborated with the SB. The independent candidate Andrzej Olechowski admitted his past collaboration and nevertheless remained fairly popular. Lech Wałęsa, who had little chance of prevailing in the election, vehemently denied collaborating. For years there had been a lingering allegation that he had signed an agreement to collaborate with the SB in 1970, but the evidence—whether for or against the Solidarity leader—remained locked in the archives. Under the new lustration law, Wałęsa finally had his day in court. The lustration court cleared him of all charges of collaboration and made public the documents that supported its verdict.[127]

Truth-Telling

In addition to the lustration law, President Kwaśniewski also proposed legislation to open the secret police files.[128] Citing the importance of the right to information, the bill recommended creating a new archive to house SB documents stemming from 1944 to 1990. The bill gave all persons the right to read materials the SB collected about them, but was careful to protect the identities of SB agents and informers. In presenting the president's legislation to the Sejm, a presidential aide spoke eloquently about the need to open the secret police files:

> This bill is about cleansing the atmosphere of public life, the satisfaction of historical justice, and equalizing the opportunity of all citizens to know the truth about the methods which were used for keeping the society in reins, and about the people who applied these methods. Every interested person should receive the right to acquaint himself with the documents which were created or collected about his person by the former security services. This truth may be bitter, it may demolish many myths, it may undermine the authority of many people. Yet it is a indispensable means of healing. For ten years we have been building democracy in our country, and we still haven't come to terms with this problem.[129]

The Sejm, again dominated by the Solidarity camp, passed a much broader law to create an Institute of National Remembrance.[130] The bill gave individuals the right to know the names of SB agents and informers, introduced the concept of "communist crime," and criminalized the denial of "communist crimes." It also gave procurators attached to the institute and archives the responsibility for investigating and prosecuting communist era crimes. Today both former victims and collaborators have the right to view their files, which are overseen by the Institute of National Remembrance. This institution, housed in a shiny, renovated building in Warsaw, carries out research into both Nazi and communist crimes, as well as providing a wealth of documents to procurators investigating these crimes.

Conclusion

While the theory of democratic transitions helps us to understand why some new democracies pursue transitional justice while others do not, the theory is not as helpful in explaining the dynamics of the issue in the years following the first free elections. Power politics is a useful explanation, elegantly simple in its assumptions and clear in its predictions. However, this theory cannot untangle the complexity of the politics of post-communist justice in Poland.

Liberal democratic ideology has shaped Poland's approach to lustration. Since 1992, Polish debates about transitional justice have centered on one key question: Is it compatible with liberal democracy? Until 1994, the liberals and leftists agreed that the answer was no. Though they were at different ends of the political spectrum, they both justified their opposition to transitional justice with liberal democratic reasons, and their common language made them surprising allies.

Later the liberals shifted their position. They were frustrated by the strategic way in which leftists appropriated liberal ideology to deny their complicity in past abuses. They also grew concerned about the many allegations and rumors that thrived on the absence of real information. In 1996, the leftists also began to appreciate the latter lesson: Allegations could bring down governments. The absence of lustration was proving a danger to democracy—the very principle they had both claimed to uphold. In addition, the leftists and liberals began to be persuaded by international experience, especially from Germany and the Council of Europe, that it might be possible to answer the key question in the affirmative. If procedures were carefully designed, it might be possible to make policies of truth and justice comport with the principles of liberal democracy. By setting up a hierarchy of values, the ideology facilitated political learning. Throughout the post-communist period, political leaders from across the spectrum professed that democracy and individual rights were primary values; however, over time the liberals and the leftists drew different conclusions about which policies would best promote these values.

Poland took nearly a decade to put in place policies of truth and justice. Legal redress and truth-telling are no panacea, as Polish liberals and the public at large have recognized. This approach does not represent a sure path to historical justice; it does not ensure stable democracy; it raises immense problems of evidence and due process. Nevertheless, Poland's "thick line" did no better job of fostering stability. Political enemies yielded to the temptation of selectively leaking information from the secret police files and, when this evidence was inaccessible, simply fabricating wild accusations. After all, it was difficult to verify such allegations when the archives remained closed. While democracy itself was not in danger as a result of the whirlwind of accusations, the recriminations confused the public and distracted its eye. This is where legal redress and truth-telling could help—by providing an orderly way for proving or disproving the validity of accusations.

The delays in adopting policies of truth and justice were costly. The lack of lustration caused unnecessary instability and distractions for a full decade. When the law was finally adopted, Poles sighed with relief that the whole matter was resolved. The country was too tired of the topic to enter into a broad public discussion about the moral and political issues surrounding collaboration with the communist era police. Quite possibly, the Polish public would have been much more eager to carry out this kind of conversation in the early years of its democratic transition. Delayed lustration does not seem to be very helpful in influencing the public's memory of the past.

The only conceivable advantage of the delay was that it contributed to a more juridically sound set of procedures. Adopted at a time when the emotions of the transition ran higher, the Czechs' lustration law did not extend a full range of procedural guarantees. Many results of the initial lustration inquiry were found to be incorrect on appeal. By that time, numerous careers had been destroyed, and the country's departure from liberal democratic norms had earned it international criticism.[131] In comparison, by 1996–97, when Poland's political parties seriously engaged with laws on lustration and secret police files, the passions of the transition had abated. The international community had taken a stance on lustration, outlining the minimal requirements for a just lustration law. The Germans' law on secret police files had proven workable and won international respect.

Poland's experience provides evidence that countries' approaches to truth and justice may converge over time. While Poland was once considered an example of a country where "forgiving and forgetting" was the rule, it later adopted policies of truth and justice quite similar to its neighbors, including Germany. The following policies were put into place:

Retribution Like its neighbors, Poland experienced almost no violence against former communists.

Trials Poland has had at least thirty trials of former state officials. The statute of limitations law was changed to facilitate the prosecution of time-barred offenses, and the parliament assigned special procurators to focus on crimes from the Stalinist era.

Lustration Poland carried out lustration of prosecutors and employees of the Ministry of Internal Affairs in 1990. In 1997, legislators finally passed a law to carry out lustration of political office-holders.

Rehabilitation The Sejm passed a law to rehabilitate individuals who had received unjust sentences during the Stalinist period, but it could not come to an agreement about rehabilitating people who were unjustly imprisoned during martial law. The ministry of justice, under Solidarity leadership, developed administrative procedures for rehabilitating these individuals.

Compensation The parliament readily agreed that people whose criminal verdicts had been reversed should receive compensation for their unjust imprisonment; however, all other aspects of compensation were very controversial. The parliament did not extend compensation to those who had been unjustly imprisoned during martial law (though these individuals could apply for compensation under the ordinary statutes). It had great difficulty in arriving at a politically and legally acceptable definition of who was eligible for the honor and privileges of combatant status. The parliament did add several categories of victims to that category, but it struggled to define which categories should be excluded.

Truth-Telling The first effort at truth-telling—the Rokita commission—provided some insight into the security apparatus's operations and led to a few trials, but it received remarkably little publicity. For nearly a decade, liberals and former communists agreed that the secret police files should not be opened. Then in 1999, the Solidarity-led Sejm passed a law to open the SB's files to former victims.

In Poland, for several years after the transition, politicians from both the former regime and opposition tried to use liberal democratic ideology to argue against policies of truth and justice. They found important resources in the ideology for this "principled forgetting," in particular the social contract and guarantees of due process. Indeed Poland's experience reminds us that liberal democracy does not offer a simple remedy to reconcile all the legal and moral dilemmas of transitional justice. The very complexity of the issues involved invites an ongoing debate. Over time Polish politicians were willing to reengage the question of transitional justice and revise their assessment of its compatibility with liberal democracy. The attempt at principled forgetting in 1989 did not foreclose further debate.

By the mid-1990s, after studying foreign experiences and learning lessons from their own mistakes, political parties—even the former communists—were ready to adopt a new approach to transitional justice, including limited trials, lustration with sufficient due process guarantees, and truth-telling with the opening of the secret police files. Principled forgetting no longer seemed compatible with liberal ideology or democratic stability.

Chapter 5
Russia's Buried Past

Introduction

The debate over the past in Russia has followed a trajectory much different than in Poland and East Germany. In Russia, the process of coming to terms with the past began in 1987, four years before the country moved from its agenda of gradual reform to a radical break with the communist system. The process started earlier than in Poland and East Germany, well before democratization seemed inevitable. During the period of *glasnost'* [openness], the media and the new independent civic organizations began telling the truth about past injustices. Truth-telling by groups outside the government became the general pattern for dealing with the legacy of the past. This public discussion about the country's dark historical moments paralleled political discussions about reforms, but it was curiously disengaged from these changes. Unlike in Poland and East Germany, Russian politicians did not make a connection between condemning past abuses and reforming the institutions responsible for them.

After *glasnost'* largely discredited the Soviet political system and the failed coup of August 1991 brought the maverick Boris Yeltsin to power, we might have expected that the new Russian leadership would drive a stake through the heart of the old system. Some of Yeltsin's early moves suggest this impulse. Yeltsin banned the Communist Party of the Soviet Union (CPSU) and promised to open the KGB archives, which would have revealed potentially shattering secrets. Procurators began criminal proceedings against the putschists. Yeltsin's tactics changed quickly, however, especially as economic reforms and the complexities of post-imperialism consumed his attention. After the communists and nationalists made strong showings in the parliamentary elections of 1993 and 1995, their ideologies shaped the understanding of the Soviet past. They were intent on recapturing its goodness and glory, rather than remembering its crimes. Thus, Russia cast aside the crimes in its history as if they had little relevance for building a democracy.

In Russia, transitional justice did not take the form characteristic of other post-communist countries: legal redress and truth-telling. Instead, after *glasnost's* brief flowering, the country opted to forget about the crimes of the Soviet state. This was not the type of forgetting attempted early in Poland's transition, where forgetting took the form of a publicly announced decision to put aside the past for the sake of a higher goal, namely national reconciliation. In Russia, forgetting set in incrementally as a way to remove a controversial, uncomfortable topic from the political agenda.

Russian politicians across the political spectrum had few incentives to raise the issue of transitional justice. The Communist Party remained stronger and more unreformed in Russia than in Poland and East Germany. By far the largest party in Russia, the communists dwarfed the congeries of puny democratic and nationalist parties, and they proudly still referred to themselves as a communist party, not a democratic socialist one. The continued good health of the Communist Party meant that it could take the offensive against anyone who dared to question its past activities. Backlash against historical revisionism began during the *glasnost'* period, and after a brief interlude following the attempted coup of August 1991, the Communist Party recovered the chutzpah to strike against any challenge to its legitimacy and good record. Democratic reformers in Poland and East Germany never needed to fear such a bold backlash by their countries' weakened and somewhat shamefaced former communist parties, so they could afford to press the point.

Furthermore, the personal history of many leading democrats included a tenure in the Communist Party and various government positions. These individuals were highly implicated in the Soviet system, even though they may not have been associated with any abuses. Too much inquiry into the past had the potential to be embarrassing for many democrats.

Whereas in Poland, the nationalist parties took a strong position in favor of transitional justice, Russia's nationalist parties were not eager to condemn the Soviet past. Of course, in Poland, the nationalists denounced the communists for collaborating with an evil foreign power in facilitating the takeover of their country. Communists, for them, were no better than traitors. In Russia, nationalists might grumble a bit about the allegedly Jewish origins of the Bolsheviks, but overall they took pride in the achievements of the Soviet empire. In elections they promised a return to past glory.

Finally, the agenda of Russia's political transition was particularly crowded. While other former communist countries had to cope with the double transition of political and economic reform, Russia had the added burden of managing the dissolution of its former empire. The leadership's attention was constantly being diverted to crises: the attempted coup of August 1991; the economic misery of 1992; the bloody confrontation between the legislature and the president in October 1993; and finally the war in Chechnya in 1994.

The frequent upheavals in Russian political life created a climate inhospitable to ideological development. As we have seen, in other countries the ideology of liberal democracy placed the issue of transitional justice on the political agenda and proposed a set of policies in response. Though the immense transformations in Russia since 1987 are referred to as a process of democratization, and Russia has indeed adopted the institutional framework of a democracy complete with representative government and free, competitive elections, Russia has not embraced the ideology of liberal democracy.[1] The terms in which other countries' politicians debated transitional justice—human rights and the rule of law—remain contentious in Russia since shared assumptions about these concepts are lacking. In the absence of an ordered way of remembering and overcoming the past, Russian politicians have chosen to forget about the crimes of the Soviet government.

Legacy of the Past

The legacy of communist rule in Russia was even more bitter than in its neighboring countries. The number of Stalin's victims may forever remain a mystery; scholars continue a morally numbing debate about how many millions died—maybe 10 mn., maybe 20 mn.[2] Executions, starvation, deportations, dekulakization—no method was too brutal in Stalin's quest to build a powerful state with himself at the helm. Yet, after Stalin's death in 1953, the Soviet state avoided these massive campaigns of cruelty. By the 1980s, only a few hundred dissidents were in prison, around 2,000 more in psychiatric hospitals.[3] As a result, few Russians have a direct memory of the gulag, and until the late 1980s, censorship meant that many people failed to develop a mature historical sensibility about Stalin's crimes.

After his death, the Soviet leadership laid the blame for past crimes squarely on Stalin's shoulders. In his secret speech to the Twentieth Party

Congress, Khrushchev suggested that Stalin's deformed character, and not the Soviet political system, was responsible for the unspeakable abuses in the past. Khrushchev established a commission to rehabilitate old Bolsheviks whom Stalin had repressed and largely obliterated. He also supported a patchwork of amnesty and rehabilitation laws that emptied the gulag and brought its prisoners back to their homes and families. Between 1954 and 1961, more than 700,000 people were rehabilitated.[4] With so many prisoners returning to their families and friends, we might have expected that their private conversations around kitchen tables would have led to a public exposure of past crimes. Yet, the former prisoners were too tired and frightened to spread information about what they had experienced.[5] The crimes of Stalinism were rarely discussed in public. The press carried reports of the rehabilitation of high-ranking political leaders, but it did not discuss the rehabilitation of ordinary people.[6] Individuals could not initiate the process of rehabilitation, since only procurators could file a protest requesting rehabilitation.[7] De-Stalinization was a process carefully defined and controlled by the communist authorities. The state never prosecuted the many people implicated in the crimes associated with Stalin's rule.

One proposal could have led to a broader social discussion of the past. At the Twenty-Second Party Congress, Khrushchev suggested building a monument to the victims of Stalinism. Given the way Russians gather at monuments to mark weddings and public holidays, such a monument could have become a focal point for discussion and remembrance. Though the state followed through on Khrushchev's proposals for removing Stalin's body from the mausoleum at Red Square and renaming all places that carried Stalin's name, it never built a monument.[8] The potential for public gatherings and protest was too threatening.

The Soviet Union changed fundamentally after Stalin's death. Violence ceased to be an ordinary tool of political competition and public control.[9] Political opponents no longer threatened to eliminate one another, which made politics a less hazardous business. The Communist Party used the stick of terror more sparingly. The KGB kept society under close surveillance. People brave enough to voice their dissent were sent to prison or psychiatric hospitals. In 1991, Freedom House estimated that the Soviet Union still had 157 political prisoners.[10] But for the most part, the state was able to rely on various carrots—better housing, job security, price stability—to win the people's quiescence, if not their support. Significantly, in polls taken in both 1991 and 1996, 80 percent of Russians said that they had never experienced injustice before *perestroika*.[11]

Gorbachev and Glasnost'

Gorbachev gradually revised the approach his predecessors had taken to the past. As early as March 1985, he spoke of the need to "expand *glasnost'* in the work of party, soviet, state, and social organizations."[12] He believed that if people were better informed about their leaders' work, they would support it more actively. Then beginning with the Twenty-Seventh Party Congress in 1986, *glasnost'* became an integral part of Gorbachev's political strategy. Although his critics urged caution in examining the country's "errors and omissions," Gorbachev boldly stated, "There may be only one response [to this concern]—a Leninist one: In all circumstances, communists need the truth."[13] He emphasized the connection between openness and economic growth. A free flow of information would promote dynamism in the country's economic and political life. Workers would take "initiative from below" and criticize inefficient practices, which would heighten productivity. A developing civil society would play an analogous role in the country's political life, holding corrupt officials accountable and suggesting superior solutions to social problems.[14] In Gorbachev's opinion, *glasnost'* would function like a high-octane social fuel; it would rev up the existing institutions and enable them to perform better.

In 1985–86, the main goals of *glasnost'* were to expose corruption and stagnation among the elites and to provide party members an opportunity to speak critically without fear of punishment. Criticisms of Soviet history were very muted in this period, yet the fact that they were uttered at all was significant. Since Khrushchev's removal from power, Soviet leaders had remained silent about the crimes of the Stalinist period. By reintroducing this theme, Gorbachev raised the question of where the acceptable boundaries of criticism would lie. In his own public pronouncements, Gorbachev did not deviate much from the line established at the Twentieth Party Congress. He lamented the "serious excesses and blunders in methods and pace" associated with collectivization, as well as other "negative aspects of socio-political life engendered by the Stalin personality cult."[15]

While Gorbachev inaugurated the process of coming to terms with the past, the party state did not actually carry out this policy. The energy for *glasnost'* was not going to come from the Communist Party, whose political imagination was spent. Instead, Gorbachev reached out to the intelligentsia to carry the banner of *glasnost'*. After Aleksander Yakovlev, a reform-oriented communist, became director of the Propaganda Department of the party, he appointed younger, more dynamic figures to leading positions in the field of culture and the media. Many of these new cultural leaders were from the generation of the *shestidesiatniki*, people who came of age politically in the 1960s after the Twentieth Party Congress. This generation marked Khrushchev's secret speech and the invasion of Czechoslovakia in 1968 as crucial turning points in their political development. In most cases they still harbored hopes for a more humane form of socialism, and they believed this could be accomplished only by completing the process of de-Stalinization, which had been initiated in their youth. The cultural intelligentsia began to probe into the past with a critical eye and to reveal the truth.

During the period of 1987–89, the boundaries of *glasnost'* expanded, and the whole country seemed to immerse itself in trying to understand Soviet history. As one observer noted, "Nothing like this has ever happened before in the history of the world. In the course of 1987 and 1988, tens of millions of Soviet citizens became passionately involved in studying their country's past, and in rethinking the principles and practice of Soviet socialism."[16]

Gorbachev initiated the process of greater openness in a meeting he held with the leaders of the mass media in February 1987. The speech is famous for Gorbachev's statement that there should be no "forgotten names or blank spots in history." Gorbachev called on the leaders of the press to support critical inquiries into the problems of Soviet society. "Criticism is a bitter medicine, but illness makes it necessary."[17] Though one might interpret the speech as encouraging the editors to shed all their political inhibitions, Gorbachev qualified his call for greater freedom. He stressed that people should continue to "treasure each year of our seventy-year Soviet history." He also alleged that the process of de-Stalinization was complete and that the party had already come to terms with the "mistakes, omissions and blunders" of the past.

What kind of criticism did Gorbachev really expect from the press at this juncture? The speech seems to indicate that he was looking for criticism of the Brezhnev period and its stagnation, corruption, and social and economic problems. This type of criticism would justify his proposals for political and economic reforms. Gorbachev's favored projects of institutional change were to transfer more power to the soviets and to introduce economic reforms. He reached out to the press to help him find public support for these projects, even in the face of conservative resistance within the party. Criticism of the party's role in stagnation would justify the transfer of power from the party to state institutions. Criticism of the planned economy's irrationalities would justify economic reforms modeled on Lenin's own New Economic Policy of the 1920s. A reassessment of Stalin did not appear to be at the forefront of

Gorbachev's mind. Indeed, it is hard to see how an exposé of Stalin could serve the interests of a moderate communist committed to gradual reforms. Stalin was an explosive topic that could provoke pointed questions about the whole Soviet project.

The media responded to Gorbachev's speech by unleashing waves of criticism. With high-level approval, publishers began to release many previously banned works of literature.[18] Banned films, such as the anti-Stalinist fable *Repentance*, made their way to the screens. Many of the works prepared "for the desk drawer" or published abroad during the years of stagnation had to do with the cruel abuses in Soviet history. During the late 1980s, Russians read Solzhenitsyn's *The Gulag Archipelago*, Rybakov's *Children of the Arbat*, and Pasternak's *Doctor Zhivago*. Compared to the powerful criticism posed in these books, Gorbachev's proposed policies—more power to the soviets, socialist rule of law, and the introduction of cooperatives—were hopelessly pallid.

Just as the Communist Party was becoming increasingly divided over how far historical criticism should go, the celebration of the October Revolution's seventieth anniversary in 1987 called for a résumé of Soviet history. The general secretary tried to navigate the middle ground and support a "dialectical" approach to history. In his speech for the anniversary, Gorbachev acknowledged that Soviet history had had its difficult moments, such as the repressions and the cult of personality. Yet, he spoke at length of the country's achievements, including collectivization, which he still justified despite its enormous human costs.

The government's approach to the rehabilitation of former political prisoners was more telling. In September 1987, the Politburo decided to establish a commission to rehabilitate the victims of the repressions. While this was certainly a step in the direction of greater historical truthfulness, the process of rehabilitation was still very constricted. Under the conservative leadership of Mikhail Solomentsev, the commission slowly began to consider the cases that it selected for itself. Individuals did not have the right to apply for rehabilitation. In its first 11 months of existence, the commission rehabilitated only 636 people, and generously reinstated 68 as members of the CPSU.[19] It continued to maintain that the state had no information about where Stalin's victims were buried.

The first major backlash against the media's revelations about Stalinism occurred when *Sovetskaya Rossiya* published a letter from Nina Andreeva, a Leningrad chemistry teacher who defended Stalin's positive contributions to the Soviet Union and minimized the terror. Whether or not Andreeva received assistance from the top echelons of power in writing her letter, she spoke for a significant group within the party and society who found the revelations about the past unseemly. Yegor Ligachev, the party's chief ideologist, later wrote of what he called the "history hysteria" of the media, "They acted like birds of prey, tearing our society to shreds, destroying the historical memory of the nation, spitting upon such sacred concepts as patriotism, and discrediting the feeling of pride in our Motherland."[20] Interestingly, this committed communist found the revelations unseemly because they were unpatriotic, not because they were anticommunist. This emerging alliance between communism and nationalism in Russia would play a major role in blocking efforts to come to terms with the past.

Three weeks after the Andreeva letter, the Politburo responded in a *Pravda* article by saying that the country needed to examine its history openly. The press recognized that for the moment, conservative forces in the Politburo were on the defensive, and journalists eagerly took up the opportunity to publish critical articles. As an observer noted, "A further major advance toward frankness occurred at this time."[21]

At the Nineteenth Party Conference in July 1988, Gorbachev again called on the media to publish the truth about all matters. The conference resolved that the Party would never permit the recurrence of events similar to those "connected with the periods of the cult of personality and stagnation, which created deep deformations in the socialist society, halted its development for whole decades, and led to many human victims and uncountable moral and ideal losses."[22] The Politburo also passed a resolution calling for the building of a memorial to the victims of the repressions, and it later set up a committee to change the names of Soviet towns whose names were connected with Stalin's henchmen.[23]

Despite all the talk about dealing with the past, the fruits of the Nineteenth Party Conference were scant. In retrospect, what did *not* happen at the conference appears to be especially pertinent. Political pluralism continued to develop at the conference, but within the framework of the clash between Mikhail Gorbachev and the renegade party boss Boris Yeltsin. Yeltsin had openly criticized the party's reforms during preparations for the seventieth anniversary celebration, and at the party conference, he again stated his major complaints: the need for direct elections with secret ballots in the party and for term limits on Politburo members.[24] Significantly, Yeltsin did not touch on questions of *glasnost'*, and throughout what would be the major political rivalry accompanying Russia's transition to democracy, coming to terms with the past would never emerge as a significant theme. This power struggle, foreshadowing later ones, was not ideological. A second lacuna was the failure to connect a condemnation of Stalin's repressions with any attempt to reform the institutions responsible for those policies. The KGB was never even mentioned at the conference.[25] This notorious organ of repression was no longer arresting dissidents, but it continued to function, unchastened and unreformed.

The Nineteenth Party Conference further emboldened the voices of *glasnost'*. Among the most vocal critics in this period was the group Memorial. The Memorial movement began in 1987 as a small group of citizens dedicated to the memory of those who perished during the repressions.[26] Prior to the party conference, Memorial had circulated a petition calling for the construction of a memorial to the victims of the repressions, and with its appeal proving successful (though Gorbachev never acknowledged Memorial's efforts), it upped the ante. The poet Evgeny Evtushenko, a member of Memorial's leadership, called for the formation of a research center to study the repressions. He emphasized that the duty of Memorial was to tell the truth about the past, not to split society:

> The task of Memorial is deprived of any vengeance. We do not stand for the physical persecution of those who were somehow mixed up in the bloody crimes of Stalinism. . . . Let their social punishment be the publication of the truth about concrete crimes and concrete people, who were participants in the war against their own people.[27]

Thus, truth-telling was the major goal of the Memorial organization. When in later years it tried to move beyond truth-telling to an agenda of institutional reform, the shift was controversial and resulted in schisms within the movement.[28]

In 1988, Memorial joined with the liberal press in organizing an exhibit called the "Week of Conscience" to illustrate just how this truth-telling would function. The Week of Conscience included a display of suggestions for a memorial to the victims of Stalinism. It also had a "Wall of Memory" where relatives and friends placed the names, rehabilitation papers, and other items belonging to the victims of Stalin's terror. Victims' relatives left notes asking others for help in determining the fate of their loved ones. Furthermore, the exhibit included a room with the names of the Chekists who directed the repressions, especially those who won awards for their activities in 1937. At the conclusion of the exhibit, which 33,000 people attended, the organizers proudly announced that "the Week of Conscience represents the beginning of a national trial of Stalin and Stalinism."[29] A few liberal journalists took up the idea of calling for a national tribunal to deal with the crimes of the Stalin era; however, it never achieved broad publicity.[30] At any rate, the Party was not prepared to allow such a step. Representatives of the state let it be known that the statute of limitations had lapsed for all crimes associated with the Stalin era, and anyway, the elderly should be allowed to live out their last days in peace.[31] Some officials even tried to argue that those responsible for the crimes under Stalin had already been prosecuted.[32] Emphatically this was not the case. A report from 1961 indicates that only 347 people were removed from the party for "violating socialist legality," and they were not prosecuted.[33]

Glasnost' could have been linked to a vision of what the country should become. But this logical connection was not forged. The historical revisionism of these years entailed a thoroughgoing criticism of the old system, but it was not clear what lessons should be drawn from the past. The lesson Gorbachev drew was that reform of some unspecified pace and vague direction—that is, *perestroika* [rebuilding]—was necessary. *Perestroika*, like a week at a Black Sea sanatorium, was supposed to be healthy in large part because it was a salutary change of pace.

The institutional reforms Gorbachev introduced took power away from the Communist Party and shifted greater responsibility to the legislative bodies and a newly created presidency. He felt that this reform was a sufficient response to the abuses committed within the Stalinist system, or perhaps he could not imagine a more complete one. Historical revisionism did not lead him to consider reforms that the ideology of liberal democracy suggests as ready correctives—reform of the criminal code, the judiciary or the secret police, institutions that had contributed to abuses in the past. Past abuses pointed out the need for reform, but without a set of ideological guidelines, it was not clear what the content of the reforms should be.

Gorbachev was not alone in failing to draw lessons from the past. Like Gorbachev, the liberal media, which relished in publishing criticisms of the Soviet Union's dark history, had only a vague notion of what would remedy the abuses. Of course, the media vowed that historical experience should inform the future. The Soviet past provided plenty of lessons about what the country should not do: It should not forcibly collectivize, build a gulag, manufacture famine, or arbitrarily imprison people. Yet, a positive vision was lacking. Liberal democracy is not necessarily the only nostrum for the ills of tyranny, but some real cure, and not another dose of political quackery, was desirable. Liberal democracy, which offers some answers to these pressing questions, did attract many members of the cultural intelligentsia; however, the "children of the twentieth party congress" still believed that socialism could be purged of its abusive elements, and they hoped for a form of socialism that protected human rights and freedoms.

The cultural intelligentsia and the emerging democratic opposition did propose a different institutional solution than Gorbachev's "all power to the Soviets." They agitated in favor of abolishing the Communist Party's constitutionally mandated leading role in society. If historical revisionism was linked to any one particular policy objective, it was the removal of this infamous Article 6 from the constitution. Andrei Sakharov led the effort. After spending years in exile, he had the moral integrity to oppose the Communist Party with credibility and charisma. He was a great unifying figure of the opposition, and the main theme of his activities in the latter part of 1989 was to abolish to Communist Party's leading role. He organized strikes and demonstrations in support of this.[34]

Thus, the cultural intelligentsia was the main proponent of historical revisionism, and it prescribed the abolition of the Communist Party's leading role as the appropriate response to the past. This web of connections had consequences for the way in which the past would inform and shape the course of reforms. When Article 6 was eliminated in 1990, the cultural intelligentsia was rudderless. Had the whole Soviet legacy been overcome in an instant? The nascent democratic movement did not have any other such paramount goals. The untimely death of Sakharov, their moral leader, compounded the loss of a sense of unity. Some members of the opposition were attracted to the ideology of liberal democracy, but socialism and nationalism also attracted adherents. Historical revisionism was no longer linked to a broad political goal. As one scholar observed, "[T]he great renewal of public morality did not take place. History was increasingly seen as irrelevant, and partly as a result of this, the great democratic reorientation of society was flawed."[35] Such a failure was not inevitable. In other countries, liberal democratic ideology provided a rationale and a structure for inquiring into the past.

After the elimination of Article 6, Gorbachev shifted toward a more conservative stance. He tried to portray himself as the protector of Soviet history. For example, he signed a decree to impose more severe punishments on those who vandalized socialist monuments.[36] Gorbachev thereby heaped heavier condemnation on the action of those people so frustrated with the regime that they defaced the country's ubiquitous statues of Lenin. He allowed a draft rehabilitation law to linger in the USSR Supreme Soviet throughout 1991 until the dissolution of the USSR made the project irrelevant.

The elimination of Article 6 also contributed to the public's loss of interest in the past. Subscriptions to the radical newspapers and journals fell off.[37] Memorial found less resonance among the populace. Apparently, its strategy of truth-telling as an end in itself did not sustain public interest. The Soviet past offered up one bleak story after another, and the negative assessments irritated citizens who were accustomed to thinking of their homeland as a great superpower. Yet, pride was not the only reason the public became less interested in the past. They were interested in the country's present—its economic problems, the threat of national separatism, and new political arrangements.

We would expect the democratic opposition to forge a link between liberal democratic ideology and criticism of the past; however, the composition and alliances of the opposition militated against this. Russia's democratic opposition during this period consisted of a rather odd alliance: between the cultural intelligentsia and reformers from the Communist Party. Together they managed to elect Boris Yeltsin to the chairmanship of the Supreme Soviet; however, they never managed to form an enduring political party. Though they cooperated in the Interregional Deputies Group to support reforms in the USSR Supreme Soviet, they did not support candidates for the Russian Congress of People's Deputies. As a result, the democrats (a loosely defined term in Russia) had to build a new organization, "Democratic Russia," which they termed "an association of deputies."[38] More than half of Democratic Russia's deputies in the Supreme Soviet were also members or former members of the CPSU.[39] During 1990–91, Democratic Russia had an opportunity to set the tone for how the country should use its past. Boris Yeltsin, whom the association supported, had the ear of the nation as the most powerful challenger to Mikhail Gorbachev, and the association had enough supporters in the Supreme Soviet to pass significant legislation. In fact though, neither Boris Yeltsin nor Democratic Russia linked an analysis of the evils of the Soviet past to the need for deep reform of the former institutions of repression, such as establishing an independent judiciary, cleaning up the police, and overhauling the KGB.

This was an ideological deficiency. The Soviet Union could have used lessons about its past to inform its reform efforts. In fact, Yurii Afanasiev, a leading historian who supported *glasnost'*, recognized this as early as 1988. He wrote, "Our task is not just to fill in the blank holes of our history. We must establish and rethink it not only on the level of events, but express it in scientific categories, consider it theoretically."[40] Russian political society did not meet this challenge. During its heyday, the cultural intelligentsia used the past to criticize the leading role of the Communist Party, but after 1990, this purpose was irrelevant. Soon the cultural intelligentsia was spent as a political force. Historical revisionism played out its role as destroyer of the old system. "[T]he democratic ideology adopted by the new parties was an expression of rebellion against the apparat and its rule rather than a programme of government."[41] It was cast away as useless when the time came to negotiate the parameters of a new system.

Rehabilitation

The Russian Supreme Soviet, locked in conflict with the USSR's legislative body, made moves to rehabilitate the victims of political repressions. However, because Russia was still not sovereign, its laws were "more symbolic and propagandistic than regulatory."[42]

The Russian draft legislation was much more extensive than the Soviet one. Its preface unreservedly condemned the political repressions of the past:

> Condemning the many years of terror and massive persecution of its own people as incompatible with the idea of law and justice, the Supreme Soviet of the RSFSR bows before the memory of the innocent who suffered and died, expresses deep sympathy to the victims of these repressions and announces its intention of achieving the removal of the consequences of these repressions, and the establishment of justice and civil rights.[43]

The Soviet draft law contained no such statement of purpose.[44] The Russia law also promised greater openness. It called for the publication of the names of those who had been rehabilitated, and it required the procurator to inform the families of the burial site of people who died while in the state's custody (Art. 8). Finally, the Russian law, unlike the Soviet one, established a compensation scheme. It gave victims the right to return to their hometowns, to receive monetary compensation, and to move back into their old apartments (Art. 15).

The Russian Supreme Soviet did not manage to pass this rehabilitation law before the August coup. It did, however, pass a law rehabilitating "repressed peoples." This law likewise began with a striking preface:

> The renewal of Soviet society in the process of its democratization and the formation of a law-based state in the country demands the cleansing of all spheres of social life from the deformations and distortions of common human values. It has created a propitious moment for rehabilitating

> peoples repressed during the years of Soviet power, who suffered genocide and defamatory attacks.[45]

This law was quite heavy on symbolism, as the language of the preface indicates. At the time the bill was rushed through the Supreme Soviet, legislators recognized, but chose not to grapple with, the extraordinary practical difficulties inherent in legislation that promises "territorial rehabilitation." This term implied that the ethnic groups deported by Stalin would have the right to return to the land they were forced to abandon nearly 50 years ago. As Boris Yeltsin emphasized in the debates on this law, the important thing was to pass the law quickly, not to perfect it.[46] The law did not set forth the level of compensation or the procedures for territorial rehabilitation. It allowed for the executive authorities to deal with each ethnic group in its particular situation. Of course, this created confusion and unequal treatment, both harbingers of greater ethnic conflict. In later years, this sketchy legislation would prove a great headache for the Russian Federation. The territorial claims it created contributed to the outbreak of conflict in Northern Ossetia, and many ethnic groups became very impatient with the Russian government's unfulfilled promises.[47]

After the 1991 Coup

Since the structure of the democratic transition is one of the best tools for predicting how a country will come to terms with its past, it is important to categorize Russia's transition properly. This is peculiarly difficult given the unique constellation of political forces during Russia's transition, and especially after the failed coup attempt of August 1991. It does not fit easily into the categories of transformation, negotiated transition or rupture.[48] Up until the coup attempt, the beginning of the transition looked like a transformation—classical reform from above. Mikhail Gorbachev, a soft-liner in the government, held the reins of an unruly, but still manageable reform process. Naturally he faced opposition from the hard-liners in the government, but somewhat unusually, his main opponent on the other side was not an opposition figure, but a "softer" soft-liner, Boris Yeltsin, who consolidated his power in Russia's governmental structures. The conflict was thus between two soft-liners—one with a claim to lead the Soviet Union and the other with a claim to lead Russia. In August 1991, the hard-liners believed they had to strike in order to prevent the devolution of greater powers to Yeltsin and other republican leaders, whose struggle for power dictated a further emaciation of Soviet institutions.

In many ways, the coup and the resistance it provoked resembled a revolutionary moment. There was a break in legality and the army was arrayed on Moscow's streets. Yet, the violence was on a very small scale, in part because the people of Moscow were weary of the use of violence as a political tool. The democratic opposition—the revolutionary force in this drama—appealed repeatedly for the capital's crowds to avoid violence and looting the Communist Party's property.[49] After Yeltsin corralled the reactionary forces, the conflict between him and Gorbachev resumed; however, Yeltsin and Russian sovereignty were now clearly on the ascendancy. The coup marks a transition to Russian sovereignty, as well as one to democracy. As Yeltsin's biographer notes, "He had taken Russia away from the Party, away from the Union, and away from Gorbachev. Most of all, from Gorbachev."[50]

The failed coup was Yeltsin's moment of triumph. At this point of ascendancy, a revolutionary would seek to punish members of the old regime for the crimes they committed. Yeltsin's revolution in the name of Russian sovereignty meant his definition of the "old regime" and its "crimes" was peculiar to this situation. The old regime consisted of the political forces that supported the coup, and its greatest crime was the attempted coup itself. Coming to terms with past injustices was reduced to a process of coming to terms with the opponents of Russian sovereignty. But avenging the crimes of the past was not Yeltsin's primary motivation in these policies; rather, Yeltsin was trying in a period of great uncertainty to consolidate his power and assert Russian sovereignty. In this tumultuous transition, even more so than in Central Europe, power considerations were primary.

During the months after the attempted coup of August 1991, Russian President Yeltsin vied with Soviet President Gorbachev to see who would hold political power. Gorbachev could reassert his authority only by salvaging the Soviet Union and its ruling party. Yeltsin could achieve political supremacy by asserting Russia's sovereignty and discrediting the Soviet Union and the CPSU. His political tactics gave rise to the logic of anticommunism in the immediate postcoup period. After a hiatus of a few years, anticommunism once again had political relevance: The goal was to assert Russian hegemony over Soviet institutions and to destroy Gorbachev's remaining bases of power.

Several policies adopted in late 1991 reflect Yeltsin's short spurt of revolutionary anti-Sovietism. Yeltsin banned the Communist Party, purged the KGB of individuals who had supported the coup, launched investigations into the coup, and authorized the arrest of the coup's participants.

In late August, Yeltsin adopted a series of decrees directed against the CPSU. He suspended the publication of several newspapers controlled by the CPSU, confiscated the party's property, and banned the CPSU as a political organization. These actions led to a strong backlash from a communist party unwilling to accept its loss of hegemony. In November, communists filed a lawsuit against the Russian government, arguing that Yeltsin's decrees were unconstitutional. In this so-called trial of the century, the CPSU was the plaintiff. The party disputed the allegation that it was responsible for the attempted coup. It argued that only some individual members of the CPSU participated in a coup attempt, but the party itself, and particularly its members in the regions, did not contribute to the preparations for the coup.[51] In a countersuit, anticommunist deputies of the Supreme Soviet argued the CPSU was an unconstitutional body because it had been involved in genocide, deportations, and inciting social enmity. The communists rebutted by emphasizing that these crimes were ancient history and that the CPSU in its current composition bore no responsibility for them.[52] Throughout the trial, the communists were brazenly unrepentant. Witnesses for the plaintiff made fabulous arguments: "The Party was the initiator of renewal of society; it was the midwife of democracy in Russia. No other party in the world did so much for the people." "Every year more people die in traffic accidents than died in the repressions."[53] The CPSU wanted to prove its innocence so that it could continue to compete in elections and to claim ownership of its property. Too much was at stake for it to use the forum of the trial to atone for the past.

Although such a trial may not encourage repentance, it could be an opportunity for historical inquiry and truth-telling. Some new information did come out during the trial, since Yeltsin released various documents—such as those describing the massacre of Polish military officers at Katyn—from his presidential archive. It was clear that this information was being released for political purposes. As one observer noted, "Delayed, piecemeal, highly censored revelations are being used—or 'misused'—as pawns in the troubled post-Soviet political arena."[54] However, most of the revelations were not news, such as the testimony that the KGB was subordinated to the CPSU.[55] The public was indifferent to this trial.

The trial reached its conclusion in November of 1992, about a year after it began. On a litigator's clock, this is relatively soon, timely enough to have shaped public opinion. The verdict was complex, finding

Yeltsin's revolutionary decrees partially constitutional. The decree that nationalized the CPSU's property was unconstitutional. While Yeltsin acted constitutionally in disbanding the central structures of the Communist Party, the court decided that the primary party organizations in Russia's cities and provinces could continue to function.[56] This allowed the Communist Party to resurrect itself from the bottom up. Commentators referred to the decision as a "political balancing act" and "a decision worthy of Solomon."[57] The decision condemned the Communist Party on the one hand, but allowed it to rebuild itself on the other. The Court dropped the anticommunists' countersuit, and it did not consider the anticommunists' allegation that the CPSU was an unconstitutional body.

The trial of the leaders of the coup failed even more miserably than the trial of the CPSU. The purpose of the trial was to sideline Yeltsin's political opponents, to condemn their attempt to seize power by unconstitutional means, and to deter such attempts in the future. The energy behind this trial petered out quickly. It failed for all the reasons that political trials often falter. First, the legal arguments for the prosecution were relatively weak. It had to prove that the putschists violated Soviet laws. Meanwhile, the putschists maintained that they had acted legally in a situation of dire necessity to protect the territorial integrity of the Soviet Union. Given the union's later demise, their argument appeared convincing. Second, the trial encountered annoying practical difficulties. The case proceeded excruciatingly slowly. A year after the coup attempt, prosecutors had questioned 2,700 witnesses, and no end was in sight. The sessions of the trial were shortened because the accused were elderly and infirm. The trial had just gotten underway in the military courts, when the procurator general and his deputy were censored for publishing material relevant to the case, which was still under investigation. The two had published a book entitled *Kremlin Conspiracy: An Account of the Investigation* in which they wrote that the defendants were guilty. The Supreme Soviet decided not to dismiss the procurator-general despite this breach of office.[58] At this point, the trial began to appear farcical. Finally, as more and more time elapsed, coming to terms with the coup was no longer a pressing political task. Yeltsin had consolidated his power vis-à-vis the forces that supported the coup, and he no longer needed to throttle them. Instead he began to face opposition in the Supreme Soviet, whose members had supported him during the coup. A new conflict had supplanted the old, and Yeltsin's attention shifted. Surely he could have drawn a connection between the two and pursued the case against the coup plotters with vigor, but he did not make that choice. Instead, Yeltsin focused on the political tactics of the here and now. In 1991 he was more interested in the putschists than in the human rights abuses committed by the Soviet government. In 1993, he shifted his attention from the illegal actions of the coup plotters to the constitutional maneuverings of his opponents in the Supreme Soviet.

Just after the failed coup, on August 24, Yeltsin signed a decree transferring the archives of the KGB and the CPSU to state control. At this point in time, the decree was symbolic, no more than a tactical threat. Since both institutions were under Soviet rather than Russian control, Yeltsin could not execute these policies. However, he was reminding these two bulwarks of Soviet rule that once he had swept power away from Gorbachev, as already seemed inevitable, he would be the master of these warehouses of information, in which were buried secrets that could jeopardize whatever legitimacy these discredited institutions still claimed. It is noteworthy that Yeltsin did not promise to give citizens access to these files, which would have signaled greater democratic openness. Instead, Yeltsin's focus was to establish the Russian Federation's control over these two powerful institutions.

Gorbachev tried to preempt these decrees. He called on the CPSU to transfer its archival materials to the local soviets, where presumably they could evade an easy takeover. He also appointed a new, more liberal head of the KGB, Vadim Bakatin, who called for a new law on the archives and ordered that no more files be destroyed.[59] The Russian Supreme Soviet then countered Gorbachev's moves, establishing a parliamentary commission to oversee the transfer of the CPSU and KGB archives to the state archives. The commission, headed by military historian Dmitry Volkogonov, did not address the question of whether the archives would be opened for public use.[60] It functioned only until mid-1992, when Viktor Barannikov, the new chief of Russia's security agency, shut it down. It had not accomplished its tasks.[61]

How much information could these archives reveal about the Soviet past? The KGB partially destroyed its archives, most intensively during the periods of 1954–55 when many files on Stalin's repressions were obliterated, and then in 1989–91 when many files on dissidents were burned. Most of the documents related to Aleksander Solzhenitsyn and Andrei Sakharov were destroyed, as were many papers and manuscripts of leading cultural figures.[62] The KGB also destroyed many documents pertaining to the August coup attempt. Yet, it is estimated that some 10.6 mn. files remain, and "any gaps which may have been created are modest compared to the evidence that was not destroyed."[63] In institutions other than the KGB, few documents were destroyed since the collapse of the Soviet Union came too quickly.[64] Alexander Yakovlev, who had access to the files as the head of the commission on rehabilitations, felt the moral burden of the immense archive. "If only the files would burn up and the men and women return to life," he wrote.[65]

Of the CPSU's rich archives, many of the most incriminating documents are locked in the presidential archive, to which only leading government officials have access. Gorbachev created this special archive in July 1990, for the purpose of protecting the party's many potentially embarrassing documents. Yeltsin did not dismantle this archive after he took over the Kremlin; he merely renamed it. Thus, the Russian president has at his disposal secret documents from throughout the Soviet period. He can release them or retain them, as seems advantageous. Yeltsin used this prerogative during the trial of the CPSU; he later released information about various international disputes in order to facilitate his foreign policy.

While Yeltsin readily put his political opponents on trial, he was not a revolutionary. He was not out to upend all the state's institutions. He pragmatically established control over them. This becomes clear if we consider what he did *not* do during the immediate postcoup period. Once he had control of the KGB, he did not undertake to remove officers who had violated human rights in the past. The officers who had been responsible for spying on dissidents and the church remained in place. The only formal purges were to remove individuals who had supported the attempted coup.[66] Yeltsin did not open the KGB's files to the public, and he did not declassify materials from the presidential archive. He did not support a lustration law to remove KGB agents from the Supreme Soviet, the judiciary, or procurator's office. He did not encourage the trials of officers who had violated human rights in the past.

Yeltsin did continue the one policy that had been inaugurated by the reformist leader before him: to rehabilitate the victims of Stalinism. The rehabilitation law did not appear as an important plank in a new approach to coming to terms with the past. Rather it seemed to finish up a piece of business started by Gorbachev and taken over by the Supreme Soviet. Even though the rehabilitation law was adopted in October 1991, just two months after the attempted coup, it did not bear the imprint of the coup or new political realities. Most of the outlines of the law had been agreed upon several months earlier.

The rehabilitation law marked a real advancement on Soviet era rehabilitations. Unlike in Soviet times, the law promised that the rehabilitations would be public knowledge. The procurator is supposed to publish lists of names of those rehabilitated in the local press (Art. 8). The law also gives individuals who had been rehabilitated (and in case of death, their families) the right to read the judicial and security files about themselves. They may receive copies of some documents. The procurator must inform surviving family members about the date and cause of death, as well as the place of burial (Art. 11). The law also sets forth more generous provisions for compensation. Rehabilitated individuals also have the right to return to the cities they lived in prior to the repression (Arts. 12–16). Finally, the law says that employees of the NKVD or the KGB who participated in political repression "are criminally responsible on the basis of existing criminal legislation." The names of those found guilty of using illegal methods of investigations will be published periodically (Art. 18).

This rehabilitation law was more legally sound than the law on rehabilitating repressed peoples. The procedures for applying for rehabilitation and compensation were more clear, and they provided for equal treatment. Nevertheless, the law contained articles that would not permit easy implementation. Few jurisdictions published the names of people who had been rehabilitated in the local press, and no lists of perpetrators ever appeared.[67] Much of the law's implementation depended on the willingness of local authorities to release information, and this varied greatly from region to region. For example, the Moscow division of the KGB began to turn over information about previously secret burial sites of the victims of Stalinism in the early 1990s in accordance with the law; however, the St. Petersburg division avoided complying with the law until the mid-1990s.[68] Since the introduction of the law, at least 4.5 mn. political prisoners have been rehabilitated.[69] This immense number indicates the pervasive injustice of the Soviet system. It also shows that despite the general tendency to forget the past, the members of the Presidential Commission for the Rehabilitation of Victims of Political Repression, headed by Alexander Yakovlev, made admirable efforts to carry out the rehabilitations with integrity.

The rehabilitation law was the only context in which Russians discussed the opening of the KGB files. Russians have not had a broad public discussion on whether the KGB files should be open to the public. In Poland and East Germany, politicians went back and forth over this divisive question for years. Each side mustered numerous arguments about the right to information versus the right to privacy. In comparison, the Russian debate has been anemic. Everything was decided in the months following the coup. Article 11 of the rehabilitation law gave persons who had been rehabilitated the right to read the materials that had led to their sentencing under the criminal or administrative code. This was not the equivalent of opening the KGB files. Private organizations and researchers cannot have access. Furthermore, people who were targets of KGB surveillance, but were never arrested and rehabilitated, do not have any access to the files the KGB collected about them.

In November 1991, the Council of Nationalities briefly considered a measure that would provide a legal basis for lustration. In discussing the "Declaration on human rights and freedoms," Deputy Mazaev proposed an amendment, which read as follows:

> Individuals who are guilty of violating the equal rights of citizens may be brought to justice on the basis of law. Officials who have committed grave violations of civil rights may not be in government service.[70]

At the request of an unidentified deputy, the chair decided that the Council would vote on each sentence separately. The first sentence—saying that individuals who violated human rights would be brought to justice on the basis of law—passed with only one dissenter. The second sentence—a basis for lustration—failed to capture a third of the votes cast.[71] This brief paragraph of debate is the only instance in which lustration was discussed in the Russian legislature. Even just two months after the attempted coup when anger against the KGB was at its peak and the statue of Feliks Dzierzhinsky, the KGB's notorious founder, in Lubianka Square had been toppled, lustration was anathema.

Unlike Germany and Poland, Russia did not form a parliamentary investigatory committee to look into the human rights abuses committed by the previous regime. Instead its legislators' attention turned to the coup attempt. The Supreme Soviet formed a committee "to study the causes and circumstances of the state coup" on September 6, 1991. Headed by Democratic Russia's Lev Ponomarev, the committee did a credible job of examining the institutions that supported the coup. It studied the role of the KGB, the military, and the CPSU in the coup, and organized open hearings on these topics. By early 1992, the committee was circulating drafts of its final reports.

The reports gave rise to recommendations that went far beyond the simple dismissal of individuals who had supported the coup. The draft reports acknowledge a link between the attempted coup and the long Soviet history of abusing individual rights. The attempted coup was a legacy of the KGB's and CPSU's extralegal status. One draft report called the KGB the "main repressive structure of the totalitarian regime" and "a tool in the genocide of its own people." The draft reports contain a full-blown agenda for coming to terms with the Soviet Union's legacy of repression. The policy recommendations included the following:

> -Apply international law to hold organizations and individuals responsible for crimes against humanity and genocide.
> -Organize specialists to study the KGB and publish a "whitebook" about its activities.
> -Establish parliamentary control over the special services.
> -Remove all KGB cadres who ignored laws while carrying out their duties.
> -"The task of quickly liberating society from the repressive institutions and their legacy puts on the agenda the question about the secret agents of the former KGB. Understanding (but not exaggerating) the complexity of this problem and at the same time the inadmissibility of maintaining in responsible posts, including in the legislative organs, people who secretly worked in the organs of force, it is necessary to begin studying this question with the goal of working out a law on lustration, for which we ask [the assistance of] the committees on legislation, human rights and security."[72]
> -Adopt a law permitting citizens to read their KGB files.[73]

Here was the liberal democratic model for dealing with past injustices: trials based on international law; lustration; a truth commission; and an opening of the secret police archives.

In March 1992, the Supreme Soviet disbanded the committee. It never reported to the Supreme Soviet, and its draft reports ended up in a jumble of cardboard boxes stuffed in the storage room of a small human rights organization started by Ponomarev. The experience of this committee shows that the investigation into the attempted coup had the potential to flower into a broader consideration of the abuses of the past. This brief foray was abruptly curtailed, however, and the auspicious moment for investigating the past never recurred.

During 1991–92, no political group challenged the government's focus on coming to terms with the coup rather than with the whole legacy of Soviet repression. No political voice raised the concerns buried in those draft committee reports. In other former communist countries, two kinds of parties regularly placed this issue on the agenda: parties of the democratic opposition that previously suffered the brunt of the state's abuses and nationalist parties critical of communist rule. In Russia the democrats were a fractious bunch, which could not unite on an issue so contentious.[74] The democrats maintained whatever unity they could by throwing themselves behind Boris Yeltsin and staying close to the circles of power. Russia did not have a serious nationalist party during the period 1991–92, so this avenue was foreclosed. Even when Vladimir Zhirinovsky's Liberal Democratic Party emerged as a formidable force after 1993, it was not virulently anticommunist, a sharp contrast to nationalist parties in Central Europe. The Russian nationalist could not utterly disparage the Soviet state: It had maintained a broad sphere of influence, conquered Nazi Germany, vied with the United States in the Cold War, and developed a mighty military–industrial complex. Like the communists themselves, Russian nationalists adopt a carefully nuanced attitude toward the past.

Ideology After the Attempted Coup

In Poland and East Germany, the upheavals of 1989 were followed by "normal time," during which political life gradually became more ordinary. As discussed in the previous chapters, the ideology of liberal democracy played an important role in shaping the debates about transitional justice in this period. Russia took a longer time in finding a political equilibrium after its transitional moment in 1991. The economic crisis, which reached greater proportions in a country that had experienced 70 years of state socialism, consumed politicians' attention, and created serious doubts about whether democracy would bring benefits to the country. The power struggle between the legislative and executive branches resulted in a bloody confrontation in October 1993, and a year later the Russian military was embroiled in an unsuccessful attempt to reassert Russian sovereignty in the breakaway republic of Chechnya.

Since ideology is more important in explaining political developments during settled times, it would be misguided to look to ideology as a major explanatory factor in understanding the country's approach to transitional justice during the great unsettledness of Russia in the early 1990s. Russian politics has not been moored to a particular ideology. For example, surveys made of the Russian population in 1995 and 1996 asked questions about broad ideas, such as whether Russia should emulate the West. Though done just a year apart, the surveys turned out very different results. The study's authors concluded that most Russians lacked an ideological framework to help them form stable political opinions.[75] Liberal democracy, so popular in other post-communist countries, has encountered ambivalence, rather than a warm embrace.

The Polish and German debates over transitional justice reflect a set of shared assumptions and commitments stemming from liberal democratic ideology, such as human rights and the rule of law. In Russia, parliamentary debates on transitional justice are scanty, but an examination of the debates on human rights instruments shows legislators' skepticism about the central concepts of liberal democracy.

In other new democracies, the term "human rights" is chanted with a convert's zeal. Human rights seem to signify all that is desirable about building a democracy. Russian lawmakers have been uncomfortable with this term, and by extension the liberal democratic tradition. When they discussed a declaration on human rights in November 1991, they were reticent about the language of even this non-binding statement of the country's aspirations in the area of human rights. Their biggest concern was that the whole catalogue of social and economic rights, such as the right to employment and housing, be included in the definition of this term.[76]

The controversy over the use of this term became more heated over time. In early 1993, the chair of the Supreme Soviet's committee on human rights, the noted democrat and former political prisoner Sergei Kovalev, made a report to his hostile colleagues. Kovalev used language and arguments that would seem natural and uncontroversial in other post-communist countries. He talked about Russia's return to the "community of civilized states," and employed a definition of human rights that focused on civil and political rights. He criticized Russia's legal culture and called for the implementation of the rule of law.[77] The response was bitter. Deputies accused Kovalev of the following sins: focusing totally on the issues important to former dissidents at the expense of ordinary Russians; ignoring the fate of the native Russian population; being rude to the average Ivan who sought help from the committee in relieving his housing problems; disregarding the effects of plunging living standards; and even using the committee to cover up shady commercial dealings. Many of these were purely *ad hominem* attacks; however, the extent to which the legislators were willing to disparage the whole idea of human rights in the process is striking. As one noted, "I am seriously bothered by the approach to human rights which Sergei Kovalev laid out for us. This is a Western European approach for rich countries, an approach to human rights which in its abstractness belongs to the liberal conception."[78]

The theme of the country's relationship to Western Europe emerged in many debates. Using the Western experience—whether in introducing trial by jury or the right of *habeas corpus*—demanded detailed explanations and half-hearted apologies. A Russian legislator did not just stand up in parliament and say: "This model from Western country x would be a good one for the following reasons." He had to search

Russian history and find some historical precedent for it.[79] While the communists and nationalists concur that Russia cannot borrow freely from Western models, they cannot agree so readily on a positive definition of Russia's path. Russia has not embraced liberal democratic ideology, but then it has not really embraced an alternative either. In fact, in 1996, President Yeltsin announced a public contest to work out a new ideology for the state.[80] This odd contest (which was never really carried out) reveals three assumptions: Russia does not have an ideology; it needs one; and, no foreign models are acceptable.

What are the consequences of losing ideological moorings? Russia had experienced 70 years of ideologically legitimated rule, and the czarist regime that preceded the communist one also had clearly articulated reasons for its rule. Now "Russian citizens cannot imagine where their country is moving and what kind of society we are building. . . . People experience nostalgia for ideology—not for Marxism-Leninism concretely, but for ideology as a factor of Stability and Order."[81] The weakness of ideology means that it is hard to tell the story of the past decade. In Poland and East Germany, the story is clear: For 40 years we lived under an authoritarian regime that violated our human rights; now we live in a liberal democracy and enjoy the protection of the rule of law. It is a story with a happy ending. In Russia, it is not clear what themes should structure public memory about the past and what should be the country's legitimate hopes for the future. The loss of empire and economic well-being means that the transition does not seem to have a storybook ending.

Transitional Justice After 1991

Once Yeltsin began to distance the democrats from power, they altered their position on transitional justice. After Prime Minister Yegor Gaidar, the democrats' darling, was forced to resign and Yeltsin replaced him with the stodgy communist Viktor Chernomyrdin, Democratic Russia decided to rethink its political strategy and move into constructive opposition to the government.[82] Its main objection to Chernomyrdin was his lack of credentials for shepherding the country's transition to a market economy. Once the movement announced its opposition to the government, however, it felt free to raise a host of other concerns about Yeltsin's political course.

Transitional justice had been absent from Democratic Russia's declarations in 1991 and early 1992. Its main declaration simply called for the "struggle against monopolism in politics."[83] However, at the Third

Congress held in December 1992, Democratic Russia adopted a declaration with much stronger language.[84] It called for Russia to "return to the path of civilized development" by undertaking radical reforms. It contended that Russia must "decommunize society" in order to create the conditions for a civil society. This would require the circulation of elites so as to remove the *nomenklatura* from positions of influence. The program called on the Supreme Soviet to adopt a lustration law (Art. 3.11).

In the first half of 1993, several committed individuals from Democratic Russia batted around the idea of a lustration law. A group worked out a draft lustration law, using the postwar Japanese law as a model. The draft law would have limited the types of government positions individuals could hold for a period of the next five to ten years if they had previously been high-ranking communist officials or if they had worked openly or secretly for the KGB. These individuals could not hold responsible positions in the executive branches (i.e., high-ranking appointed positions), and they could not teach in middle and higher educational institutions. They would remain free to hold elected positions.[85]

Within the circles of Democratic Russia, the proposed law was quite controversial. The fault line between advocates of substantive justice and of procedural justice emerged, just as it had in other new democracies. A series of articles in *Moskovskie Novosti* counterpoised Galina Starovoitova and Sergei Kovalev. Starovoitova argued that the country needed to acknowledge openly the cleavages Russia's difficult history had left imprinted in its society. She believed a Victorian silence would only gloss over the real differences in society, but do nothing to lay a foundation of trust. Lustration would reveal the truth about the influence of the KGB in the past, and ensure that those who had caused harm would not enjoy the fruits of service in the new system. Lustration was the path to truth and justice. Meanwhile, Kovalev, the leader of the Supreme Soviet's human rights committee, held that dividing society into the "clean" and "unclean" would only exacerbate tensions.[86] It would be extremely difficult, if not impossible, to delineate between the guilty and the innocent, and ultimately the process would violate citizens' rights. Lustration was impracticable and illiberal.

Later the philosopher Aleksander Tsipko weighed in with the argument that in Russian society the good and the wicked were so mixed up together as to be inseparable. The communists themselves had made the decision to transform the political system and had thus atoned for their past misdeeds. Furthermore, "after a year the current helpless government has lost its right to judge the old one."[87] Yeltsin might have been able to push through a lustration agenda in 1991. (The brief debate in the Supreme Soviet in November showed that the legislature was not ready to take the initiative in this matter. Nevertheless, given Yeltsin's authority, it might have responded to a prodding.) A year later, though, the situation was different. Already Yeltsin's own shortcomings were becoming apparent: Economic production and living standards had plunged, and Russia's stature as a great power had diminished. Yeltsin had already squandered some of the moral authority he had accumulated during the heady days of August 1991.

Democratic Russia had initiated a classic liberal democratic debate over lustration. Their debates took place only within the press, however, and not in parliament. And the debates were among two wings of a small democratic movement. This germ of a debate was soon suffocated. All talk of lustration came to an end in October 1993 when the conflict between Yeltsin and the Supreme Soviet escalated from political bickering to the use of guns and tanks. With the Supreme Soviet refusing to be dissolved and trying to seize control of the state-run television station, Yeltsin used force to remove the recalcitrant deputies from the White House. Just two years earlier the White House had been the symbol of Russia's resistance to the communist-inspired coup. After Yeltsin ordered the military's attack, its smoldering hulk could conjure up only the dashed promise of Russian democracy.

This time Yeltsin capitalized on his opponents' weakness and pushed for the adoption of a new constitution, which would give the executive branch significant powers. In December 1993, voters chose members of a new legislative body—the Russian State Duma—and approved a referendum on the new constitution. With a new legislature and a new constitution, Russia had an opportunity for a fresh beginning.

Given the communists' and nationalists' success in the parliamentary elections, there could be no thought of introducing legislation regarding transitional justice. A debate on lustration was impossible. Indeed the democrats did not raise the issue of lustration again after the sketchy initiatives of early 1993. In the aftermath of the events of October 1993, coming to terms with the past took on a more contemporary meaning, which had little to do with the attempted coup of 1991 or the entire legacy of Soviet rule. Coming to terms with the past meant dealing with the aftermath of October 1993.

One of the Duma's first official acts was to set up a parliamentary committee to investigate the events of October 1993. If protracted, this investigation could poison again the relationship between the president and the parliament. At the same time, deputies introduced legislation calling for an amnesty of both the 1991 coup leaders and the Supreme Soviet deputies jailed after the October events. The Communist, Agrarian, and Zhirinovsky's misnamed Liberal Democratic parties joined together in supporting the amnesty law. Supporters said it was time to "draw a line behind the past."[88] The leader of the Communist Party issued a program for national reconciliation. Among other things the program called for the removal of "odious figures" from the government, the development of a "national state doctrine which takes into consideration the entire 1000-year history and does not divide it into halves," and the "rejection of historical revenge."[89] In effect, he was calling for an unambiguous moratorium on coming to terms with the past.

Yeltsin's supporters opposed the amnesty law, especially as it applied to the events of October 1993. They did not want to offer an amnesty until the individuals had been found guilty of particular criminal acts. One individual even tried to make a connection between the country's failure to come to terms with the Soviet past and the conflict of October 1993. A deputy from Russia's Choice, then the incarnation of the democratic forces, argued that since the crimes of the communist regime went unpunished for 70 years, people did not believe they would be punished for any political crimes.[90] A Liberal Democratic deputy retorted by quipping that the tsar had started it all by opening fire on demonstrators in 1905. Such relativizing statements are typical fare in Russian discussions about the crimes of the past.[91]

Yeltsin eventually compromised. He agreed to an amnesty of his political opponents from both 1991 and 1993, if the Duma disbanded its committee on investigating the events of October 1993. Vladimir Zhirinovsky, flush from his party's surprising success in the December elections, declared, "Today we can close the dark, troubling pages in the history of Russian government and begin a new page. . . . We can break from our past, so to speak, and we will not blacken it, nor will we judge."[92]

National reconciliation was nothing more than ephemeral political rhetoric, and soon the muted tones of political reconciliation rose to the usual shrill pitch of Russia's rough-and-ready democracy. Conflict between the legislative and executive branches became a central feature of politics in the Yeltsin era.

Though the amnesty law did not set the stage for a grand reconciliation, it did effectively remove the issue of transitional justice from the political agenda for good. Yeltsin had no interest in reopening the question of past human rights abuses when he knew that any such move would result in adroit counter-investigations into his own questionable policies. After the disastrous failure of his policy in Chechnya in 1994–95, Yeltsin stood on even shakier ground.

Anticommunist rhetoric did not entirely disappear, however. Yeltsin employed it during his campaign for reelection in 1996, packing the state-run television stations' nightly line-up with historical documentaries about the Bolsheviks' crimes and running a campaign advertisement with damning Soviet era footage accompanied by the warning: "The communists haven't even changed their name. They won't change their methods. It's not too late to prevent civil war and famine."[93] Reminding voters how bad communism was helped to distract them from criticizing the failings of his own regime—a clever campaign strategy. Criticism of the past was tied to the political goal of winning an election, rather than that of reforming the former institutions of repression or creating a sense of historical justice. Yeltsin's sharp rhetoric was not accompanied by any of the serious policy initiatives one might expect from someone who criticizes the past regime's crimes, for example, to reform the police, former KGB, or judicial system; to open the secret police files; to make a formal apology to the nation. After winning the 1996 election, Yeltsin did not advocate any policies of truth and justice.

Truth-Telling by Civic Organizations

While remembrance of past injustices has no resonance in national-level politics, the public has not entirely lost interest in the past. Various civic organizations, especially the widespread branches of Memorial and the Association of the Victims of Political Repressions, attempted to keep alive the memory of the past. Two kinds of projects have been the focus of their attention: the building of memorials to the victims of the repressions and the publication of *Books of Memory* [*Knigi pamiati*], listing the names of all people who had been repressed and later rehabilitated in a given region. In both of these projects, civic organizations took the initiative, and frequently they were able to enlist the financial support of local government authorities.

Since the beginning of *glasnost'*, at least 102 memorials to the victims of the repressions have been erected on the territory of the Russian Federation.[94] Of these, 27 were built entirely by civic organizations, while a further 52 resulted from collaboration between the government and civic organizations. The government sponsored only 17 of these projects on its own initiative. The typical memorial involves placing a cross or a slab of granite at a place where political prisoners were executed or buried. However, some regions, especially Siberia where so many perished, have undertaken more elaborate and costly projects. The Memorial group in Perm' formed a museum on the site of the Soviet Union's last labor camp for political prisoners, and the sculptor Ernst Neizvestny designed a trio of massive sculptures honoring the victims of repressions in Vorkuta, Ekaterinburg, and Magadan.[95]

Thirty-two memorials were erected during 1991–93, and a further 47 went up during 1994–96. This shows that civic organizations did not lose interest in the past after 1990. They continued to work steadily on projects at the local level. The pace at which these memorials were being erected began to slacken only in 1998, by which time many of the key sites were already marked.

As noted earlier, the 1991 rehabilitation law stated that the names of all individuals rehabilitated by the authorities should be published in the local press. This occurred only sporadically. Once again civic organizations seized the initiative. Many chapters of Memorial and the Association of Victims of Political Repressions began to compile such lists. Their members requested information from the KGB archives and procurator's office, and in many cases, they developed cooperative relationships with the state institutions. As they gained additional financing, usually from the local government, many regions began to publish their own *Books of Memory*.[96] Typically such a book includes basic biographical information about the victims of Stalinism as well as the information about their fate in the machine of terror. In some regions, the list fits in a single volume, whereas other regions had to issue several tomes, numbing in their meticulous cataloguing of victims.

As in the case of the monuments, the role of civic organizations is quite significant in the publication of these lists. Only 30 books explain clearly how they came to be published. Half of these involved extensive cooperation between civic organizations and government organs, as well as financing from the local governments. Local governments published only seven of the books on their own initiative, while civic organizations published eight without government financing.[97] Despite the letter of the law, it is clear that most of these lists would not have been published without the civic organizations' steady pressure and lively initiative at the local level. Their pressure seems to have been particularly effective beginning in 1995, when the country celebrated the fiftieth anniversary of the Soviet victory in the Great Patriotic War. In conjunction with the celebrations many regions published *Books of Memory* listing their casualties in that calamitous war. After issuing these volumes, many local governments decided to put their resources behind the publication of *Books of Memory* for the repressions. In some cases the same editorial board just shifted gears into the new work.[98] Of the 45 *Books of Memory* for which I found publication dates, 33 were published in the period 1995–99. This is further evidence that many activists had not forgotten about the abuses of the past. They found, however, that they were better able to articulate their concerns by participating in local projects rather than in politics on the national scale.

However laudable, these local efforts by civic organizations cannot substitute for the state's action. They have had but a small impact on the popular imagination, as apathy about the crimes of the Soviet past has spread.[99] Only the state can officially acknowledge that past abuses occurred and offer an apology. Only the state can ensure that abuses are never repeated: by punishing the perpetrators, releasing information about the crimes from archives, and, most importantly, reforming the institutions that permitted the abuses in the first place. Instead of taking these steps, Russia has chosen to forget its past. The results turn up in survey data about past political figures. In early 2003, 36 percent of Russians said they thought Stalin did more good than bad for the country.[100] More than half of Russians thought he played a positive role in history.[101]

Conclusion

Russia's approach to transitional justice has assumed unique outlines. During a period of liberalization from above, an extensive public conversation about the abuses of the past took place. The liberal media and emerging civic organizations led the effort to reveal the truth about the country's difficult history. The results included a wave of interest in previously banned literature, probing news stories, and the Memorial movement. Such was Russia's promising start to the process of coming to terms with its past.

Yet, interest in the past peaked early (too early perhaps), and all of society's interest in the past translated poorly into political action. Initially, Sakharov and the Inter-Regional Group of Deputies connected criticism of the past to the abolition of Article 6 from the constitution. After this succeeded, transitional justice disappeared from the political agenda for many months.

The coup attempt in Russia led to a transition by rupture, which would lead us to expect high levels of retribution. Indeed, Russian President Yeltsin did adopt some retributive policies just after the coup: He organized trials of the coup's organizers, banned the CPSU, and threatened to take over the KGB's archives. However, it is important to note against whom this retribution was directed. Yeltsin did not threaten to punish people who had violated human rights in the past; rather, he sought to remove from public life those who had organized the coup and sought to perpetuate Soviet hegemony. Yeltsin's retribution was a tool in his quest for power.

Only one policy represented an effort to come to terms with human rights abuses committed by the Soviet regime: the rehabilitation law, which had been framed long before the coup. Subsequently, democratic factions made efforts to place transitional justice on the political agenda. Ponamarev's commission developed a liberal democratic agenda for transitional justice in 1991–92, but the commission was disbanded before its reports were made public. Later, the democrats broached the topic of lustration, but the upheaval in autumn 1993 brought this discussion to a precipitate end.

In sum, then, these were Russia's policies of transitional justice:

Violent Retribution There was no violence between communists and anticommunists, but Russia's transition to democracy has not been altogether peaceful. The street clashes in August 1991, the attack on the White House in October 1993, and the ethnic war in Chechnya have marred the process of democratization.

Trials Russia's few trials directed toward those responsible for the coup attempt ultimately ended with an amnesty. Perversely, the most significant trial involved the Communist Party as a plaintiff trying to rehabilitate itself.

Lustration Russia has had no lustration, except the removal of some KGB officials who supported the coup.

Rehabilitation Two major laws—for repressed ethnic groups and political prisoners—rehabilitated the victims of past human rights abuses. Both laws were in place by October 1991.

Compensation The rehabilitation laws provided for compensation, which turned out to be a paltry sum in the context of the country's galloping inflation.

Truth-Telling The government did not sponsor any effort at truth-telling. The government appears to have forgotten about the abuses of the past. Meanwhile, civic organizations organized efforts to reveal the truth about Soviet history.

Glasnost', Gorbachev's preferred approach to dealing with the past, turned out to be an enduring precedent. In Russia, the media and local civic organizations carried out the work of coming to terms with the past. They built public monuments and published the names of the victims, so that the past would not be forgotten. It is not true that Russians have lost interest in their painful history. Rather, coming to terms with the past has not emerged as an issue of national-level politics, as it did in Germany and Poland.

Transitional justice was absent from the national political agenda in Russia because it lacked a strong political advocate. Neither communists nor nationalists would support policies of truth and justice. The democrats were too small and fractious to push through this agenda. Furthermore, Russian politicians could not agree on the values that would organize a debate about the Soviet past. In Poland and Germany, liberal democratic ideology provided a conceptual framework within which politicians could analyze the past. It contributed key words that made discussion of the past possible; it set flexible, but definite boundaries to how far the debate could range. In Russia, competing political forces knew no so such consensus. In the absence of shared values, politics was reduced to the battle of "*kto-kogo*" [who gets whom]. Politics is a quest for power, in which one of necessity sullies his hands. Remembering the sins of the past would engage all political forces in mutual recrimination, which would spiral into the distant past. And the Russian past would yield a ripe "harvest of sorrows," for which no one wishes to assume responsibility.[102]

Instead of taking responsibility for the past, Russian political forces have agreed to forget. Forgetting is not just inadvertent; it is based on an agreement forged after the events of autumn 1993. Only a few isolated voices—such as Memorial—challenge this political amnesia. Significantly, Memorial's commitment to transitional justice has inspired them to fight for justice in post-communist Russia, especially by criticizing the government's human rights record in Chechnya. Their concern for victims of abuse in the past led them to a concern for present-day victims. This is an indication that a commitment to transitional justice, especially if it leads to serious institutional reforms, can teach important political lessons. If the state had learned these lessons, the human rights record in the Russian Federation might be considerably stronger. Nevertheless, despite criticism from a small group of human rights activists, the agreement to forget past crimes survives since it continues to serve most political interests. It is likely that only a new generation of politicians, men and women unstained by the past, will dare to challenge it.

Conclusion: Liberal Democracy's Shortcomings and Overriding Advantage

Ideology is like a plot formula for politics. A recipe for a romance novel provides the author with an ending (happily ever after) and a set of ordinary means toward that end (man rescues woman). Likewise, an ideology organizes our thoughts about politics over time. It defines an end (the political good) and the means for attaining it (e.g., revolution, war, or negotiations). Ideology is thus as useful to politicians as the plot formula is to the budding novelist. It helps to economize on effort and to focus the imagination. A certain end is given, and the acceptable means are outlined. This hardly means that ideology is a rigid template for political action. One plot formula gives rise to shelf upon shelf of variations on the theme, as any trip to the public library will attest. Similarly, ideology awaits the creative politician and the interpretive public. It is flexible and malleable, though not limitlessly so.

Liberal democracy is the key ideology of our times. It provides an explanation for the suffering under an illiberal regime: The regime did not respect civil rights or allow citizens an opportunity to participate in decision-making. This led to an abuse of power and the crushing of threatening dissent. Liberal democracy also outlines the desired ends. All people will be included in the new democracy, regardless of their past. Political life will be organized so as to limit the state's power and guarantee civil liberties. This liberal democratic regime will promote justice so that each individual is respected and given his due. It also will promote truth: Free speech and a free press will discuss public issues without hindrance. The story of liberal democracy begins with its ends—liberty, truth, and justice.

Of these, truth and justice are most relevant to countries in the midst of trying to come to terms with past human rights abuses. The people who hope for liberal democracy have faith that these promises will be their inheritance, their "happily ever after." They long for justice, that those who caused suffering will themselves suffer punishment and that those who suffered in the past will find their vindication. Retribution upon the perpetrators and restoration to the victims will be among the fruits of liberal democracy. Furthermore, the people hope that in a liberal democracy, the truth about the past will be uttered freely and probed deeply. Whereas the dictators of the past obfuscated and concealed the truth, liberal democracy obligates the government to openness and allows people to speak about their suffering. Truth-telling also involves the public acknowledgment of events that shaped individuals' personal histories.

At the same time, with its model of the social contract, the ideology contains a seemingly contradictory emphasis on inclusivity and forward-looking justice. In the name of these values, some have argued that a new democratic regime should take a principled decision to forget about past abuses.[1] This position does not reflect the complexity of liberal democratic ideology, which includes important competing elements. The contribution of social contract theory in this context is more modest: To remind us that securing a just future for everyone is of paramount importance. Consolidating a liberal democratic regime is the overriding political goal. If efforts to obtain truth and justice for past abuses imperil democracy, for example, by instigating a coup, then they are inappropriate. The survival of democracy is the key to ensuring justice for the next generation. Nevertheless, justice for the future does not require foregoing justice for past crimes. The trade-off—in most cases—is not so stark.

Democratization is a teleological process of attaining these political ends—liberty, justice, and truth. In addition to defining the ends, the ideology also constrains the political means involved in democratization. Violence in general is anathema, but in particular, the illegal use of force is discouraged. Instead, the ideology promotes nonviolent, legal change to the existing political structures.

Liberal democracy also establishes the acceptable means for attaining truth and justice. The ideology insists on procedural justice, that is, it sets limits on how the state can use its massive coercive powers with respect to the individual. Power must be exercised in accordance with law. The rule of law prohibits the state from retroactively deeming an individual's acts illegal. The state must abide by norms of due process whenever it exercises its coercive powers against the individual. Individuals must be given a "fair shake" when they face the state as their adversary. They must be given protection against prolonged pretrial detentions, illegal searches and seizures, and notice of the evidence against them. They must have the right to legal counsel, a chance to speak or be silent, a fair trial before an impartial judge, and an opportunity to appeal a decision they believe to be incorrect.[2]

The ideology of liberal democracy thus sets forth the substantive ends for dealing with past human rights abuses: Do justice and tell the truth without jeopardizing democracy. It also establishes the acceptable means for achieving those ends, namely procedural justice. The contradiction in the ideology is that the prescribed means often seem insufficient for achieving the prescribed ends. There is no perfect liberal democratic solution to the dilemmas of transitional justice. The ideology sets up competing values, which must be resolved by political compromises and ideological balancing.

The debates on transitional justice in Poland and East Germany show that liberal democratic ideology accommodates a number of political voices. Procedural justice is the rallying cry of the former communists. They argue that the main lesson of communist rule is that law, not political will, must regulate the exercise of power. They therefore advocate procedural justice at the expense of substantive ends. Of course, this policy protects them and their cronies from retribution, keeps the state from making a costly restoration to the victims, and conceals the truth about their own misdeeds. The former communists are also likely to draw on the social contract metaphor to argue for their right to participate in the new democracy. Altogether it is a convenient position.

When the democratic opposition is in power, they often join the former communists in advocating procedural justice at the expense of substantive justice. They may believe that the simple fact that they now control the levers of power represents true justice, and they are reluctant to step into the hypocritical position of exceeding the state's powers in order to seek retribution against the criminals of the past. Moreover, especially in the early stages of the transition, they may fear that any attempts to undertake policies of truth and justice would only invite retaliation, which could lead to social unrest and the derailing of democracy. They are willing to be magnanimous with the former communists, referring to the theory of the social contract to justify inclusivity and forward-looking justice. However, when the democratic opposition is out of power, they tend to shift toward the other pole, emphasizing the importance of substantive justice. They suspect that at heart the advocates of procedural justice may have little interest in justice at all. While it may be acceptable for them to forget the past, they certainly do not want the former communists to grow forgetful. Instead they stress that the government must take responsibility for the crimes of the past by adopting policies of truth and justice.

In the post-communist setting, the advocates of policies of truth and justice often come from groups with nationalist leanings. They want to reveal how the previous regime collaborated with a foreign power, and they want the collaborators to suffer punishment. They believe these policies will help to solidify the national character of the new liberal democratic regime. Logically, we might expect the former victims to support the nationalists who pursue the substantive ends of liberal democracy. They have a personal interest in the retribution against their enemies and the restitution of their lost honor. Often, though, the victims are among the most whole-hearted supporters of the ideology of liberal democracy. They have suffered in the past, and they have looked for an explanation of their suffering and an alternative to it. Ideologically aware, they recognize the conflict between the substantive ends and procedural justice; cautious about the possibility of the abuse of the state's power, they are reluctant to advocate the state overreaching its bounds.

The dynamics of the debates in Poland and East Germany indicate an ongoing concern with the appropriate balance between forgetting and taking political responsibility, and between substantive and procedural justice. In both countries, the democratic opposition emphasized forgetting and procedural justice during the early days of the transition. They urged political inclusion rather than retribution and insisted on carrying out a transition by legal means, rather than by force. In both countries, the opposition feared that some individuals might resort to violence and thereby threaten the legitimacy of their liberal democratic identity. Violence might threaten the entire transition by provoking retaliation from the military or police. Punishing those guilty of past abuses was not worth the risk of jeopardizing democracy.

Compared to Poland's Solidarity movement, East Germany's opposition was less strongly committed to the rules of procedural justice. Unlike Solidarity, the citizens' movements did not have a rich intellectual history of theorizing about a self-limiting revolution; thus, they were more willing to adopt a new stance as one threat disappeared and another loomed. The main reason that the East German opposition shifted its attention to political responsibility and substantive justice, was its rapid loss of political control. As early as the Volkskammer elections in March 1990, the opposition was thrust outside the political mainstream. The major political parties from West Germany established themselves in the East, and the drive toward unification became unstoppable. With its loss of power, East Germany's opposition focused increasingly on political responsibility, substantive justice and truth. They did not trust Western politicians who lacked a personal experience of life under communist rule to come to terms with the past. East Germans assumed that for the West transitional justice would be a low priority given the unified Germany's strapped budget, competing priorities, and diluted connection to the communist past.

The East Germans were apparently correct in their assessment of the Kohl government, which was eager to set aside the past in the interests of a smooth unification process. It wanted the Stasi files to disappear into the vast Federal Archives, and it made discouraging noises about the prospects of lustration. The all-German Bundestag, however, began a series of nuanced debates about how to establish political responsibility balancing substantive and procedural justice. The debates were very legalistic, leading some commentators to lament the "juridification" of the political discourse surrounding transitional justice. The legal discourse, despite its technicality and dryness, has the advantage of permitting several perspectives and encouraging compromise. In this climate, the Bundestag put together a legislative program for transitional justice relatively quickly; the major laws on truth and justice were in place by 1993.

In Poland, Solidarity's intellectuals had a firmer belief that forgetting the past was necessary for building an inclusive democratic government; they were sticklers for procedural justice. Their writings throughout the 1980s had emphasized the desirability of a political transition based entirely on legal means, and the experience of negotiations with the communists throughout 1989 only reinforced this commitment. The democratic transition left this group at the helm of the state, where they were quite self-conscious about the possibility of abusing their powers. If they violated due process, even in minor ways to facilitate retribution against communist era criminals, they would fall into the ready jaws of hypocrisy. The Solidarity-led government of Tadeusz Mazowiecki was reluctant to support any lustration, even in the secret police; however, once again, the deliberative body—the Sejm—worked out a compromise to allow lustration of the secret police and the procurators.

Even when the liberal democratic wing of Solidarity was not in power, they were slow to shift to a position advocating more substantive justice for past abuses. They moved to the periphery of power after the October 1991 elections, and then lost power to the former communists in fall 1993; however, their frustration with procedural justice did not begin to set in until 1995. The change of heart occurred largely because the liberals sensed that the former communists were exploiting procedural justice to distort the truth about the past. By 1996, the liberals were willing to support a lustration law, and a year later, when they had a greater influence on the country's coalition government, they supported an opening of the secret police files.

Both Poland and German have gradually worked through the conflict between substantive and procedural justice, arriving at a set of very similar compromises. Both have taken political responsibility for the abuses committed by the communist regimes. They have apportioned blame to the communist leaders, some of whom have been prosecuted, while many more have lost their positions and influence through lustration. The countries have also assigned a more diffuse blame to the state as a whole, which has borne the financial burden of rehabilitation and compensation of the victims. Both states have attempted to compile the facts that tell the true story of the past through opening archives and holding parliamentary inquiries. The main difference between these two countries' approaches to transitional justice is that the Poland's path was much longer and more tumultuous, leaving in its wake two governments and bitter allegations. Many of the debates in Poland had more emotional fume than substance, and they only postponed the compromises finally agreed upon. Poland's experience teaches us that the issue of transitional justice does not arise only in the year or two of dramatic political change, but can linger on the political agenda, creating more problems if left unresolved. It is preferable to have these debates early and resolve the dilemmas of transitional justice rather than letting the questions fester.

Once Poland and Germany had determined that political responsibility was preferable to forgetting, the debates turned on legal issues: How can liberal democracy reconcile its substantive ends with its procedural guarantees? In framing the question in that way, politicians anticipated a set of characteristic outcomes. In both countries, retribution was weak. They carried out some trials to achieve substantive justice. They attempted to use international law or domestic precedents to get around the procedural protections offered by the statute of limitations; however, numerous due process guarantees hindered the state's ability to carry out trials. Both countries permitted some lustration, but they did not allow lustration to escalate into political purges. Again, due process constrained the policy. Policies of restorative justice also involved procedural limitations. The parliaments debated heatedly whom they should rehabilitate, how much compensation should be paid, and how to compare victims of the communist regime to other classes of victims.

In theory, restorative justice, being less fettered by procedural limitations, should be the preferred method of coming to terms with the past. If the state cannot exact retribution upon the perpetrators, the least it can do is to provide rehabilitation and ample compensation to the victims. Surprisingly, though, Poland and Germany paid relatively scant attention to restorative justice. Germany spent little money compensating individuals wrongly imprisoned by the state socialist regime, especially in comparison to what it spent on the restitution of property. It was very slow to allow rehabilitation of those who lost their employment for political or religious reasons. Poland could not find a legal solution to its veterans' law, so many former secret police agents were eligible for the benefits while former victims were excluded. It never did pass a law to rehabilitate those wrongly imprisoned after 1956; the procurator's office carried out this rehabilitation on its own initiative.

The lack of attention to restorative justice comes in part because the victims' organizations in both countries failed to unify. Splintered as they were, the victims' movements never really emerged on the political scene, and they never developed a connection with a single party to act as their mouthpiece. With victims' perspectives marginalized, parliaments in both countries devoted more effort to retributive policies. Retribution affects the high and mighty, those who are visible to the public eye, and the stakes are high—deprivation of liberty or loss of high government positions. Toppling the former pinnacle of power involves great drama, and the visibility and drama contribute to a strong educational effect. Retribution teaches people that those who commit crimes in the name of the state will not enjoy impunity.

Meanwhile, restorative justice affects many people, but these are the ordinary people who protested against the government, tried to escape across the border, or simply said the wrong thing at the wrong time. Rehabilitating and compensating them involves thousands of little administrative acts—reviewing files, sending out certificates and modest checks, signing up people for pension benefits, and allowing them to reapply for their former jobs. While retribution is more legally complex than restorative justice, the latter is a greater administrative headache. Furthermore, restoration is relatively invisible to the public eye. The former victims are for the most part nameless, and when they receive their certificate and check, the newspapers do not run headlines. Little public learning occurs as a result of restoration. When governments carry out restoration, for the most part they are joylessly going through with what they perceive to be a duty, an exercise of political responsibility.

With its several competing, sometimes contradictory values, the liberal democratic approach to transitional justice is highly imperfect. There is no determinate model for other countries to copy. Each country must grope its way to a solution by applying the ideology's central concepts, and the set of compromises may please no one. In particular, an exclusive focus on procedural justice may lead some—such as nationalists and former victims—to believe that liberal democracy does not yield substantive justice. It is merely an empty set of hallowed promises. At times the East German opposition has voiced a disappointment with liberal democracy's shortcomings; however, there is no evidence that the lack of substantive justice has seriously discredited the ideology.

In fact, the ideology's complexity and indeterminacy are its great political assets. They encourage a serious debate about transitional justice and accommodate a wide range of political voices. In East Germany and Poland, former communists, liberal democrats, and nationalists alike have framed their positions in terms of the ideology. An ideology that allows parties across the spectrum to share a conceptual framework encourages continuing dialogue and eventual compromise. It keeps potentially dangerous groups inside the established political system, rather than encouraging them to attack it from the outside. A group can voice its dissent without upending the democratic transition. After all, establishing and then preserving democracy must be the paramount goals in these times of rapid change, even at the cost of substantive justice.[3] Liberal democratic ideology encourages moderation among the democratic opposition and the participation of communists. These values augur well for peaceful, negotiated change, rather than a violent revolution.

The desire to take political responsibility for the past while respecting the boundaries of procedural justice has led to a search for a way of dealing with the past without encountering legal barriers. The result has been increased attention to truth-telling in various forms, including opening archives and carrying out parliamentary inquiries. If substantive justice cannot be achieved because of procedural restrictions, then at least the truth about the past can be revealed. Truth-telling is an attractive solution to the problem of transitional justice. It contains elements both of retribution, such as exposing the perpetrators' misbegotten deeds, and restoration, by proclaiming the victims' innocence, even their heroism. Carried out by a public commission, truth-telling can also be in the center of the public eye. A truth commission can be the supreme act of assuming political responsibility for past injustices, for it allows a society to debate openly the apportioning of blame, perhaps even inviting citizens to consider how their own acts and omissions contributed to the harm.

Drawing Russia into the comparative study only highlights the similarities between East Germany and Poland. We might have expected that transitional justice in Russia would go further than in its western neighbors. It had experienced a more repressive regime, and early in the years of *glasnost'*, understanding the past was seen as a crucial step on the road to a more open government. However, as the transition progressed, the question of transitional justice was lost in a churning sea of other problems, and no significant political grouping took an interest in the question. Instead of having a serious, ideologically informed debate about policies of truth and justice, Russia had no debate at all.

Russia exemplifies the paradox noted by other students of transitional justice—that those countries which most need to come to terms with their past have the hardest time in doing so.[4] With its previous lack of democratic experience and its history of harsh political repression and tight secrecy, Russia could benefit from an open accounting with the crimes of the Soviet period. However, these very factors make it difficult to begin the debate.

Does Russia's failure to adopt policies of truth and justice bode ill for its democracy? The experience of other countries—Spain is a favorite example—shows that transitional justice is not necessary for the consolidation of democracy.[5] Indeed by themselves, trials, lustration, open archives, and rehabilitation programs do not do much to ensure free elections and civil liberties. They are most meaningful in acting as the catalyst for institutional reforms that will ensure democratic stability.[6] Trials can contribute to the end of the climate of impunity, which allowed political, military, and police officials to commit abuses without any threat of punishment. Lustration can be one aspect of deep reforms of the former institutions of repression, which leave the police and military firmly under democratic, civilian control. Truth-telling, along with rehabilitation and compensation, can help eradicate the habits of secrecy that thrived under authoritarian rule and pave the way for more open, accountable government. Transitional justice can be the beginning of these important reforms, which may ultimately impact the survival of democracy. Policies of truth and justice set a valuable precedent of concern about the state's power to oppress individuals.

Of course, these reforms can be undertaken in the absence of policies of truth and justice. In Spain, where policies of truth and justice would have been very controversial after Franco's death, most of the key institutional reforms took place—quietly, gradually, and without unduly agitating the military and pro-Franco political elite. The fact that transitional justice was avoided as a politically explosive issue meant that the reforms took nearly a decade to put in place and that significant "pockets of undemocratic decision-making" remained a part of Spanish political institutions.[7] Nevertheless, Spanish democracy was consolidated, and these shortcomings must be measured against the good of a peaceful transition to democracy.

Russia has not followed the Spanish model as closely as one might hope. The key institutional reforms are not in place. A climate of impunity persists, with the military committing serious abuses in

Chechnya, the police harassing and extorting people in Moscow, and politicians engaging in spectacular corruption.[8] The institutions formerly involved in repression—the military, judiciary, secret police, and procuracy—have not been reformed sufficiently to ensure that they adhere to the law rather than to executive power.[9] Indeed under President Putin's leadership the FSB (the post-communist KGB) gained strength in influencing political affairs.[10] Finally, the atmosphere of secrecy is still too much a part of Russian politics, with scandal, blackmail, conspiracy and rumors of conspiracy contributing to the public distaste for politics. As one observer lamented, "The past does not haunt Russia's secret police, Russia's judges, Russia's politicians or Russia's business elite."[11] Transitional justice would not have cured all these ills, but an open debate about policies of truth and justice for past abuses may have set an agenda for the necessary reforms and a powerful precedent for holding government officials accountable for their actions.

In the wave of recent transitions to democracy, Russia is unusual. Most countries have adopted policies of truth and justice broadly similar to those adopted in Poland and Germany.[12] South Africa had its truth commission, as did several Latin American countries. In Yugoslavia, Rwanda, and later Sierra Leone, the international community established tribunals to facilitate the prosecution of those guilty of human rights abuses in the past.[13] These have paved the way for the development of an International Criminal Court with jurisdiction over war crimes and crimes against humanity. The arrest of Chilean General Pinochet in England on charges leveled by a Spanish prosecutor marked the international community's readiness to end the impunity that former dictators enjoyed. After torturing their own citizens, dictators should not be free to roam the globe in search of superior medical treatment or luxury accommodations. The international community is showing an increasing willingness to reconsider the norm of state sovereignty and decide that no state has the right to commit certain kinds of crimes against its own citizens.

International law applies, however, only to the most serious crimes (and, most likely, only to those committed by weaker states). It will still be up to the individual states to decide how to proceed with the trials of less serious offenses. Even matters like torture are likely to come under the purview of domestic courts. International law can reach perpetrators only if they travel abroad or their home country extradites them. A country can still harbor its own former dictator and grant him immunity from prosecution. Thus, a democratizing state still has choices to make about what to do with the former dictator—whether to prosecute, extradite, or grant immunity.

International law is helpful in that it sets a precedent favoring prosecution and establishes a positive law to facilitate prosecution. Opponents of trials can no longer argue that the prosecutions are time-barred acts of political revenge. The statute of limitations has disappeared for the most serious crimes, and trials of leaders accused of abuses are seen as a step along the path to justice, not an unhealthy distraction from more pressing political decisions. In the future, an International Criminal Court will provide a venue for trying cases too difficult to administer impartially at home. This would ease the pressure upon the fragile institutions of young democracies. Where the police, prosecutors, and the judiciary were formerly under the thumb of dictatorial rule, these institutions often lack the credibility and will to carry out fair trials.[14] If these institutions must be reformed before the perpetrators can be brought to justice, then justice is inevitably delayed.

Coming to terms with the past is not simply a matter of trials. New democracies ready to accept political responsibility for the abuses of the past must also reach decisions about lustration, rehabilitation, compensation, and truth commissions. International law offers little guidance in these matters, but liberal democratic ideology does. In countries where this ideology shapes the political imagination, politicians are likely to debate these issues broadly and to find careful legal compromises between the ideology's competing values. Like Poland and Germany, they will find a moderate approach to transitional justice to accompany their peaceful transitions to democracy—a limited round of trials with ample due process guarantees accorded to the defendants; some lustration, also with guarantees that prevent them from becoming political purges; rehabilitation and compensation of the victims; and state-sponsored truth-telling. This is quite in the spirit of liberal democracy.

Appendix—Trials of Former Communist Officials in Poland

[*This list includes only cases in which indictments were made.*]

Defendant	*Allegation/Outcome*	*Source*
1. 6 Security Service agents	Kidnapping in 1984; guilty	Rzeczpospolita 11/6/91
2. 24 interior ministry officers	Shooting of 9 miners at Wujek; not guilty	Gazeta Wyborcza 7/30/96
3. 7 former (MO officers)	Shooting of strikers at Lubin; not guilty	Rokita Commission[1]
4. Wlodzimierz J. (MO officer)	Beating of Wojciech Cieslewicz; not guilty	Rokita Commission
5. Andrzej Augustyn	Murder of Bogdan Wlosik; guilty	Rokita Commission
6. Jan Zurek (MO officer)	Murder of Stanislaw Kulki; guilty	Rokita Commission
7. Leon Szypillo (MO officer)	Murder of Mirsolaw Adamczyk; guilty	Rokita Commission
8. 2 MO officers	Beating of Ryszard Slusarski; not guilty	Rokita Commission
9. 2 MO officers	Beating of Stanislaw Kot; not guilty	Rokita Commission
10. 1 MO officer	Manslaughter of K. Struski; not guilty	Rokita Commission
11. 3 MO officers	Perjury; amnesty	Rokita Commission
12. 4 MO officers	Beating of M. Rokitowski; guilty	Rokita Commission
13. 2 military intelligence officers	Harrassment of priest; amnesty	Rokita commission
14. Wladyslaw C. and Zenon P.	Ordering murder of Fr. Popieluszkounder appeal	BBC Monitoring 3/18/98
15. 3 SB officers	Burning car; guilty	Rzeczpospolita 6/9/92
16. 6 SB agents	Kidnapping; guilty, partial amnesty	Rzeczpospolita 9/2/94
17. 3 internal affairs directors	Destruction of files; not guilty	Rzeczpospolita 12/7/92
18. 12 MO officers (+ Jaruzelski)	Ordering the shooting at the Baltic Coast (1970), ongoing	Rzeczpospolita 3/28/96
19. 2 MO officers	Kidnapping of 6 activists; amnesty	Rzeczpospolita 12/8/94

Defendant	*Allegation/Outcome*	*Source*
20. 6 WSW officials	Destruction of files; guilty	Slowo 3/11/96
21. Arkadiusz Denkiewicz (MO)	Beating G. Przemyk; guilty	Jan Ordynski 6/4/97[2]
Kazimierz Otlowski (MO)	Destruction of files; guilty	Jan Ordynski 6/4/97
Stalinist Era Crimes		
22. Adam Humer and ten others	Torture; guilty	Rzeczpospolita 3/9–10/96
23. Marian Nowak (UB)	Torture; guilty	Zycie Warszawy 3/19/96
24. Judge Maria G.	Murder; indicted	Prawo i zycie 5/25/96
25. Zdzislaw B. (UBP)	Torture; indicted	Gazeta Wyborcza 4/3/96
26. Stanislaw Z. (mil. procurator)	Murder; too ill to stand trial	Zycie Warszawy 4/2/96
27. Jozef N. (WUBP)	Torture; indicted	Rzeczpospolita 6/7/96
28. Mieczyslaw H. (WUBP)	Torture; indicted	Rzeczpospolita 1/26/95
29. Stanislaw P (UB)	Murder; indicted	Rzeczpospolita 2/21/96
30. Zygmunt T. (UB)	Torture; indicted	Rzeczpospolita 11/18/96

Notes

1. Informacje o stanie spraw przekazanych przez Sejmowa Komisje Nadzwyczajna do Zbadania Dzialalnosci MSW, Akty Sekretariatu Posiedzen Sejmu, session 55, Zalacznik do odpowiedzi na interpelacje, July 12, 1995.
2. Interview with Jan Ordynski, legal affairs correspondent for *Rzeczpospolita*, June 4, 1997.

Notes

Introduction

1. Vladimir Lenin, *The State and Revolution*, in *The Lenin Anthology*, ed. Robert C. Tucker (New York: W.W. Norton, 1975), 317.
2. Samantha Power, "Bystanders to Genocide," *The Atlantic Monthly*, 288, 2 (September 2001): 84–108.
3. The term "policies of truth and justice" is employed in a useful volume by Alexandra Barahona de Brito, Carmen Gonzalez-Enriquez, and Paloma Aguilar, eds., *The Politics of Memory: Transitional Justice in Democratizing Societies* (Oxford: Oxford University Press, 2001).
4. Herbert R. Lottman, *The Purge* (New York: William Morrow, 1986), 274. Hans Woller, "Ausgebliebene Säuberung? Die Abrechnung mit dem Faschismus in Italien," in *Politische Säuberung in Europa: Die Abrechnung mit Faschismus und Kollaboration nach dem Zweiten Weltkrieg*, ed. Klaus-Dietmar Henke and Hans Woller (Munich: Deutscher Taschenbuch Verlag, 1991), 182.
5. Hugh McCullum, *The Angels Have Left Us: The Rwanda Tragedy and the Churches* (Geneva: WCC Publications, n.d.), 2–5.
6. Peter Siani-Davies, "The Revolution After the Revolution," chap. 1 in *Post-Communist Romania: Coming to Terms with Transition*, ed. Duncan Light and David Phinnemore (New York: Palgrave, 2001), 17–22.
7. Henry Rousso, *The Vichy Syndrome: History and Memory in France since 1944*, trans. by Arthur Goldhammer (Cambridge: Harvard University Press, 1991).
8. Tony Judt, "Epilogue," in *The Politics of Retribution in Europe*, ed. Istvan Deak, Jan T. Gross, and Tony Judt (Princeton: Princeton University Press, 2000), 304.
9. Ibid., 299.
10. Eric Foner, *Reconstruction: America's Unfinished Revolution, 1863–1877* (New York: Harper and Row, 1988), 603–604, 612.
11. Paloma Aguilar, "Justice, Politics and Memory in the Spanish Transition," chap. 3 in Barahona de Brito et al., *The Politics of Memory*, 92–118.
12. For speculation along these lines, see "An Awkward Case," *The Economist*, December 1, 2001; "The Chagrin and the Belated Pity," *The Economist*, May 12, 2001.
13. See Human Rights Watch, "The Dirty War in Chechnya: Forced Disappearances, Torture and Summary Executions" (March 2001).
14. Foner, *Reconstruction*, 504.

15. Claus Offe, "Coming to Terms with Past Injustices: An Introduction to Legal Strategies Available in Post-Communist Societies," *Archives europeennes de sociologie,* 23 (1992): 195–201.
16. Unlike Offe, I include rehabilitation as an instance of criminal law being applied to the victim.
17. George Sher, "Ancient Wrongs and Modern Rights," *Philosophy and Public Affairs* 10, 1 (Winter 1981): 6.
18. Karl Jaspers, *The Question of German Guilt,* trans. by E.B. Ashton (New York: The Dial Press, 1947), 36, 73.
19. Geoffrey Robertson, *Crimes Against Humanity: The Struggle for Global Justice,* second edition (London: Penguin, 2002), 340–341.
20. Douglas Farah, "Sierra Leone Court May Offer Model for War Crimes Cases," *Washington Post* (April 15, 2003); Human Rights Watch, "Serious Flaws: Why the U.N. General Assembly Should Require Changes to the Draft Khmer Rouge Tribunal Agreement" (April 30, 2003).
21. Robertson, *Crimes Against Humanity,* 346–392.
22. Bass similarly argues that liberal states are more likely to pursue a foreign policy that involves seeking justice for foreign victims of war crimes. It is logical that liberal democratic ideology would influence political elites' choices about policies of truth and justice in both foreign and domestic affairs. See Gary Jonathan Bass, *Stay the Hand of Vengeance: The Politics of War Crimes Tribunals* (Princeton: Princeton University Press, 2002).

Chapter 1 The Politics of Transitional Justice

1. Barrington Moore, Jr., *The Social Origins of Dictatorship and Democracy: Lord and Peasant in the Making of the Modern World* (Boston: Beacon Press, 1966), 20, 505–508.
2. Theda Skocpol, *States and Social Revolutions: A Comparative Analysis of France, Russia, and China* (Cambridge: Cambridge University Press, 1979), 163–164.
3. Dick Howard, "Toward a Politics of Judgement," *Constellations,* 1, 2 (1994): 290.
4. Kay Trimberger, *Revolution from Above: Military Bureaucrats in Development in Japan, Turkey, Egypt, and Peru* (New Brunswick, NJ: Transaction Books, 1978), 2. See also Michael Walzer, *Regicide and Revolution* (New York: Columbia University Press, 1992).
5. George J. Szablowski and Hans-Ulrich Derlien, "East European Transitions, Elites, Bureaucracies, and the European Community," *Governance,* 6, 3 (July 1993): 308. The degree to which the Romanian revolutionary leadership ultimately reshaped society is quite debatable, however.
6. Samuel P. Huntington, *The Third Wave: Democratization in the Late Twentieth Century* (Norman: University of Oklahoma Press, 1991), 215–216, 228.
7. Alexandra Barahona de Brito, Carmen Gonzalez-Enriquez, and Paloma Aguilar, *The Politics of Memory: Transitional Justice in Democratizing Societies* (Oxford: Oxford University Press, 2001), 11–14; Huntington, *The Third Wave,* 228.

8. Vera Tolz, "New Situation for CPSU and KGB Archives," *Radio Liberty*, 3, 38 (September 28, 1991): 1–4, and Carla Thorson, "Has the Communist Party Been Legally Suspended?" *Radio Liberty*, 3, 40 (October 4, 1991): 4–8.
9. Manuel Antonio Garreton writes that a political logic dominates the transition, but a moral–ethical logic leads to conflict between the state and society after the democratic leadership has been installed. See his article "Human Rights in Processes of Democratisation," *Journal of Latin American Studies*, 26 (1994): 221–234.
10. This is the approach adopted by Barahona de Brito in an important comparative study of transitional justice in Uruguay and Chile. She examines how several political factors affected the outcomes in those countries: the nature and strength of human rights movements; the relationship between the opposition party and the human rights organizations; the degree of opposition party unity; and the role of the democratically elected executive. She argues that a series of complex interactions among these factors yields the different outcomes in the two countries she studies. See Alexandra Barahona de Brito, *Human Rights and Democratization in Latin America: Uruguay and Chile* (Oxford: Oxford University Press, 1997).
11. Kathryn Sikkink, "Human Rights, Principled Issue-Networks, and Sovereignty in Latin America," *International Organization*, 47, 3 (Summer 1993): 416.
12. Ibid., 438–439, and Susan E. Waltz, *Human Rights and Reform: Changing the Face of North African Politics* (Berkeley: University of California Press, 1995), 21–30.
13. Jack A. Goldstone, *Revolution and Rebellion in the Early Modern World* (Berkeley: University of California Press, 1991), 49, emphasis in original.
14. Ann Swidler, "Culture in Action: Symbols and Strategies," *American Sociological Review*, 51, 2 (April 1986): 278.
15. Norman Fairclough and Ruth Wodak, "Critical Discourse Analysis," chap. 10 in *Discourse as Social Interaction* vol. 2, *Discourse Studies: A Multidisciplinary Approach*, ed. Teun A. Van Dijk (London: Sage Publications, 1997), 271.
16. Paul Chilton and Christina Schaeffner, "Discourse and Politics," chap. 8 in *Discourse as Social Interaction* (London: Sage Publications, 1997), vol. 2, *Discourse Studies: A Multidisciplinary Approach*, ed. Teun A. Van Dijk, 214–222. Teun A. Van Dijk, "Discourse as Interaction in Society," chap. 1 in *Discourse as Social Interaction* (London: Sage Publications, 1997), vol. 2, *Discourse Studies: A Multidisciplinary Approach*, ed. Teun A. Van Dijk, 214–222. Michel Foucault, "The Order of Discourse," chap. 7 in *Language and Politics*, ed. Michael J. Shapiro (New York: New York University Press, 1984), 116. Robert Wuthnow, *Communities of Discourse: Ideology and Social Structure in the Reformation, the Enlightenment, and European Socialism* (Cambridge: Harvard University Press, 1989), 13–16.
17. Ludwig Wittgenstein also makes an analogy between language and a toolkit. See Hanna Fenichel Pitkin, *Wittgenstein and Justice: On the Significance of Ludwig Wittgenstein for Social and Political Thought* (Berkeley: University of California Press, 1972), 36–37.
18. Murray Edelman, *Constructing the Political Spectacle* (Chicago: University of Chicago Press, 1988), 12; John A. Robinson and Linda Hawpe, "Narrative

Thinking as a Heuristic Process," chap. 6 in *Narrative Psychology: The Storied Nature of Human Conduct*, ed. Theodore R. Sarbin (New York: Praeger, 1986), 113.

19. Mary Ann Glendon, *Rights Talk: The Impoverishment of Political Discourse* (New York: Free Press, 1991).
20. Richard Ashcraft, *Revolutionary Politics and Locke's Two Treatises of Government* (Princeton: Princeton University Press, 1986), 5.
21. Walter R. Fisher, "Narrative, Reason, and Community," chap. 14 in *Memory, Identity, Community: The Idea of Narrative in the Human Sciences*, ed. Lewis P. Hinchman and Sandra K. Hinchman (Albany: State University of New York Press, 1997), 314.
22. Seyla Benhabib, "Deliberative Rationality and Models of Democratic Legitimacy," *Constellations*, 1, 1 (1994): 32–33.
23. The idea that ideology plays different roles in various stages of regime transition is discussed in Goldstone, *Revolution and Rebellion*, 419–457; Swidler, "Culture in Action," 278–282; and Giovanni Sartori, *The Theory of Democracy Revisited* (Chatham, NJ: Chatham House Publishers, 1987), 69–70.
24. Goldstone, *Revolution and Rebellion*, 425.
25. In Poland, commentators frequently use phrases like "coming back to normal" or "borrowing from the tested models" to describe their country's embrace of liberal democratic norms. See Wojciech Sokolewicz, "The Relevance of Western Models for Constitution-Building in Poland," chap. 11 in *Constitutional Policy and Change in Europe*, ed. Joachim Jens Hesse and Nevil Johnson (Oxford: Oxford University Press, 1995), 250.
26. Barahona de Brito, *Human Rights and Democratization in Latin America*, 33.
27. Adam Przeworski calls democracy a "system for processing conflicts without killing one another." See his *Democracy and the Market* (Cambridge: Cambridge University Press, 1991), 95.
28. Guillermo O'Donnell and Philippe C. Schmitter, *Transitions from Authoritarian Rule: Tentative Conclusions about Uncertain Democracies* (Baltimore: Johns Hopkins University Press, 1986); see also Przeworski, *Democracy and the Market*.
29. See Jon Elster, ed., *The Roundtable Talks and the Breakdown of Communism* (Chicago: University of Chicago Press, 1996).
30. Mansoor Moaddel, *Class, Politics and Ideology in the Iranian Revolution* (New York: Columbia University Press, 1993), 272.
31. Goldstone, *Revolution and Rebellion*, 419–420.
32. Stephen Holmes, "Precommitment and the Paradox of Democracy," chap. 7 in *Constitutionalism and Democracy*, ed. Jon Elster and Rune Slagstad (Cambridge: Cambridge University Press, 1988), 195.
33. Andrew Arato, *From New-Marxism to Democratic Theory: Essays on the Critical Theory of Soviet-Type Societies* (Armonk, NY: M.E. Sharpe, 1993), 298–303.
34. Seyla Benhabib, "Hannah Arendt and the Redemptive Power of Narrative," chap. 5 in *Hannah Arendt: Critical Essays*, ed. Lewis P. Hinchman and Sandra K. Hinchman (Albany: State University of New York Press, 1994), 127.
35. Charles Taylor, *Philosophy and the Human Sciences* (Cambridge: Cambridge University Press, 1985), 19. A caveat is in order because while we can easily

verify whether or not a particular policy has been adopted as a matter of law, we might still disagree on whether the policies were implemented and whether they had significant consequences.

36. See Ole R. Holsti, *Content Analysis for the Social Sciences and Humanities* (Reading, MA: Addison-Wesley Publishing Company, 1969) and Martha Cooper, *Analyzing Public Discourse* (Prospect Heights, IL: Waveland Press, 1989).
37. Taylor, *Philosophy and the Human Sciences*, 15.
38. Giuseppe Di Palma, *To Craft Democracies: An Essay on Democratic Transitions* (Berkeley: University of California Press, 1990), 109.

Chapter 2 Liberal Democratic Ideology and Transitional Justice

1. J.M. Kelly, *A Short History of Western Legal Theory* (Oxford: Clarendon Press, 1992), 13.
2. John Locke, "The Second Treatise of Government," *in Two Treatises of Government*, ed. Peter Laslett, rev. ed. (Cambridge: Cambridge University Press, 1960), 404.
3. Anthony Arblaster, *The Rise and Decline of Western Liberalism* (Oxford: Basil Blackwell, 1984), 73.
4. Ibid., 78.
5. Thomas Hobbes, *Leviathan*, ed. C.B. Macpherson (London: Penguin Books, 1968), 186.
6. Mark J. Osiel, "Ever Again: Legal Remembrance of Administrative Massacre," *University of Pennsylvania Law Review*, 144, 2 (December 1995): 587.
7. See Louis Hartz, The *Liberal Tradition in America: An Interpretation of American Political Thought Since the Revolution* (San Diego: Harcourt Brace Jovanovic, 1983).
8. Arato, *From New-Marxism to Democratic Theory*, 103.
9. Kelly, *A Short History of Western Legal Theory*, 131.
10. Walzer, *Regicide and Revolution*, 79.
11. Luc Huyse, "Justice after Transition: On the Choices Successor Elites Make in Dealing with the Past," *Law and Social Inquiry* (1995): 60.
12. Ibid.
13. Ibid., 60–62.
14. See Noel Calhoun, "The Statute of Limitations and the Prosecution of Human Rights Violations," in *1989–1999 Transformations: Triumph or Tragedy?* (New York: Harriman Institute, 2000).
15. On the political and legal drawbacks of repressing political organizations, see Otto Kirchheimer, *Political Justice* (Princeton: Princeton University Press, 1961), chap. 4.
16. Ruti G. Teitel, *Transitional Justice* (New York: Oxford University Press, 2000), 40–44.
17. Juan E. Mendez, "In Defense of Transitional Justice," chap. 1 in A. James McAdams, ed., *Transitional Justice and the Rule of Law in New Democracies* (Notre Dame, IN: University of Notre Dame Press, 1997), 7–8.

18. Huntington, *The Third Wave*, 231.
19. The latter is a tempting political advantage since it opens up jobs for the new elite's supporters. The appearance of expediency may call the process of lustration into disrepute.
20. Bruce Ackerman, *The Future of Liberal Revolution* (New Haven: Yale University Press, 1992), 96.
21. Huyse, "Justice after Transition," 62–63.
22. Teitel, *Transitional Justice*, 166–167.
23. John W. Chapman, ed., *Compensatory Justice*, Nomos XXXIII (New York: New York University Press, 1991), 126.
24. Anne Sa'adah, *Germany's Second Chance: Trust, Justice, and Democratization* (Cambridge, MA: Harvard University Press, 1998), 1–3, 238.
25. Arthur L. Stinchcombe, "Lustration as a Problem of the Social Basis of Constitutionalism," *Law and Social Inquiry* (1995): 261.
26. Kirchheimer, *Political Justice*, 136.
27. Hannah Arendt, *The Origins of Totalitarianism*, new edition (New York: Harcourt, Brace And World, 1966), 385.
28. Hannah Arendt, *Between Past and Future* (New York: Penguin, 1993).
29. David A. Welch, *Justice and the Genesis of War* (Cambridge: Cambridge University Press, 1993), 19.
30. Judith N. Shklar, *The Faces of Injustice* (New Haven: Yale University Press, 1990), 107.
31. John Stuart Mill, *On Liberty*, with an introduction by Gertrude Himmelfarb (New York: Penguin, 1988), 141.
32. Diane Orentlicher, "Settling Accounts: The Duty to Punish Human Rights Violations of a Prior Regime" in *Transitional Justice*, v. I, ed. Neil Kritz (Washington, DC: United States Institute of Peace Press, 1995).
33. Ibid., 392.
34. Hannah Arendt, *Eichmann in Jerusalem* (New York: Penguin, 1994), 298.
35. Marina Thode, "Towards Democracy: Criminal Law, Criminal Justice and the Reunification of Germany," in *Democracy, Market Economy, and the Law: Legal, Economic, and Political Problems of Transition to Democracy*, ed. Werner F. Ebke and Detlev F. Vagts (Heidelberg: Verlag Recht und Wirtschaft GmbH, 1995). In German the quotation reads: "Wir wollten Gerechtigkeit und haben den Rechtsstaat bekommen."
36. Sa'adah, *Germany's Second Chance*, 281.
37. Michael Rosenfeld, "Restitution, Retribution, Political Justice and the Rule of Law," *Constellations*, 2, 3 (January 1996): 309. Walzer writes (in *Regicide and Revolution*, 248) that the problem of political justice is "how to vindicate the rule of law in spite of, or even against, the rules of pure procedural justice."
38. Some indeed believe this assumption is true. See, e.g., John Borneman, *Settling Accounts: Violence, Justice, and Accountability in Postsocialist Europe* (Princeton: Princeton University Press, 1997). Despite its moral persuasiveness, the evidence does not support the assumption that retributive justice is a necessary condition for the health of democracy. Though trials have been few in post-communist Europe, democracy is taking root.

39. See Chapman, *Compensatory Justice*, 128; Stinchcombe, "Lustration as a Problem," 249; Ackerman, *The Future of Liberal Revolution*, 70–98.

Chapter 3 Germany Comes to Terms with the Past, Again

1. Claus Offe, *Der Tunnel am Ende des Lichts* (Frankfurt: Campus Verlag, 1995), 193; Jürgen Habermas, "Burdens of a Double Past," *Dissent* (Fall 1994): 513–517; Eberhard Jäckel, "Die doppelte Vergangenheit," *Der Spiegel*, 51 (1991): 39–43.
2. See the chapters by Uwe-Jens Heuer and Detlef Joseph in "*Unrechtsstaat*?"*—Politische Justiz und die Aufarbeitung der DDR-Vergangenheit*, ed. Lothar Bisky, Uwe-Jens Heuer, and Michael Schumann (Hamburg: VSA-Verlag, 1994). In 1991, 63% of East Germans agreed with the statement that "the West Germans have conquered the GDR in a colonial style." "Spiegel-Umfrage," *Der Spiegel*, 30 (1991): 28.
3. Wolfgang Rüddenklau, "Bekämpfung feindlich negativer Kräfte," *Horch und Guck*, 3 (1992): 11–13.
4. Lothar Probst, "Die Entwicklung der Bürgerbewegungen im Prozess der Vereinigung," *Forschungsjournal NSB*, 1 (January 1992): 50; *Junge Welt*, December 9, 1989, 6. Reprinted in Ute Reuter and Thomas Schulte, *Dokumentation zur Entwicklung der neuen Parteien und Bürgerrechtsgruppen in der DDR* (Bonn: Gesamtdeutsches Institut, 1990): 100–101.
5. Probst, "Die Entwicklung," 50–51.
6. Protesters in Leipzig, the city of the largest demonstrations, demanded the legalization of New Forum. Kurt Mühler and Steffen H. Wilsdorf, "Meinungstrends in der Leipziger Montagsdemonstration," in *Leipzig im Oktober: Kirchen und alternative Gruppen im Umbruch*, ed. Jürgen Grabner et al. (Berlin: Wichern, 1990), 160.
7. Mary Fulbrook, *Anatomy of a Dictatorship: Inside the GDR, 1949–1989* (Oxford: Oxford University Press, 1995), 236–240. See also Rüddenklau "Bekämpfung feindlich negativer kräfre."
8. Jonathon Osmond, *German Reunification: A Reference Guide and Commentary* (Essex: Longman, 1992), 34–35.
9. *Die Andere*, 2 (February 1, 1990).
10. Mühler and Wilsdorf, "Meinungstrends in der Leipziger," 160.
11. Fulbrook, "Anatomy of a Dictatorship," 259–262.
12. Frank Petzold, "Betrachtungen zur Auflösung des Ministeriums für Staatssicherheit unter der Regierung Modrow," Teil I, *Horch und Guck*, Heft 9 (1993): 8–11.
13. For the role of New Forum in occupying Stasi offices, see Bürgerkomitee Leipzig, ed., *Stasi Intern: Macht und Banalität* (Leipzig: Forum, 1991), 22; Justus Werdin, *Unter Uns: Die Stasi. Berichte der Bürgerkomitees zur Auflösung der Staatssicherheit im Bezirk Frankfurt (Oder)* (Berlin: Basis, 1990), 9.
14. Anne Worst, *Das Ende eines Geheimdienstes. Oder: Wie lebendig ist die Stasi*? (Berlin: LinksDruck, 1991), 26; Walter Süss, "Entmachtung und Verfall der Staatssicherheit," *BF informiert*, Abteilung Bildung und Forschung,

Der Bundesbeauftragte für die Unterlagen des Staatssicherheitsdienstes der ehemaligen DDR, 5 (1994): 56–57.

15. Karl Wilhelm Fricke, "Entmachtung und Erblast des MfS," *Deutschland Archiv*, 23, 12 (1990): 1883–1884; Hans-Georg Golz, "Seriöse Zahlen zum IM-Bestand," *Deutschland Archiv*, 27, 4 (1994): 343–344.
16. David Gill and Ulrich Schröter, *Das Ministerium für Staatssicherheit: Anatomie des Mielke-Imperiums* (Berlin: Rowohlt, 1991), 184; Bürgerkomitee Leipzig, *Stasi Intern*, 33, 359; Werdin, *Unter Uns*, 29.
17. Süss, "Entmachtung und Verfall der Staatssicherheit," 61.
18. Werdin, *Unter Uns*, 25.
19. Bürgerkomitee Leipzig, *Stasi Intern*, 26, 362.
20. See the Beschlüsse der 1. Sitzung des Rundtischgespräches, in Helmut Herles and Ewald Rose, eds., *Vom Runden Tisch zum Parlament* (Bonn: Bouvier, 1990), 26.
21. Worst, *Das Ende lines Geheimdienstes*, 31.
22. "No violence." Hans Modrow's declaration before the Round Table, session 7, January 15, 1990. In Herles and Rose, Vom Runden Tischzum Parlament, 55.
23. Frank Petzold, "Betrachtungen zur Auflösung des Ministeriums für Staatssicherheit unter der Regierung Modrow," Teil II, *Horch und Guck*, Heft 10 (1993): 16.
24. Ibid., 16–17. Many people believe that the destruction of property was a Stasi conspiracy to discredit the citizens' committees. They point out that the demonstrators entered only the least significant of the buildings, where no personal files were destroyed. They also note that people began flinging files out of the windows at the top of the building almost as soon as the door was opened, much more quickly than demonstrators could have reached these floors. Despite this testimony, no hard evidence of a Stasi conspiracy has emerged. See Uwe Thaysen, *Der Runde Tisch. Oder: Wo blieb das Volk*? (Opladen: Westdeutscher, 1990), 70; Worst, *Das Ende eines Geheimdienstes*, 33–39.
25. Festlegungsprotokoll der Beratung der AG Sicherheit, January 30, 1990, File 17150501, Archiv des 15. Januar, Berlin.
26. Werner Fischer, member of the group of four, "Information zur Arbeitsstruktur und Arbeitsweise für den Runden Tisch," dated February 5, 1990. Excerpted in Gill and Schröter, *Das Ministerium*, 191–203.
27. Fischer's report, in Gill and Schröter, *Das Ministerium*, 194.
28. Round Table resolution of January 22, 1990 (proposed by New Forum), in Herles and Rose, Vom Runden Tisch Zum Parlament, 84.
29. Round Table resolution of January 22, 1990 (proposed by the Green Party), in ibid., 86.
30. The fears of former Stasi employees are recounted in the dissolution reports ("*Auflösungsberichte*") of the various district offices of the Stasi. See the reports in file 171520, Auflösungsberichte, January 7, 1990, Archiv des 15. Januar, Berlin. See also the Protokollvermerk zur Beratung des Staatssekretärs Halbritter mit den Regierungsbeauftragten in den Bezirken, January 29, 1990, file 17150701, Archiv des 15. Januar, Berlin.

31. Resolution of the Round Table "Zu Fragen der Sicherheit," on January 15, 1990, in Herles and Rose, Vom Runden Tischzum Parlament, 69.
32. Fischer's report, in Gill and Schröter, *Das Ministeriun,* 196–197.
33. See Auflösungsberichte, January 7, 1990, file 171520, Archiv des 15. Januar, Berlin. The Berlin and Cottbus reports stated that citizens' committees favored the destruction of files, while reports from Leipzig, Dresden, and Potsdam said that the committees opposed destruction.
34. Ibid. The confusion about what the citizens' committees really wanted to do with the files is also evident in a report of a meeting between Hans Modrow and the Round Table's commissioners on dismantling the Stasi. Modrow unsuccessfully attempted to discern whether the committees wanted the files destroyed or stored. See "Niederschrift zur Beratung des Ministerpräsidenten mit den Beauftragten des Runden Tisches zur Auflösung des ehemaligen MfS" (January 24, 1990), file 171507, Archiv des 15. Januar, Berlin.
35. Round Table resolution of January 22, 1990 (proposed by the Green Party), in Herles and Rose, Von Runden Tisch Zum Parlament, 86.
36. Information Nr. 8, Round Table, session 7, January 15, 1990. File 171505, Archiv des 15. Januar, Berlin.
37. Petzold, Teie II 19; "Zum weitern Umgang mit den Unterlagen des ehemaligen MfS," Neues Forum Schwerin, February 15, 1990, file 171704, Archiv des 15. Januar, Berlin.
38. Bericht der Arbeitsgruppe Sicherheit vor dem Zentralen Runden Tisch der DDR, March 12, 1990, in Gill and Schröter, 244–245.
39. Ibid., 247.
40. Petzold, Teie II 20–21.
41. Beschluß der Bürgerkomitees der Bezirke, March 22, 1990, file Bezirkskoordinierungsgruppe, Archiv des 15. Januar, Berlin.
42. *Der Spiegel*, nr. 14, April 2 1990, 18–20.
43. *Volkskammer der DDR*, electoral period 10, session 2 (April 12, 1990), 24–27.
44. Report of Peter Hildebrand, *Volkskammer der DDR*, electoral period 10, session 37 (September 28, 1990), 1811.
45. See speeches of Haschke (DSU), Birthler (B90/G), and Hönicke (CDU/DA) in ibid., 1816–1818.
46. See the speeches by Dr. Opitz (FDP), Dr. Viehweger (Minister for Construction), Dr. Schiffner (CDU/DA), Frönicke (CDU/DA), in ibid., 1828–1841.
47. Deputy Birthler (B90/G) made this point in ibid., 1842.
48. Section 13(4), Richtergesetz (July 5, 1990), *GBl.* I 42.
49. Speech of deputy Hacker, *Volkskammer der DDR*, electoral period 10, session 27 (July 22, 1990), 1255.
50. Section 30(2), Richtergesetz (July 5, 1990), *GBl.* I 42.
51. Anlage I zum Einigungsvertrag, Kap. XIX, Abschn. III, Ziff. 1 (7). Application of the general rule might have made it impossible to reappoint any of the GDR's judges.
52. Herwig Roggemann, *Fragen und Wege zur Rechtseinheit in Deutschland* (Berlin: Arno Spitz, 1995), 146, 154–160. It should also be pointed out that many judges, including several high-ranking members of the profession, left

their positions during the year 1989–90; thus, they did not even apply for lustration. See Annette Weinke, "Die DDR-Justiz im Jahr der 'Wende'," *Deutschland Archiv*, 30, 1 (1997): 53.

53. *Die Andere*, nr. 34 (September 12, 1990), 4.
54. *Volkskammer der DDR*, electoral period 10, session 31 (August 23, 1990), 1428–1431.
55. *Volkskammer der DDR*, electoral period 10, session 32 (August 24, 1990), 1504.
56. Anlage I zum Einigungsvertrag, Kap. XIX, Abschn. III, Ziff. 5.
57. Wolfgang Schäuble, *Der Vertrag* (Stuttgart: Knaur, 1991), 268.
58. Press conference by Minster of Interior Dr. Diestel (May 16, 1990), file Bezirkskoordinierungsgruppe, Archiv des 15. Januar, Berlin.
59. Thomas Schmidt, speaker of the citizens' committees, and Dr. M. Kummer, representative of the citizens' committees in the consultative commission of the interior minister, "Zum weiteren Umgang mit den Unterlagen des ehemaligen MfS," draft letter (June 11, 1990), file Bezirkskoordinierungsgruppe, Archiv des 15. Januar, Berlin.
60. Worst, *Das Ende evnes Geheimdienstes,* 116–122.
61. *Volkskammer der DDR*, electoral period 10, session 35 (September 13, 1990): 1690–1698.
62. Schäuble, *Der Vertrag,* 273.
63. Letter from Dr. Eckhard Werthebach to MdI Abteilung Recht Professor Dr. Shüssler (August 21, 1990), IS 2–620 220/19, in file 171514, Archiv des 15. Januar, Berlin.
64. Gesetz über die Sicherung und Nutzung der personenbezogenen Daten des ehemaligen Ministeriums für Staatssicherheit/Amtes für Nationale Sicherheit (August 24, 1990), *GBl.* I58.
65. See speeches of Geisthardt (CDU/DA) and Brinksmeier (SPD) in *Volkskammer der DDR*, electoral period 10, session 32 (August 24, 1990), 1455.
66. Speech of Heuer (PDS) in ibid., 1456.
67. Speech of Joachim Gauck in ibid., 1453.
68. *Volkskammer der DDR*, electoral period 10, session 33 (August 30, 1990), 1540–1543; Schäuble, *Der Vertrag,* 277.
69. *Die Andere*, nr. 34 (September 12, 1990): 3–4.
70. Art. I, Vereinbarung zwischen der BRD und der DDR zur Durchführung und Auslegung des am 31. August 1990 in Berlin unterzeichneten Vertrage zwischen der BRD und der DDR über die Herstellung der Einheit Deutschlands, September 18, 1990.
71. Anlage I zum Einigungsvertrag, Kap. II, Sach. B, Abschn. II, Ziff. 2.
72. Speech by Dr. Nissel, state secretary in the ministry of justice, *Volkskammer der DDR*, electoral period 10, session 26 (July 20, 1990), 1134.
73. Rehabilitierungsgesetz, *GBl.* I69 (September 18, 1990).
74. Schäuble, *Der Vertrag,* 280–281.
75. Anlage II zum Einigungsvertrag, Kap. III, Sach. C, Abschn. II, Ziff. 2. However, Article 19 of the Unification Treaty added that the administrative acts of the the GDR could be overturned if they violated the principles of a law-based state.

76. Bundesbeauftragte für die Unterlagen des Staatssicherheitsdienstes der ehemaligen DDR, *Erster Tätigkeitsbericht des Bundesbeauftragten für die Unterlagen des Staatssicherheitsdienstes der ehemaligen DDR* (Berlin: Abteilung Bildung und Forschung, 1993), 11.
77. Arbeitsgruppe der Bürgerkomitees, "Ohne Aufarbeitung des Stasi-Systems kein gesellschaftlicher Neuanfang," *Die Kontinuität des Wegsehens und Mitmachens: Stasi-Akten oder die schwierige Bewältigung der DDR-Vergangenheit* (Cologne: Heinrich-Böll Stiftung, 1991), 14.
78. Poll by the Ifep-Institute taken in April 1990, *Spiegel*, 17 (April 23, 1990): 100–103.
79. *die tageszeitung* (November 17, 1990), reprinted in Silke Schumann, *Vernichten oder Offenlegen? Zur Entstehung des Stasi-Unterlagen-Gesetzes: Eine Dokumentation der öffentlichen Debatte 1990/1991*, Reihe A: Dokumente Nr. 1/1995 (Berlin: Der Bundesbeauftragte für die Unterlagen des Staatssicherheitsdienstes der DDR), 125.
80. Speech of Wolfgang Schäuble, *Verhandlungen des Deutschen Bundestages*, electoral period 12, session 21 (April 18, 1991): 1326.
81. Speech of Rolf Schwanitz (SPD), *Verhandlungen des Deutschen Bundestages*, electoral period 12, session 31 (June 13, 1991): 2362. See also the speeches of Hartmut Bütter (CDU/CSU), 2372, and Burkhard Hirsch (FDP), 2375.
82. Article. 2, §1 of the Basic Law. Everyone shall have the right to the free development of his personality insofar as he does not violate the rights of others or offend against the constitutional order or the moral code.
83. Speech of Angelika Barbe (SPD), *Verhandlungen des Deutschen Bundestages*, electoral period 12, session 31 (June 13, 1991): 2373.
84. Speech of Hartmut Büttner (CDU/CSU), *Verhandlungen des Deutschen Bundestages*, electoral period 12, session 31 (June 13, 1991): 2373.
85. Sec. 1, Gesetz über die Unterlagen des Staatssicherheitsdienstes der ehemaligen Deutschen Demokratischen Republik (December 20, 1991), *BGBl.* I 2272.
86. *Erster Tätigkeitsbericht des Bundesbeauftragten*, 8.
87. Bundesbeauftragte für die Unterlagen des Staatssicherheitsdienstes der ehemaligen DDR, *Zweiter Tätigkeitsbericht des Bundesbeauftragten für die Unterlagen des Staatssicherheitsdienstes der ehemaligen Deutschen Demokratischen Republic* (Berlin: Abteilung Bildung und Forschung, 1995), 4, 92–94.
88. Poll of 197 individuals who had read their Stasi files. Administered by the psychological institute of Hamburg University. See ibid., 16–17.
89. Ibid., 18.
90. Speech of Gerald Häfner (Buendnis 90/Die Grünen), *Verhandlungen des Deutschen Bundestages*, electoral period 13, session 98 (April 18, 1996): 8726.
91. Section 20, Gesetz über die Unterlagen des Staatssicherheitsdienstes der ehemaligen Deutschen Demokratischen Republik (December 20, 1991), *BGBl.* I 2272.
92. Drucksache 12/284 (March 20, 1991): 1–2.
93. Speech of Jürgen Schmieder (FDP) in ibid., 13,096.

94. See Drucksache 12/1942 (January 16, 1992); Speeches of Rolf Schwanitz (SPD) and Martin Göttsching (CDU/CSU) in *Verhandlungen des Deutschen Bundestages*, electoral period 12, session 152 (April 22, 1993): 13,094–13,095.
95. *Zweiter Tätigkeitsbericht*, 21.
96. Ibid., 7.
97. Ibid., 7–8.
98. Ibid., 23–24.
99. Interestingly, the PDS also supported the call for mandatory lustration in the Bundestag. They had little to lose since the Stasi did not recruit high-ranking communist party officials as agents. This put the former communists in a good position to try to portray themselves as "anti-Stasi." They also relied on the former opposition's argument that everyone must be treated equally.
100. Speech of Monika Brudlewsky (CDU/CSU) in *Verhandlungen des Deutschen Bundestages*, electoral period 12, session 64 (December 5, 1991): 5479. See also session 31 (June 13, 1991): 2474–2479.
101. Since the commission on the files continued to add materials to its archive, it made sense to double check.
102. Drucksache 13/2994 (November 14, 1995): 1–2.
103. Christoph Schäfgen, "Die Strafverfolgung von Regeriungskriminalitaet der DDR," in *Eine Diktatur vor Gericht: Aufarbeitung von SED-Unrecht durch die Justiz*, ed. Jürgen Weber and Michael Piazolo (Munich: Olzog, 1995), 60–61.
104. *Zentrale Ermittlungsstelle Regierungs-und Vereinigungskriminalität* (Berlin: Polizeipräsident, 1994), 8–9.
105. *Associated Press*, November 26, 1996. The number is higher not only because two more years had elapsed, but because the figure includes a larger range of crimes, such as the so-called unification crimes, which included illegal profiteering during the unification period.
106. Schäfgen,"Die Strafverfolgung," 62–63.
107. *Associated Press*, November 26, 1996.
108. Article 103(2) of the Basic Law reads, "An act may be punished only if it was defined by a law as a criminal offense before the act was committed."
109. See Herwig Roggemann, *Systemunrecht und Strafrecht am Beispiel der Mauerschützen in der ehemaligen DDR* (Berlin: Berlin Verlag, 1993), 56–58.
110. See the discussion in Klaus Lüderssen, *Der Staat geht unter-das Unrecht bleibt? Regierungskriminalität in der ehemaligen DDR* (Frankfurt am Main: Suhrkamp, 1992), 27–67.
111. Gary Anderson, "The Mauerschützenprozesse and the Principle of *Nullum Crimen Sine Lege*," *German Politics*, 7, 2 (August 1998): 52.
112. Adrienne M. Quill, "To Prosecute or Not To Prosecute: Problems Encountered in the Prosecution of Former Communist Officials in Germany, Czechoslovakia, and the Czech Republic," *Indiana International and Comparative Law Review*, 7 (1996): 165.
113. Micah Goodman, "After the Wall: The Legal Ramifications of the East German Border Guard Trials in Unified Germany," *Cornell International Law Journal*, 29 (1996): 737.

114. Ibid., 741.
115. *Deutsche Presse-Agentur*, October 30, 1998.
116. For a general account of the trial, see Uwe Wesel, *Der Honecker-Prozess: Ein Staat vor Gericht* (Frankfurt am Main: Eichborn, 1994). For the details of the jurisdictional question, see Michael Sachs, "Verfassungsrechtliche Anmerkungen zum Strafverfahren gegen Erich Honecker," *Zeitschrift für Politik*, 40, 2 (1993).
117. On the Mielke trial, see Peter Jochen Winters, "Der Mielke-Prozeß," in *Eine Diktatur vor Gericht*, ed. Weber and Piazolo, 101–113.
118. *Deutsche Presse-Agentur*, October 30, 1998.
119. *The Times* (London), August 26, 1997. Günther Kleiber, a former economic adviser to the Politburo, Günter Schabowski, head of the SED in Berlin, and Egon Krenz, former head of state and general secretary of the SED received sentences. *Financial Times* (London), November 9, 1999, 10.
120. Roggemann, *Systemunrecht und Strafrecht*, 8.
121. R.A. Monson, "West German Statute of Limitations on Murder: A Political, Legal and Historical Exposition," *American Journal of Comparative Law*, 30 (1982): 611.
122. Ibid., 615–624.
123. "Gesetz über das Ruhen der Verjährung bei SED-Unrechtstaten," *BGBl.* I (March 26, 1993): 392.
124. Wilhelm Tappert, *Die Wiedergutmachung von Staatsunrecht der SBZ/DDR durch die Bundesrepublik Deutschland nach der Wiedervereinigung* (Berlin: Arno Spitz, 1995), 69–71.
125. See especially the speeches of Klaus Kinkel (minister of justice), Norbert Geis (CDU/CSU), and Jörg van Essen (FDP) in *Verhandlungen des deutschen Bundestags*, electoral period 12, session 64 (December 5, 1991): 5369–5372, 5378–5379, 5382.
126. For a list of organizations, see "Gerechtigkeit den Opfern der kommunistischen Diktatur," *Deutschland Archiv*, 24, 7 (July 1991): 760.
127. Tappert, *Die Wiedergutmachung* 285. See also the speech of Gerald Häfner (Bündnis 90) in *Verhandlungen des deutschen Bundestags*, electoral period 13, session 71 (November 23, 1995): 6323.
128. Drucksache 12/1608, "Entwurf eines Ersten Gesetzes zur Bereinigung von SED-Unrecht" (November 15, 1991).
129. Ibid.
130. Drucksache 12/2820, "Beschlußempfehlung und Bericht des Rechtsausschußes" (June 16, 1992). Thus, if Stasi agents were held in jail and then released, they would receive compensation at the level of 600 DM per month in jail. This contrast irked many of the victims.
131. Ibid.; Drucksache 13/3038, "Entwurf eines Gesetzes zur Verbesserung der Rechtsstellung der Opfer der SED-Diktatur" (November 21, 1995).
132. Drucksache 12/3281, "Beschlußempfehlung des Vermittlungsausschußes" (September 23, 1992).
133. Drucksache 12/1608 (November 15, 1991). The federal government paid 65 percent the rehabilitation budget, while the Länder were responsible for the other 35 percent.

134. Speech by Rainer Funke (state secretary, ministry of justice) in *Verhandlungen des deutschen Bundestags*, electoral period 13, session 103 (August 5, 1996): 9036–9037.
135. Jürgen Roth et al., "Das Zweite SED-Unrechtsbereinigungsgesetz," *Deutschland Archiv*, 27, 5 (May 1994): 450–451.
136. Drucksache 12/4994, "Entwurf eines Zweiten Gesetzes zur Bereinigung von SED-Unrecht" (May 19, 1993).
137. Drucksache 13/3038, "Entwurf eines Gesetzes zur Verbesserung der Rechtsstellung der Opfer der SED-Diktatur" (November 21, 1995).
138. See Drucksache 13/4568, "Verbesserung der Rehabiliteriung und Entschädigung von Opfern der politischen Verfolgung in der ehemaligen DDR" (May 8, 1996).
139. Drucksache 13/3038, "Entwurf eines Gesetzes zur Verbesserung der Rechtsstellung der Opfer der SED-Diktatur" (November 21, 1995).
140. Speeches of Jörg van Essen (FDP) and Norbert Geis (CDU/CSU) in *Verhandlungen des deutschen Bundestags*, electoral period 12, session 64 (December 5, 1991): 5382, 5379.
141. Wolfgang Thierse, "Ein Plädoyer für die selbstkritische Bewältigung unserer Geschichte," Friedrich Schorlemmer, "Das Dilemma des Rechtsstaats," and Wolfgang Ullmann, "Köningsprozess oder Nürnberger Tribunal?" in *Ein Volk am Pranger? Die Deutschen auf der Suche nach einer neuen politischen Kultur*, ed. Albrecht Schönherr (Berlin: Aufbau Taschenbuch, 1992), 13–39.
142. Jaspers, *The Question of German Guilt*, 31, 36.
143. See Petra Bock, "Von der Tribunal-Idee zur Enquete-Kommission," *Deutschland Archiv*, 28, 11 (November 1995): 1175.
144. Drucksache 12/2597 (May 14, 1992).
145. Speech by Dirk Hansen (FDP) and Hartmut Koschyk (CDU/CSU) in *Verhandlungen des Deutschen Bundestages*, electoral period 12, session 234 (June 17, 1994): 20,444, 20,455.
146. Speech of Rainer Eppelmann (CDU/CSU) in ibid., 20,440.
147. Ibid., 20,449; Drucksache 12/7820 (May 31, 1994): 11–12.

Chapter 4 Poland's Long Search for Justice

Portions of this chapter were previously published as an article in *East European Politics and Societies*, 16, 2 (2002).

1. Huntington, *The Third Wave*, 211–231.
2. Scholars giving this opinion include: Andrzej Walicki, "Transitional Justice and the Political Struggles of Post-Communist Poland," chap. 7 in *Transitional Justice and the Rule of Law in New Democracies*, ed. A. James McAdams (Notre Dame, IN: University of Notre Dame Press, 1997), 187; Jacek Wasilewski, "Towards New Political Elites in Poland," chap. 3 in *Post-Communist Poland: From Totalitariansm to Democracy?* ed. Jacques Coenen-Huther and Brunon Synak (Commack, NY: Nova Science, 1993), 44. Politicians include: Jerzy Dziewulski (SLD), interview by author, July 19, 2000; Bogdan Pęk (PSL), interview by author, July 19, 2000; Andrzej Potocki (UW), interview by author, July 19, 2000.

3. Mark Osiel, *Mass Atrocity, Collective Memory, and the Law* (New Brunswick: Transaction, 1997), 111.
4. Raymond D. Gastil, *Freedom in the World* (New York: Freedom House, 1989), 53–54, 58.
5. Jan Kubik, *The Power of Symbols Against the Symbols of Power: The Rise of Solidarity and the Fall of State Socialism in Poland* (University Park, PA: Pennsylvania State University Press, 1994), 163–168, 200–206; Grzegorz Ekiert, *The State Against Society: Political Crises and Their Aftermath in East Central Europe* (Princeton, NJ: Princeton University Press, 1996), 269–270.
6. Jan Skorzynski, *Ugoda i Rewolucja: Władza i opozycja 1985–1989* (Warsaw: Rzeczpospolita, 1995), 202.
7. Wiktor Osiatynski, "The Roundtable Talks in Poland," in *The Roundtable Talks and the Breakdown of Communism*, ed. Jon Elster (Chicago: University of Chicago Press, 1996), 53. Janusz Reykowski was a member of the Politburo and the PZPR's cochairman of the political reform table.
8. Krzysztof Dubinski, *Magdalenka: Transakcja epoki* (Warsaw: Sylwa, 1990), 20.
9. Osiatynski, "The Roundtable Talks in Poland," 44.
10. Ibid.
11. *Tygodnik Mazowsze*, November 23, 1988. Quoted in Skorzynski, 154.
12. Interview with Tadeusz Mazowiecki's son and adviser, Wojciech Mazowiecki, Cambridge, MA, June 17, 1996.
13. "Telewizyjno-radiowe wystąpienie premiera T. Mazowieckiego w opinii społecznej," Centrum Badania Opinii Społecznej, BD/229/50/89 (November 1989): 2.
14. The speech is printed in *Sprawozdanie stenograficzne Sejmu PRL*, session 6 (August 24, 1989): 84–86.
15. This point was made by Tadeusz Mazowiecki's son and advisor, Wojciech Mazowiecki, interview by author, Cambridge, MA, June 17, 1996; and by Dariusz Wójcik (KPN), interview by author, Warsaw, July 13, 2000.
16. This is the perspective of Adam Michnik, see *The New York Times*, November 7, 1999, 71. Interestingly, Pope John Paul II also seems to have this perspective. See Aleksander Hall, *Pierwsza Taka Dekada* (Poznań: "W drodze," 2000), 181–183.
17. Maria Łoś, "Lustration and Truth Claims: Unfinished Revolutions in Central Europe," *Law and Social Inquiry*, 19 (1995): 157.
18. Jerzy Holzer, "The Communist Poland: The Role of a Concept of the Polish History for the Transformation to Democracy," in *After Communism: A Multidisciplinary Approach to Radical Social Change*, ed. Edmund Wnuk-Lipinski (Warsaw: Institute of Political Studies, 1995), 70.
19. Osiel (1997), 48–51.
20. *Sprawozdanie stenograficzne Sejmu PRL*, session 8 (September 29, 1989): 84–87; session 9 (October 13, 1989): 87–93.
21. See the remarks of Andrzej Rozmarynowicz, Ryszard Juszkiewicz, and Adam Stanowski in *Sprawozdania Stenograficzne Senatu PRL*, session 13 (December 1, 1989): 19, 25, 44.
22. *Sprawozdania Stenograficzne Senatu PRL*, session 15 (December 30, 1989): 134–135.

23. Remarks by Leszek Piotrowski, *Sprawozdania Stenograficzne Senatu PRL*, session 15 (December 30, 1989): 143.
24. Ibid., 147.
25. Protests were held in Białystok, łódź, Warsaw, and Gdańsk. See *Rzeczpospolita*, January 10, January 24, January 30, 1989.
26. *Rzeczpospolita*, January 30, 1990.
27. *Sprawozdanie stenograficzne Sejmu PRL*, session 19 (January 26, 1990): 165–166.
28. Speech of Jan Rokita (OKP), *Sprawozdanie stenograficzne Sejmu PRL*, session 21 (February 9, 1990): 33.
29. Interview with Prof. Jerzy Holzer, Institute of History, Warsaw University, November 25, 1996.
30. *Rzeczpospolita*, April 30–May 1, 1990, 3.
31. Report of a press conference held by Andrzej Milczanowski, deputy head of the UOP, in *Rzeczpospolita*, June 16–17, 1990, 1.
32. *Rzeczpospolita*, April 7, 1993, 1. Antoni Zielinksi, the director of the UOP's archive, similarly estimated that between 40 and 50 percent of the archive had been destroyed. See his testimony before the lustration subcommission in *Biuletyn*, Komisja Nadzwyczajna do rozpatrzenia projektów ustaw lustracyjnych, nr. 2931 (September 25, 1996): 9.
33. Speech of Minister Jerzy Kaminski, *Sprawozdanie stenograficzne Sejmu RP*, session 44 (May 17, 1993): 137.
34. *Rzeczpospolita*, July 22, 1993, 9.
35. *Rzeczpospolita*, October 23, 1996, 15. The director of military intelligence, General Edmund Buła, received a two-year suspended sentence.
36. Speech of Zbigniew Pudysz, secretary of state of the ministry of internal affairs, *Sprawozdanie stenograficzne Sejmu PRL*, session 21 (February 9, 1990): 40.
37. *Biuletyń*, Komisja Administracji i Spraw Wewnętrznych, nr. 333 (March 7, 1990): 6.
38. Ibid., 9.
39. Article 131, "O Urzędzie Ochrony Państwa," April 6, 1990, *Dziennik Ustaw*, nr. 30, poz. 180.
40. Article 8.1, Uchwala Nr. 69 Rady Ministrow of May 21, 1990, *Monitor Polski*, no. 20, poz. 159.
41. See interpellation by Marek Boral in *Sprawozdanie stenograficzne Sejmu PRL*, session 38 (September 13, 1990): 193; and *Biuletyń*, Rzecznik Praw Obywatelskich, nr. 2, 1991, poz. 80a: 17.
42. Interview with Jan Widacki, under-secretary of state, ministry of internal affairs, *Rzeczpospolita*, September 3, 1990, 1.
43. Ibid., and *Biuletyń*, Rzecznik Praw Obywatelskich, nr. 2, 1991, poz. 80a: 10.
44. Speech of justice minister Włodzimierz Cimoszewicz in *Sprawozdanie stenograficzne Sejmu RP*, session 11 (February 4, 1994): 24–25.
45. *Rzeczpospolita*, September 29–30, 1990, 1.
46. *Rzeczpospolita*, October 9, 1990, 1. See also Jan B. de Weydenthal, "Inquiry into the Murder of Father Popieluszko Reopened," *Report on Eastern Europe* (August 17, 1990): 12–15.

47. Speech of Stanisław Rogowski, *Sprawozdanie stenograficzne Sejmu RP*, session 55 (April 4, 1991): 128.
48. *Orzecznictwo Trybunłu Konstytucyjnego* 1991, poz. 34, 290–294.
49. *Rzeczpospolita*, September 11, 1990, 1.
50. In comparison, 84 extraordinary revisions involving rehabilitation were carried out in 1989, and only 4 in 1988. See Maria Stanowska, "Orzecznictwo Sadu Najwyzszego w sprawach rehabilitacyjnych w latach 1988–1991," *Archiwum Kryminologii*, v. 19 (1993): 134.
51. Article 21.4.b of "O kombatantach oraz niektorych osobach bedących ofiarami represji wojennych i okresu powojennego," January 24, 1991, *Dziennik Ustaw* nr. 17, poz. 75.
52. Speech of Ignacy Czeżyk (OKP), *Sprawozdanie stenograficzne Sejmu PRL*, session 44 (November 23, 1990): 242.
53. Speech of Jozef Hennelowa, *Sprawozdanie stenograficzne Sejmu PRL*, session 44 (November 23, 1990): 239.
54. Articles 1–4 of "O kombatantach oraz niektorych osobach bedących ofiarami represji wojennych i okresu powojennego," January 24, 1991, *Dziennik Ustaw* nr. 17, poz. 75.
55. *Dariusz Sejmowy*, session 90 (October 11, 1996): 47–55; *Rzeczpospolita*, October 8, 1996, 14.
56. *Sprawozdanie stenograficzne Sejmu RP*, session 52 (February 23, 1991): 360–365.
57. Speech of Lech Paprzycki, *Sprawozdanie stenograficzne Sejmu RP*, session 52 (February 23, 1991): 368.
58. Ustawa z 23.02.91 . . . , Ministerstwo Sprawiedliwości, Department Organizacji i Informatyki, Wydział Sprawozdawczości i Statystyki, undated document.
59. Kowalczyk made his accusation in *Sprawozdanie Stenograficzne Sejmu PRL*, session 3 (July 10, 1989): 68; the undersecretary of state of the ministry of internal affairs, Zbigniew Pudysz, responded in session 4 (August 2, 1989): 297, 301.
60. *Sprawozdanie Stenograficzne Sejmu PRL*, session 4 (August 2, 1989): 304.
61. Of the commission's 23 original members, only 13 really participated. Of the ten who did not participate, 7 were members of the PZPR. See "Sprawozdanie Komisji Nadzwyczajnej do Zbadania Działalności MSW z działalności w okresie X kadencji Seju RP (1989–1991)," Druk nr. 1104 (September 25, 1991): 1–2; *Biuletyń*, nr. 708/ X Kad., Komisja Nadzwyczajna do zbadania działalności MSW (October 9, 1990): 16, 42.
62. When the commission investigated the events associated with the pacification of the strikes at Lubin and Wujek, many military officers and PZPR functionaries simply refused to show up. The deputies questioned a few bystanders who agreed to testify. See *Biuletyń*, nr. 762/ X Kad., Komisja Nadzwyczajna . . . (October 30, 1990) and *Biuletyń*, nr. 1051/ X Kad., Komisja Nadzwyczajna . . . (March 2, 1991).
63. *Biuletyń*, nr. 343/ X Kad., Komisja Nadzwyczajna . . . (March 13, 1990): 34–35.

64. As minister of justice, Aleksander Bentkowski advocated rehabilitating people who had been falsely imprisoned in the past and reinstating procurators and judges who had lost their position during martial law. See the open letter by Bentkowski in *Gazeta Prawnicza*, nr. 21 (November 1, 1989): 1.
65. "Sprawozdanie Komisji Nadzwyczajnej do Zbadania Działalności MSW z działalności w okresie X Kadencji Sejmu RP (1989–1991)," Druk nr. 1104 (September 25, 1991): 10–11.
66. Ibid., 235.
67. Ibid.
68. Ibid., 236.
69. Speeches of Stanisław Gabrielski (PKLD) and Jerzy Karpacz (PKLD) in *Sprawozdanie stenograficzne Sejmu RP*, session 76 (October 4, 1991): 277–280, 315–318.
70. Speech of Jacek Kuron in *Sprawozdanie stenograficzne Sejmu RP*, session 76 (October 4, 1991): 300.
71. "Pakt dla Polski," brochure published by the National Bureau of Democratic Union in May 1991, printed in Inka Słodkowska, *Programy Partii i Ugrupowań Parlamentarnych, 1989–1991*, v. 2 (Warsaw: Instytut Studiow Politycznych, 1995): 233.
72. "O Naprawie Rzeczypospolitej," *Biuletyń PC* nr. 12, May 27, 1991, printed in Słodkowska, 138.
73. *Rzeczpospolita*, January 21, 1992, 1.
74. Interview with press secretary of the ministry of internal affairs, Tomasz Tywonek, in *Rzeczpospolita*, May 5, 1992, 2; Jacek Stefański, *Polska 1988–1993* (Kolbuszowa: Biblioteka Publiczna Miasta I Gminy w Kolbuszowej, 1995), 157.
75. *Sprawozdanie stenograficzne Sejmu RP*, session 16 (May 28, 1992): 37–40.
76. Ibid., 41.
77. Wiktor Osiatyński, "Agent Wałęsa?" *East European Constitutional Review* 1, 2 (Summer 1992): 28–30.
78. The law is critiqued extensively in "Sprawozdanie Komisji do badania wykonywania przez Ministra Spraw Wewnętrznych uchwały Sejmu RP z dnia 28 maja 1992 r." Druk nr. 363 (1992).
79. Speech of Włozimierz Cimoszewicz (SLD) in *Sprawozdanie stenograficzne Sejmu RP*, session 19 (July 4, 1992): 324.
80. Speeches of Jan Rokita (UD) in *Sprawozdanie stenograficzne Sejmu RP*, session 17 (June 6, 1992): 167 and Jacek Taylor (UD) in session 19 (July 4, 1992): 340–341.
81. Speech of Jacek Maziarski (PC) in *Sprawozdanie stenograficzne Sejmu RP*, session 17 (June 6, 1992): 172.
82. Speeches of Andrzej Wielowieyski, Jacek Taylor, and Maria Dumochowska (UD) in *Sprawozdanie stenograficzne Sejmu RP*, session 23 (September 5, 1992): 178–179, 193, 205.
83. Speeches of Józef Oleksy (SLD) and Włodzimierz Cimoszewicz (SLD) in ibid.: 180, 194.
84. Ibid.

85. Speech of Paweł Abramski (KLD) in *Sprawozdanie stenograficzne Sejmu RP*, session 23 (September 5, 1992): 169. Members of the UD, SLD, PSL, and UP also raised various practical difficulties of carrying out lustration: the inaccuracy of the files, the reliance on the testimony and administrative assistance of former Security Service officers, and the necessity of retaining qualified cadres despite their past political activities. However, these parties did not offer support to any of the lustration bills, even the KLD's, and they recommended not sending the bills to committee. Their larger point was that lustration is inherently incompatible with liberal democracy.
86. Speech of Krzysztof Kamiński (KPN) in *Sprawozdanie stenograficzne Sejmu RP*, session 23 (September 5, 1992): 165.
87. Speeches of Marek Markiewicz (NSZZ "S"), Bartłomiej Kołodziej (PC), and Alojzy Pietrzyk (NSZZ "S") in *Sprawozdanie stenograficzne Sejmu RP*, session 23 (September 5, 1992): 170, 173, 188.
88. Speeches of Krzysztof Kamiński (KPN), Marek Markiewicz (NSZZ "S"), and Jan Piątkowski (ZChN) in ibid., 165–166, 170–171, 182–183.
89. *Rzeczpospolita*, January 7, 1993, 2.
90. Jacek Kurski and Piotr Semka, *Lewy Czerwcowy* (Warsaw: Editions Spotkania, 1993), 36.
91. Anna Sabbat-Swidlicka, "Crisis in the Polish Justice Ministry," *Radio Free Europe/Radio Liberty Research Report*, 2, 15 (April 9, 1993): 14.
92. Ryszard Bugaj in *Rzeczpospolita*, June 4, 1993, 3.
93. *Rzeczpospolita*, March 10, 1993, 2.
94. Interview with Adam W. Kieruj, procurator, Głowna Komisja Badania Zbrodni Przeciwko Narodowi Polskiemu, Warsaw, November 14, 1996.
95. *Rzeczpospolita*, August 6, 1992, 3; October 2, 1992, 3.
96. Report by Aleksander Herzog, advisor to the ministry of justice, "Informacja o wynikach przeglądu spraw o przestepstwa z dekretu o stanie wojennym i z innych przepisow związanych z opozycyjną działalnością polityczną w latach 1981–1989," PR I 070/24/92 (March 25, 1994). The data on the number of people involved in each case is incomplete.
97. *Gazeta Wyborcza*, November 10–11, 1993, 1, 3.
98. *Rzeczpospolita*, April 7, 1994, 2.
99. Orzeczenie (K. 15/93), February 15, 1994, *Orzecznictwo Trybułu Konstytucyjnego w roku 1994*, poz. 4.
100. Speech of Marek Dyduch (SLD), *Sprawozdanie stenograficzne Sejmu RP*, session 35 (November 16, 1994): 40.
101. Speech of Olga Krzyżanowska (UW) in *Sprawozdanie stenograficzne Sejmu RP*, session 53 (June 30, 1995): 270.
102. Speech of Andrzej Milczanowski, minister of internal affairs, *Sprawozdanie stenograficzne Sejmu RP*, session 25 (July 7, 1994): 157.
103. *Sprawozdanie stenograficzne Sejmu RP*, session 35 (November 16, 1994): 122.
104. Jan Lityński (UW), interview by author, Warsaw, July 12, 2000.
105. Edmund Wnuk-Lipiński, *Gazeta Wyborcza*, July 5, 1994, 10–11.
106. Article 108.2, Kodeks Karny.
107. Speech of Krzysztof Baszczyński (SLD) in *Sprawozdanie stenograficzne Sejmu RP*, session 44 (March 2, 1995): 109.

108. Speech of Jan Rokita (UW) in *Sprawozdanie stenograficzne Sejmu RP*, session 44 (March 2, 1995): 118.
109. Ibid., 117.
110. See Article 25.b in *Dziennik Ustaw*, poz. 475, August 19, 1995.
111. *Rzeczpospolita*, March 9–10, 1996, 1.
112. See appendix I for a list of these trials.
113. *Rzeczpospolita*, February 7, 1996, 5.
114. This point is made by politicians of both the left and the right. Stefan Niesiołowski (AWS), interview by author, Warsaw, July 11, 2000; Jerzy Dziewulski (SLD), interview by author, Warsaw, July 19, 2000.
115. "Lustracja – Problem wciąż aktualny," Centrum Badania Opinii Społecznej BS/34/34/96 (Warsaw: February, 1996): 2, 4. This number had not changed significantly since the poll in 1993, which asked whether people thought that "individuals holding certain functions in the state should have to undergo lustration." A total of 64 percent responded affirmatively. See "Oczekiwania i obawy związane z lustracją," Centrum Badania Opinii Społecznej BS/38/29/93 (Warsaw: March, 1993): 1.
116. "Lustracja – Problem wciąż aktualny," 16.
117. See Druk Nr. 1534, "O wyodrębnieniu, przechowywaniu oraz udostępnianiu informacji o pracownikach i tajnych wspólpracownikach organów bezpieczeństwa państwa w latach 1944–1989" (January 31, 1996); *Rzeczpospolita*, October 10, 1996, 2.
118. *Dziennik Ustaw*, nr. 70, poz. 443 (April 11, 1997).
119. Speech by Jerzy Dziewulski (SLD) in "Biuletyń z posiedzenia Komisji Nadzwyczajnej do rozpatrzenia projektów ustaw lustracyjnych," nr. 3027 (October 23, 1996): 23.
120. Speech of Jan Lityński (UW) in ibid., 20.
121. German organizations in Warsaw put on two conferences in fall 1996 to present the Poles with the German experience of transitional justice. Prominent Polish politicians, including members of the lustration subcommission heard Joachim Gauck, the head of the Stasi archive, speak at both conferences. The conference entitled "Aufarbeitung der Geschichte–eine Herausforderung für Europa" sponsored by the Friedrich Ebert Stiftung was held at Warsaw University on October 18–19, 1996. The conference entitled "Ochrona danych w Polsce i w Niemczech–koncepcje, praktyka, polityka" sponsored by the Friedrich-Naumann-Stiftung was held in Warsaw on October 10–11, 1996.
122. Resolution 1096, "On measures to dismantle the heritage of former communist totalitarian regimes" (June 27, 1996). Available at http://stars.coe.fr/ta/ta96/ERES1096.HTM.
123. The omission of the latter provision is somewhat surprising, since it seems that liberals, rather than leftists, would have an interest in supporting free access to information. The liberals' reticence concerning the opening of the files probably stemmed from their lingering concern that the information in the files could "unleash a new avalanche of denunciations and slander." (Adam Michnik, *Gazeta Wyborcza*, June 19, 1997, 2.) These were more likely to harm the former opposition than the former communists.

124. *Gazeta Wyborcza*, June 30, 1997, 4; July 7, 1997, 3. One admitted collaborator—Jerzy Szteliga (SLD)—won election to the Sejm.
125. *The Washington Post*, September 9, 1999.
126. *BBC Monitoring Europe*, September 17, 1999; November 19, 1999; November 23, 1999. PAP Polish Press Agency, January 18, 2000; *Nowy Dziennik*, June 15, 2000, 1.
127. *Rzeczpospolita*, August 21, 2000.
128. Druk 31 (November 13, 1997).
129. Speech by Marek Siwiec, secretary of state in the presidential chancellery and leader of the Bureau of National Security, *Sprawozdanie stenograficzne Sejmu RP*, 3 kadencja, session 15 (April 2, 1998).
130. Druk nr. 252 (March 24, 1998).
131. See Lawrence Weschler, "The Velvet Purge: The Trials of Jan Kavan," *The New Yorker* (October 19, 1992), 66–96.

Chapter 5 Russia's Buried Past

1. For discussion of liberal democratic ideology in Russia, see Ken Jowitt, "Undemocratic Past, Unnamed Present, Undecided Future," *Demokratizatsiya*, 4, 3 (Summer 1996): 409–419; Roundtable discussion, "The Russian Historical Tradition and Prospects of Liberal Reforms," *Russian Social Science Review*, 40, 2 (March–April 1999): 48–76.
2. Robert Conquest, *The Great Terror: A Reassessment* (New York: Oxford University Press, 1990), 485–486; Anne Applebaum, *Gulag: A History of the Soviet Camps* (New York: Random House, 2003), 515–522; Alexander N. Yakovlev, *A Century of Violence in Soviet Russia*, with a foreword by Paul Hollander, trans. Anthony Austin (New Haven and London: Yale University Press, 2002), 233–234.
3. Applebaum, Gulag, 499–500.
4. Aleksander Yakovlev, ed., *Reabilitatsia: Politicheskie protsessy 30-50-x godov* (Moscow: Izdatel'stvo politicheskoi literatury, 1991), 7.
5. In many cases, former political prisoners are still too frightened tell their stories. The Sakharov Museum has attempted to gather the oral histories of Stalinist era survivors, but many people are unwilling to have their stories recorded for fear of reprisals.
6. Albert P. van Goudoever, *The Limits of Destalinization in the Soviet Union: Political Rehabilitations in the Soviet Union since Stalin*, trans. Frans Hijkoop (London: Croom Helm, 1986), 3, 77. See also Stephen G. Wheatcroft, "Glasnost' and Rehabilitations," in *Facing Up to the Past: Soviet Historiography under Perestroika*, ed. Takayuki Ito (Sapporo, Japan: Slavic Research Center, Hokkaido University, 1989), 199–200.
7. van Goudoever, *The Limits of Destalinization*, 41.
8. N.F. Katkov, "Vosstanovlenie istoricheskoi pravdy i spravedlivosti," *Voprosy istorii KPSS*, 9 (1991): 85.
9. See Peter Hauslohner, "Politics before Gorbachev: De-Stalinization and the Roots of Reform," chap. 2 in *Politics, Society, and Nationality Inside Gorbachev's Russia*, ed. Seweryn Bialer (Boulder: Westview, 1989), 46–48.

10. Peter Juviler, *Freedom's Ordeal: The Struggle for Human Rights and Democratization in Post-Soviet States* (Philadelphia: University of Pennsylvania Press, 1998), 57.
11. David S. Mason and Svetlana Sidorenko-Stephenson, "Public Opinion and the 1996 Elections in Russia: Nostalgic and Statist, Yet Pro-Market and Pro-Yeltsin," *Slavic Review*, 56, 4 (Winter 1997): 711.
12. Gorbachev's speech at the extraordinary plenum of the Central Committee, March 11, 1985. Mikhail Gorbachev, *Izbrannye rechi i stat'i*, v. 2 (Moscow: Izdatel'stvo politicheskoi literatury, 1987), 130.
13. Speech at the Twenty-Seventh Party Congress, February 25, 1986, in ibid., 241.
14. See Murray Yanowitch, *Controversies in Soviet Social Thought: Democratization, Social Justice and the Erosion of Official Ideology* (Armonk, NY: M.E. Sharpe, 1991), 28, 58–59.
15. Mikhail Gorbachev, *Perestroika: New Thinking for Our Country and the World* (New York: Harper & Row, 1987), 40, 43.
16. Robert William Davies, *Soviet History in the Gorbachev Revolution* (Bloomington: Indiana University Press, 1989), vii.
17. Gorbachev, *Izbrannye rechi i stat'i*, v. 4, 371.
18. Rosalind Marsh, *History and Literature in Contemporary Russia* (London: Macmillan, 1995), 41.
19. Interview with Mikhail Solomentsev in *Pravda*, August 19, 1988.
20. Yegor Ligachev, *Inside Gorbachev's Kremlin*, with an introduction by Stephen F. Cohen, trans. Catherine Fitzpatrick et al. (New York: Random House, 1993), 294, 287.
21. Davies, *Soviet History,* 141–151.
22. *Pravda*, July 5, 1988, 1–2.
23. Ibid. Like Khrushchev, Gorbachev never actually built a monument to the victims of Stalinism. He had better success in pushing through some more name changes.
24. Speech by Boris Yeltsin, *Pravda*, July 2, 1988, 10.
25. For this point, see Seweryn Bialer, "The Changing Soviet Political System: The Nineteenth Party Conference and After," chap. 7 in *Politics, Society, and Nationality Inside Gorbachev's Russia*, ed. Seweryn Bialer (Boulder: Westview, 1989), 236.
26. On the development of Memorial, see Dov B. Yaroshevski, "Political Participation and Public Memory: The Memorial Movement in the USSR, 1987–1989," *History and Memory*, 2, 2 (Winter 1990): 5–31; Kathleen Smith, *Remembering Stalin's Victims: Popular Memory and the End of the USSR* (Ithaca: Cornell University Press, 1996), 78–104.
27. *Literaturnaya gazeta*, 44 (November 2, 1988), 2.
28. Smith, *Remembering Stalin's Victims*, 183.
29. *Ogoniek*, 49 (December 3–10, 1988): 32–33.
30. Walter Laquer, *Stalin: The Glasnost' Revelations* (New York: Macmillan, 1990), 264–265. See also the call for a trial of Stalinism in *Moskovskie novosti*, August 27, 1989, 4.
31. This point was made by Solomentsev and V. Pirozhkov, deputy head of the KGB in ibid., 166. See also the interview with Boris Viktorov, former deputy

head of the USSR Military Procuracy in *Sovetskaya kultura*, October 1, 1988, 7; interview with Vladimir Provotorov, chief of department of Major-General of Justice, in *Sovetskaya kultura*, February 25, 1989, 8.

32. See the remarks by Viktorov and Pirozhkov.
33. "Otchet of rabote komiteta partiinogo kontrolia pri TsK KPSS za period s XX po XXII s'ezd KPSS (1956–1961)," excerpted in Yakovlev, *Reabilitatsiia*, 88.
34. Andrei Sakharov, *Moscow and Beyond, 1986–1989*, trans. Antonina Bouis (New York: Alfred A. Knopf, 1991), 152–153; Giulietto Chiesa, *Transition to Democracy: Political Change in the Soviet Union, 1987–1991* (Hanover, NH: University Press of New England, 1993), 124–125.
35. Judith Devlin, *The Rise of the Russian Democrats: The Causes and Consequences of the Elite Revolution* (Hants: Edward Elgar, 1995), 68.
36. Ukaz "O presechenii nadrugatel'stva nad pamiatnikami, sviazannymi s istoriei gosudarstva i ego simvolami" in *Pravda*, October 14, 1990, 2.
37. Marsh, *History and Literature in Contemporary Russia*, 22.
38. Jerry F. Hough, *Democratization and Revolution in the USSR, 1985–1991* (Washington, DC: Brookings Institution, 1997), 300.
39. Devlin, *The Rise of the Russian Democrats,* 172.
40. Yurii Afanasiev, "Perestroika i istoricheskoe znanie" in *Inogo ne dano* (Moscow: Progress, 1988), 499.
41. Devlin, *The Rise of the Russian Democrats*, 213.
42. Hough, *Democratization and Revolution*, 337.
43. RSFSR draft law, Committee on Human Rights, "O reabilitatsii zhertv politicheskikh represii," April 1991.
44. USSR draft law, "O reabilitatsii zhertv politicheskikh repressii i poriadke vosstanovlenia prav reabilitirovannykh," April 30, 1991.
45. RSFSR law, "O reabilitatsii repressovannykh narodov," April 26, 1991, *Vedomosti s'ezda narodnykh deputatov RSFSR i Verkhovnogo Soveta RSFSR*, 18 (1991).
46. "O proekte zakona RSFSR o reabilitatsii repressirovannykh narodov Rossii," Tretiia Sessiia Verkhovnogo Soveta RSFSR, Sovmestnogo Zasedaniia, *Biulleten'*, 25 (April 26, 1991): 6.
47. "O khode ispolneniia Zakona RSFSR: O reabilitatsii repressirovannykh narodov ot 26 aprelia 1991g." *Materialy parlamentskikh slushanii* (Moscow: State Duma, 1995), 4–6 and passim. This parliamentary hearing was held on May 25, 1995.
48. See chapter 1.
49. Leon Aron, *Boris Yeltsin: A Revolutionary Life* (London: HarperCollins, 2000), 466–468.
50. Ibid., 481.
51. *Nezavisimaya gazeta*, May 26, 1992. Translated in *Current Digest of the Soviet Press* [*CDSP*], 44, 21 (1992): 12–13.
52. *Izvestiia*, July 3, 1992, 2. Translated in *CDSP*, 44, 27 (1992): 18.
53. *Izvestiia*, July 3, 1992, 3. Translated in ibid., 19–20.
54. Patricia Kennedy Grimsted, "Russian Archives in Transition: Caught between Political Crossfire and Economic Crisis," *The American Archivist*, 56, 5 (Fall 1993): 617.

55. *Izvestiia*, July 28, 1992, 2. Translated in *CDSP*, 44, 30 (1992): 23.
56. *Kuranty*, December 1, 1992, 1. Translated in *CDSP*, 44, 48 (1992): 11.
57. *Nezavisimaya gazeta*, December 1, 1992, 1–2. Translated in ibid., 11–12; *Rossisskie vesti*, December 2, 1992, 1. Translated in ibid., 13.
58. *Nezavisimaya gazeta*, June 4, 1993, 1. Translated in *CDSP*, 45, 22 (1993): 18.
59. Vadim Bakatin, *Izbavlenie ot KGB* (Moscow: Novosti, 1992), 150–151.
60. Amy Knight, *Spies Without Cloaks: The KGB's Successors* (Princeton: Princeton University Press, 1996), 199.
61. Interview with Dmitry Yurasov, "Hinter sieben Siegeln," *Deutschland Archiv*, 26, 7 (July 1993), 869; Mark Kramer, "Archival Research in Moscow: Progress and Pitfalls," *Cold War International History Project Bulletin*, 1 (Fall 1993): 23.
62. Knight, *Spies Without Cloaks*, 194; Bakatin, *Izbavlenie of KGB*, 159–161; Vitaly Shentalinsky, *The KGB's Literary Archive*, with an introduction by Robert Conquest, trans. John Crowfoot (London: Harvill, 1995), 285.
63. Bakatin, *Izbavlenie of KGB*, 149; Kramer, "Archival Research in Moscow," 20, 23.
64. Kramer, "Archival Research in Moscow," 19.
65. Yakovlev, *Century of Violence*, 3.
66. Nikita Petrov, specialist on the KGB and Memorial activist, interview by author, June 8, 1999, Moscow.
67. Ibid.
68. Yurii Vdovin, "Grazhdansky kontrol,'" *Vestnik Memoriala*, 1, 7 (May 1993): 14.
69. Applebaum, *Gulag*, 507.
70. *Biulleten'*, Zasedaniia soveta national'nostei, 9 (November 27, 1991): 16.
71. Ibid.
72. "Zakliuchenie po rezultatam otkrytykh parlamentskikh slushanii: O roli repressivnykh organov byvshego SSSR v podgotovke i provedenii gosudarstvennogo perevorota v SSSR" (February 4, 1992): 3.
73. These recommendations are found in ibid., as well as the following documents: Lev Ponomarev, "Vyvody i rekomendatsii po rezul'tatam raboty" (January 13, 1992); Lev Ponomarev, "Otchet o rabote deputatskoi komissii dlia parlamentskogo rassledovaniia prichin i obstoiatel'stv gosudarstvennogo perevorota" (undated document).
74. For a history of the early splits in the democratic camp, see *Malaia entsiklopediia Rossiiskoi politiki: Osnovyne partii I dvizheniia zaregistrirovannye Ministrom iustitsii* (Moscow: Supreme Soviet, 1992), 25–27.
75. Timothy J. Colton, *Transitional Citizens: Voters and What Influences Them in the New Russia* (Cambridge: Harvard University Press, 2000), 149–150, 172.
76. "Chetvertaia sessiia Verkhovnogo Soveta RSFSR," *Biulleten'*, 14 (November 22, 1991): 39.
77. "Shestaia sessiia Verkhovnogo Soveta RSFSR," *Biulleten'*, 47, pt. 2 (July 3, 1993): 35–36, 38.
78. Speech by N.A. Pavlov in ibid., 41.
79. See the debate on habeas corpus in Chetvertaia sessiia Verkhovnogo Soveta RSFSR, *Biulleten'*, 43 (March 13, 1992): 41–44; on judicial reform, see *Biulleten'*, 10 (October 24, 1991): 25–27.

80. On Russia's search for an ideology, see B.V. Mezhuev, "Poniatie 'nazional'nyi interes' v Rossiiskoi obshchestvenno-politicheskoi mysli," *Polis*, 1 (January 1997): 5–31; T.A. Alekseev et al., "Kakovy ideologicheskie usloviia obshchestvennogo soglasiia v Rossii?" *Polis*, 3 (March 1997): 16–52; Wayne Allensworth, *The Russian Question: Nationalism, Modernization, and Post-Communist Russia* (Lanham, MD: Rowman and Littlefield, 1988).
81. Eduard Batalov, "Chem zapolnim ideinyi vakkum?" *Svobodnaia mysl'*, 11 (1996): 4, 7.
82. Democratic Russia, "Ob izmenenii strategii demokraticheskogo dvizheniia v novykh usloviiakh" (undated mimeo).
83. "Ustav Dvizheniia Demoktraticheskogo Rossii" (November 10, 1991).
84. See "Programma Dvizheniia Demokraticheskaia Rossiia" (December 1992).
85. The draft law is printed in *Moskovskie Novosti*, 5 (January 3, 1993): 8. If it had been passed, Vladimir Putin would have had the right to be elected president, but not to teach judo in a secondary school.
86. Ibid., 8–9.
87. Aleksander Tsipko, "Liustratsiia ili kapituliatsiia," *Moskovskie novosti*, 8 (February 21, 1993): 8.
88. Gosudarstvennaia Duma, *Stenogramma zasedanii*, 2 (February 17, 1994), 493.
89. Speech by Gennadii Ziuganov in Gosudarstvennaia Duma, *Stenogramma zasedanii*, 3 (February 23, 1994), 27–28.
90. Speech by A.E. Shabad in *Stenogramma zasedanii*, 2 (February 17, 1994), 501.
91. For a similar exchange, see the debate concerning a new constitutional law on state symbols, in *Stenogramma zasedanii*, 11 (December 7, 1994), 217–219.
92. *Stenogramma zasedanii*, 3 (February 23, 1994), 29–31.
93. Aron, *Boris Yeltsin*, 623.
94. The information on memorials comes from a database called "Pamiat' o bespravii," compiled by Tatiana Gromova at the Sakharov Museum. The database contains information on nearly 200 such memorials throughout the former Soviet Union. Tatiana Gromova, interview by author, June 12, 1999, Moscow.
95. Memorial'nyi muzei istorii politicheskikh repressii i totalitarizma, Otchet, 1994/95.
96. There is no comprehensive listing of all the Books of Memory that have been published. Memorial's website lists the Books of Memory in its library (see www.memo.ru), and I suppplemented this with the collection at the Sakharov Library. I have counted 45 books listing names of people who were repressed on the territory of the Russian Federation. Similar books have been published in the other former Soviet republics.
97. The Russian Orthodox Church, ethnic organizations, and a few energetic individuals managed to publish books without state financing. Memorial and the Association of Victims of Political Repressions usually cooperated with the local government.
98. See N.E. Popkov and V.N. Miasnikov, *Samarskaia oblast'*: Belaia kniga o zhertvakh politicheskikh repressii, *1 (Samara: Samarsky Dom pechati, 1997), 6; Yu. A. Dem'iachenko and P.E. Stepanov,* Ne predat'zabveniiu*: Kniga Pamiati zhertv politicheskikh repressii*, 1 (Pskov: 1996), 6.

99. Smith, *Remembering Stalin's Victims*, 174–193.
100. *Interfax*, February 27, 2003.
101. *Reuters*, March 5, 2003.
102. Robert Conquest, *The Harvest of Sorrow: Soviet Collectivization and the Terror-Famine* (New York: Oxford University Press, 1986).

Chapter 6 Liberal Democracy's Shortcomings and Overriding Advantage

1. See Ackerman, *The Future of Liberal Revolution*, 70–98; Jon Elster, "On Doing What One Can: An Argument against Postcommunist Restitution and Retribution," *Eastern European Constitutional Review*, 1, 2 (1992): 15–17.
2. Barton L. Ingraham, *The Structure of Criminal Procedure: Laws and Practice of France, the Soviet Union, China, and the United States* (New York: Greenwood, 1987), 61.
3. For a similar argument, see Carlos Santiago Nino, *Radical Evil on Trial* (New Haven: Yale University Press, 1996), 187–189.
4. Barahona de Brito et al., *The Politics of Memory*, 311–312; O'Donnell and Schmitter, *Transitions from Authoritarian Rule*, 30.
5. See, e.g., Barahona de Brito et al., *The Politics of Memory*, 312–314.
6. On the importance of institutional reforms, see Garreton, "Human Rights in Processes of Democratization," 232.
7. Paloma Aguilar, "Justice, Politics and Memory in the Spanish Transition," chap. 3 in *The Politics of Memory: Transitional Justice in Democratizing Societies*, ed. Alexandria Barahona de Brito, Carmen Gonzalez-Enriquez, and Paloma Aguilar (Oxford: Oxford University Press), 115–118.
8. On the abuses in Chechnya and the climate of impunity, see Human Rights Watch, "Last Seen . . .: Continued Disappearances in Chechnya" (April 2002) and "Swept Under: Torture, Forced Disappearances and Extrajudicial Killings during Sweep Operations in Chechnya" (February 2002); on impunity among the police, see Amnesty International, "Dokumenty! Discrimination on Grounds of Race in the Russian Federation" (London: Amnesty International Publications, 2003); on corruption, see David E. Hoffman, *The Oligarchs: Wealth and Power in the New Russia* (New York: PublicAffairs, 2002).
9. See Gordon B. Smith, *Reforming the Russian Legal System* (New York: Cambridge University Press, 1996); Dale R. Herspring, "Putin and Military Reform: Some First Hesitant Steps," *Russia and Eurasia Review*, 1, 7 (September 10, 2002) at www.jamestown.org.
10. Timothy J. Colton and Michael McFaul, "Russian Democracy Under Putin," *Problems of Post-Communism*, 50, 4 (July/August 2003).
11. Applebaum, Gulag, 512.
12. See the collected volumes on transitional justice around the world, e.g., McAdams *Transitional Justice*; Kritz, *Transitional Justice*; Barahona de Brito et al., *The Politics of Memory*; Henry Steiner, ed., *Truth Commissions: A Comparative Assessment* (Cambridge, MA: Harvard Law School Human Rights Program, 1997).

13. See Bass, *Crimes Against Humanity*; Robertson *Stay the Hand of Vengeance*, Douglas Farah, "Sierra Leone Court May Offer Model for War Crimes Cases," *Washington Post* (April 15, 2003).
14. This is a major factor complicating the prospect of carrying out trials of members of the Pol Pot regime in Cambodia. See Human Rights Watch, "Serious Flaws."

Bibliography

General

Ackerman, Bruce. *The Future of Liberal Revolution*. New Haven: Yale University Press, 1992.

Aguilar, Paloma. "Justice, Politics and Memory in the Spanish Transition." In *The Politics of Memory: Transitional Justice in Democratizing Societies*, ed. Alexandria Barahona de Brito, Carmen Gonzalez-Enriquez, and Paloma Aguilar. Oxford: Oxford University Press, 2001.

Arato, Andrew. *From New-Marxism to Democratic Theory: Essays on the Critical Theory of Soviet-Type Societies*. Armonk, NY: M.E. Sharpe, 1993.

Arblaster, Anthony. *The Rise and Decline of Western Liberalism*. Oxford: Basil Blackwell, 1984.

Arendt, Hannah. *Between Past and Future*. New York: Penguin, 1993.

———. *Eichmann in Jerusalem*. New York: Penguin, 1994.

———. *The Origins of Totalitarianism*, new edition. New York: Harcourt, Brace and World, 1966.

Barahona De Brito, Alexandria. *Human Rights and Democratization in Latin America: Uruguay and Chile*. Oxford: Oxford University Press, 1997.

Barahona De Brito, Alexandria, Carmen Gonzalez-Enriquez, and Paloma Aguilar, eds. *The Politics of Memory: Transitional Justice in Democratizing Societies*. Oxford: Oxford University Press, 2001.

Bass, Gary Jonathan. *Stay the Hand of Vengeance: The Politics of War Crimes Tribunals*. Princeton: Princeton University Press, 2002.

Benhabib, Seyla. "Deliberative Rationality and Models of Democratic Legitimacy." *Constellations* 1, 1 (1994): 26–52.

———. "Hannah Arendt and the Redemptive Power of Narrative." In *Hannah Arendt: Critical Essays*, ed. Lewis P. Hinchman and Sandra K. Hinchman. Albany: State University of New York Press, 1994.

Borneman, John. *Settling Accounts: Violence, Justice, and Accountability in Postsocialist Europe*. Princeton: Princeton University Press, 1997.

Calhoun, Noel. "The Statute of Limitations and the Prosecution of Human Rights Violations." In *1989–1999 Transformations: Triumph or Tragedy?* (New York: Harriman Institute, 2000).

Chapman, John W., ed. *Compensatory Justice*. Nomos XXXIII. New York: New York University Press, 1991.

Chilton, Paul and Christina Schaeffner. "Discourse and Politics." In *Discourse Studies: A Multidisciplinary Approach*, ed. Teun A. Van Dijk. London: Sage Publications, 1997.

Cooper, Martha. *Analyzing Public Discourse*. Prospect Heights, IL: Waveland Press, 1989.

Di Palma, Giuseppe. *To Craft Democracies: An Essay on Democratic Transitions*. Berkeley: University of California Press, 1990.

Elster, Jon. "On Doing What One Can: An Argument against Postcommunist Restitution And Retribution." *Eastern European Constitutional Review* 1, 2 (1992): 15–17.

———, ed. *The Roundtable Talks and the Breakdown of Communism*. Chicago: University of Chicago Press, 1996.

Fairclough, Norman and Ruth Wodak. "Critical Discourse Analysis." In *Discourse Studies: A Multidisciplinary Approach*, ed. Teun A. Van Dijk. London: Sage Publications, 1997.

Fisher, Walter R. "Narrative, Reason, and Community." In *Memory, Identity, Community: The Idea of Narrative in the Human Sciences*, ed. Lewis P. Hinchman and Sandra K. Hinchman. Albany: State University of New York Press, 1997.

Foner, Eric. *Reconstruction: America's Unfinished Revolution, 1863–1877*. New York: Harper and Row, 1988.

Foucault, Michel. "The Order of Discourse." In *Language and Politics*, ed. Michael J. Shapiro. New York: New York University Press, 1984.

Garreton, Manuel Antonio. "Human Rights in Processes of Democratisation." *Journal of Latin American Studies* 26 (1994): 221–234.

Gastil, Raymond D. *Freedom in the World*. New York: Freedom House, 1989.

Glendon, Mary Ann. *Rights Talk: The Impoverishment of Political Discourse*. New York: Free Press, 1991.

Goldstone, Jack A. *Revolution and Rebellion in the Early Modern World*. Berkeley: University of California Press, 1991.

Hartz, Louis. The *Liberal Tradition in America: An Interpretation of American Political Thought Since the Revolution*. San Diego: Harcourt Brace Jovanovic, 1983.

Henke, Klaus-Dietmar and Hans Woller, eds. *Politische Säuberung in Europa: Die Abrechnung mit Faschismus und Kollaboration nach dem Zweiten Weltkrieg*. Munich: Deutscher Taschenbuch Verlag, 1991.

Hobbes, Thomas. *Leviathan*, ed. C.B. Macpherson. London: Penguin Books, 1968.

Holmes, Stephen. "Precommitment and the Paradox of Democracy." In *Constitutionalism and Democracy*, ed. Jon Elster and Rune Slagstad. Cambridge: Cambridge University Press, 1988.

Holsti, Ole R. *Content Analysis for the Social Sciences and Humanities*. Reading, MA: Addison-Wesley, 1969.

Howard, Dick. "Towards a Politics of Judgement." *Constellations* 1, 2 (1994): 286–305.

Human Rights Watch. "Serious Flaws: Why the U.N. General Assembly Should Require Changes to the Draft Khmer Rouge Tribunal Agreement" (April 30, 2003).

Huntington, Samuel P. *The Third Wave: Democratization in the Late Twentieth Century*. Norman: University of Oklahoma Press, 1991.

Huyse, Luc. "Justice after Transition: On the Choices Successor Elites Make in Dealing With the Past." *Law and Social Inquiry* 19 (1995): 51–78.

Ingraham, Barton L. *The Structure of Criminal Procedure: Laws and Practice of France, the Soviet Union, China, and the United States*. New York: Greenwood, 1987.

Jaspers, Karl. *The Question of German Guilt*. Translated by E.B. Ashton. New York: The Dial Press, 1947.

Judt, Tony. "Epilogue." In *The Politics of Retribution in Europe*, ed. Istvan Deak, Jan T. Gross, and Tony Judt. Princeton: Princeton University Press, 2000.

Kelly, J.M. *A Short History of Western Legal Theory*. Oxford: Clarendon Press, 1992.

Kirchheimer, Otto. *Political Justice*. Princeton: Princeton University Press, 1961.

Kritz, Neil J., ed. *Transitional Justice: How Emerging Democracies Reckon With Former Regimes*. Three volumes. Washington, DC: United States Institute of Peace Press, 1995.

Locke, John. "The Second Treatise of Government." In *Two Treatises of Government*, ed. Peter Laslett. Cambridge: Cambridge University Press, 1960.

Lottman, Herbert R. *The Purge*. New York: William Morrow, 1986.

McAdams, A. James, ed. *Transitional Justice and the Rule of Law in New Democracies*. Notre Dame, IN: University of Notre Dame Press, 1997.

McCullum, Hugh. *The Angels Have Left Us: The Rwanda Tragedy and the Churches*. Geneva: WCC Publications, n.d.

Mendez, Juan E. "In Defense of Transitional Justice." In *Transitional Justice and the Rule of Law in New Democracies*, ed. A. James McAdams. Notre Dame, IN: University of Notre Dame Press, 1997.

Mill, John Stuart. *On Liberty*. With a foreword by Gertrude Himmelfarb. London: Penguin, 1988.

Moaddel, Mansoor. *Class, Politics and Ideology in the Iranian Revolution*. New York: Columbia University Press, 1993.

Moore, Barrington, Jr. *The Social Origins of Dictatorship and Democracy: Lord and Peasant in the Making of the Modern World*. Boston: Beacon Press, 1966.

Nino, Carlos Santiago. *Radical Evil on Trial*. New Haven: Yale University Press, 1996.

O'Donnell, Guillermo and Philippe C. Schmitter. *Transitions from Authoritarian Rule: Tentative Conclusions About Uncertain Democracies*. Baltimore: Johns Hopkins University Press, 1986.

Offe, Claus. "Coming to Terms with Past Injustices: An Introduction to Legal Strategies Available in Post-Communist Societies." *Archives europeennes de sociologie* 23 (1992).

Orentlicher, Diane. "Settling Accounts: The Duty to Punish Human Rights Violations of a Prior Regime." In *Transitional Justice*, vol. 1, ed. Neil Kritz. Washington, DC: United States Institute of Peace, 1995.

Osiel, Mark J. "Ever Again: Legal Remembrance of Administrative Massacre." *University of Pennsylvania Law Review* 144, 2 (December 1995): 463–704.x

———. *Mass Atrocity, Collective Memory, and the Law*. New Brunswick: Transaction, 1997.

Pitkin, Hanna Fenichel. *Wittgenstein and Justice: On the Significance of Ludwig Wittgenstein for Social and Political Thought*. Berkeley: University of California Press, 1972.

Power, Samantha. "Bystanders to Genocide." *The Atlantic Monthly* 288, 2 (September 2001): 84–108.

Przeworski, Adam. *Democracy and the Market*. Cambridge: Cambridge University Press, 1991.

Robertson, Geoffrey. *Crimes Against Humanity: The Struggle for Global Justice*, second edition. London: Penguin Books, 2002.

Robinson, John A. and Linda Hawpe. "Narrative Thinking as a Heuristic Process." In *Narrative Psychology: The Storied Nature of Human Conduct*, ed. Theodore R. Sarbin. New York: Praeger, 1986.

Rosenfeld, Michael. "Restitution, Retribution, Political Justice and the Rule of Law." *Constellations* 2, 3 (January 1996): 309–332.

Rousso, Henry. *The Vichy Syndrome: History and Memory in France Since 1944*. Translated by Arthur Goldhammer. Cambridge, MA: Harvard University Press, 1991.

Sartori, Giovanni. *The Theory of Democracy Revisited*. Chatham, NJ: Chatham House Publishers, 1987.

Sher, George. "Ancient Wrongs and Modern Rights." *Philosophy and Public Affairs* 10, 1 (Winter 1981): 3–17.

Shklar, Judith N. *The Faces of Injustice*. New Haven: Yale University Press, 1990.

Siani-Davies, Peter. "The Revolution After the Revolution." In *Post-Communist Romania: Coming to Terms with Transition*, ed. Duncan Light and David Phinnemore. New York: Palgrave, 2001.

Sikkink, Kathryn. "Human Rights, Principled Issue-Networks, and Sovereignty in Latin America." *International Organization* 47, 3 (Summer 1993): 411–441.

Skocpol, Theda. *States and Social Revolutions: A Comparative Analysis of France, Russia, and China*. Cambridge: Cambridge University Press, 1979.

Steiner, Henry, ed. *Truth Commissions: A Comparative Assessment*. Cambridge, MA: Harvard Law School Human Rights Program, 1997.

Stinchcombe, Arthur L. "Lustration as a Problem of the Social Basis of Constitutionalism." *Law and Social Inquiry* (1995): 245–273.

Swidler, Ann. "Culture in Action: Symbols and Strategies." *American Sociological Review* 51, 2 (April 1986): 273–286.

Szablowski, George J. and Hans-Ulrich Derlien. "East European Transitions, Elites, Bureaucracies, and the European Community." *Governance* 6, 3 (July 1993): 304–324.

Taylor, Charles. *Philosophy and the Human Sciences*. Cambridge: Cambridge University Press, 1985.

Teitel, Ruti G. *Transitional Justice*. New York: Oxford University Press, 2000.

Trimberger, Kay. *Revolution from Above: Military Bureaucrats in Development in Japan, Turkey, Egypt, and Peru*. New Brunswick, NJ: Transaction Books, 1978.

Tucker, Robert, ed. *The Lenin Anthology*. New York: W.W. Norton, 1975.

———, ed. *The Marx-Engels Reader*. New York: W.W. Norton, 1978.

Van Dijk, Teun A. "Discourse as Interaction in Society." In *Discourse as Social Interaction*, vol. 2, *Discourse Studies: A Multidisciplinary Approach*, ed. Teun A. Van Dijk, London: Sage Publications, 1997.

Waltz, Susan E. *Human Rights and Reform: Changing the Face of North African Politics*. Berkeley: University of California Press, 1995.

Walzer, Michael. *Regicide and Revolution*. New York: Columbia University Press, 1992.

Welch, David A. *Justice and the Genesis of War*. Cambridge: Cambridge University Press, 1993.

Weschler, Lawrence. "The Velvet Purge: The Trials of Jan Kavan." *The New Yorker* (October 19, 1992): 66–96.

Woller, Hans. "Ausgebliebene Säuberung? Die Abrechnung mit dem Faschismus in Italien." In *Politische Säuberung in Europa: Die Abrechnung mit Faschismus und Kollaboration nach dem Zweiten Weltkrieg*, ed Klaus-Dietmar Henke and Hans Woller. Münich: Deutscher Taschenbuch Verlag, 1982.

Wuthnow, Robert. *Communities of Discourse: Ideology and Social Structure in the Reformation, the Enlightenment, and European Socialism*. Cambridge, MA: Harvard University Press, 1989.

Germany

Anderson, Gary. "The Mauerschützenprozesse and the Principle of *Nullum Crimen Sine Lege*." *German Politics* 7, 2 (August 1998): 47–63.

Arbeitsgruppe der Bürgerkomitees. "Ohne Aurarbeitung des Stasi-Systems kein gesellschaftlicher Neuanfang." In *Die Kontinuität des Wegsehens und Mitmachens: Stasi-Akten oder die schwierige Bewältigung der DDR-Vergangenheit*. Cologne: Henrich-Böll Stiftung, 1991.

Binsky, Lothar, Uwe-Jens Heuer and Michael Schumann, eds. "*Unrechtsstaat?*"—*Politische Justiz und die Aufarbeitung der DDR-Vergangenheit*. Hamburg: VSA-Verlag, 1994.

Bock, Petra. "Von der Tribunal-Idee zur Enquete-Kommission." *Deutschland Archiv* 28 (November 1995): 1171–1183.

Bürgerkomitee Leipzig, ed. *Stasi intern: Macht und Banalität*. Leipzig: Forum, 1991.

Bundesbeauftragte für die Unterlagen des Staatssicherheitsdienstes der ehemaligen DDR, *Erster Tätigkeitsbericht*. Berlin: Abteilung Bildung und Forschung, 1993.

———. *Zweiter Tätigkeitsbericht*. Berlin: Abteilung Bildung und Forschung, 1995.

Fricke, Karl Wilhelm. "Entmachtung und Erblast des MfS." *Deutschland Archiv* 23, 12 (1990): 1881–1890.

Fulbrook, Mary. *Anatomy of a Dictatorship: Inside the GDR, 1949–1989*. Oxford: Oxford University Press, 1995.

Gill, David, and Ulrich Schröter. *Das Ministerium für Staatssicherheit: Anatomie des Mielke-Imperiums*. Berlin: Rowohlt, 1991.

Goodman, Micah. "After the Wall: The Legal Ramifications of the East German Border Guard Trials in Unified Germany." *Cornell International Law Journal* 29 (1996): 727–765.

Golz, Hans-Georg. "Seriöse Zahlen zum IM-Bestand." *Deutschland Archiv* 27, 4 (1994): 343–344.

Habermas, Jürgen. "Burdens of a Double Past." *Dissent* (Fall 1994): 513–517.

Herles, Helmut and Ewald Rose, eds. *Vom Runden Tisch zum Parlament.* Bonn: Bouvier, 1990.

Jäckel, Eberhard. "Die doppelte Vergangenheit." *Der Spiegel* 51 (1991): 39–43.

Lüderssen, Klaus. *Der Staat geht unter-das Unrecht bleibt? Regierungskriminalität in der ehemaligen DDR.* Frankfurt/Main: Suhrkamp, 1992.

Monson, R.A. "West German Statute of Limitations on Murder: A Political, Legal and Historical Exposition." *American Journal of Comparative Law* 30 (1982): 605–625.

Mühler, Kurt and Steffen H. Wilsdorf. "Meinungstrends in der Leipziger Montagsdemonstration." In *Leipzig im Oktober: Kirchen und alternative Gruppen im Umbruch*, ed. Jürgen Grabner et al. Berlin: Wichern, 1990.

Offe, Claus. *Der Tunnel am Ende des Lichts.* Frankfurt: Campus Verlag, 1995.

Osmond, Jonathon. *German Reunification: A Reference Guide and Commentary.* Essex: Longman, 1992.

Petzold, Frank. "Betrachtungen zur Auflösung des Ministeriums für Staatssicherheit unter der Regierung Modrow, Teil I." *Horch und Guck* 9 (1993): 3–16.

———. "Betrachtungen zur Auflösung des Ministeriums für Staatssicherheit unter der Regierung Modrow, Teil II." *Horch und Guck* 10 (1993): 15–24.

Probst, Lothar. "Die Entwicklung der Bürgerbewegungen im Prozess der Vereinigung." *Forschungsjournal NSB*, 1 (January 1992): 47–60.

Quill, Adrienne M. "To Prosecute or Not To Prosecute: Problems Encountered in the Prosecution of Former Communist Officials in Germany, Czechoslovakia, and the Czech Republic." *Indiana International and Comparative Law Review* 7 (1996): 165–183.

Reuter, Ute and Thomas Schulte. *Dokumentation zur Entwicklung der neuen Parteien und Bürgerrechtsgruppen in der DDR.* Bonn: Gesamtdeutsches Institut, 1990.

———. *Systemunrecht und Strafrecht am Beispiel dier Mauerschützen in der ehe-maligen DDR.* Berlin: Berlin Verlag, 1993.

Roggemann, Herwig. *Fragen und Wege zur Rechtseinheit in Deutschland.* Belin: Arno Spitz, 1995.

Roth, Jürgen et al. "Das Zweite SED-Unrechtsbereinigungsgesetz." *Deutschland Archiv* 27 (May 1994): 449–456.

Rüddenklau, Wolfgang. "Bekämpfung feindlich negativer Kräfte." *Horch und Guck* 3 (1992): 7–15.

Sa'adah, Anne. *Germany's Second Chance: Trust, Justice, and Democratization.* Cambridge, MA: Harvard University Press, 1998.

Sachs, Michael. "Verfassungsrechtliche Anmerkungen zum Strafverfahren gegen Erich Honecker." *Zeitschrift für Politik* 40, 2 (1993): 121–137.

Schäfgen, Christoph. "Die Strafverfolgung von Regierungskriminalität der DDR." In *Eine Diktatur vor Gericht: Aufarbeitung von SED-Unrecht durch die Justiz*, ed. Jürgen Weber and Michael Piazolo. Munich: Olzog, 1995.

Schäuble, Wolfgang. *Der Vertrag.* Stuttgart: Knaur, 1991.

Schönherr, Albrecht, ed. *Ein Volk am Pranger? Die Deutschen auf der Suche nach einer neuen politischen Kultur.* Berlin: Aufbau Taschenbuch, 1992.

Schumann, Silke. *Vernichten oder Offenlegen? Zur Entstehung des Stasi-Unterlagen-Gesetzes: Eine Dokumentation der öffentlichen Debatte 1990/1991.* Berlin: Der Bundesbeauftragte für die Unterlagen des Staatssicherheitsdienstes der DDR, 1995.

Süss, Walter. "Entmachtung und Verfall der Staatssicherheit." *BF informiert* 5 (1994): 49–73.

Tappert, Wilhelm. *Die Wiedergutmachung von Staatsunrecht der SBZ/DDR durch die Bundesrepublik Deutschland nach der Wiedervereinigung.* Berlin: Arno Spitz, 1995.

Thaysen, Uwe. *Der Runde Tisch. Oder: Wo blieb das Volk?* Opladen: Westdeutscher, 1990.

Thode, Marina. "Towards Democracy: Criminal Law, Criminal Justice and the Reunification of Germany." In *Democracy, Market Economy, and the Law: Legal, Economic, and Political Problems of Transition to Democracy*, ed. Werner F. Ebke and Detlev F. Vegts. Heidelberg: Verlag Recht und Wirtschaft, 1995.

Weber, Jürgen and Michael Piazolo, eds. *Eine Diktatur vor Gericht: Aufarbeitung von SED-Unrecht durch die Justiz.* Munich: Olzog, 1995.

Weinke, Annette. "Die DDR-Justiz im Jahr der 'Wende'." *Deutschland Archiv* 30, 1 (1997): 41–62.

Werdin, Justus. *Unter Uns: Die Stasi. Berichte der Bürgerkomitees zur Auflösung der Staatssicherheit im Bezirk Frankfurt (Oder).* Berlin: Basis, 1990.

Wesel, Uwe. *Der Honecker-Prozess: Ein Staat vor Gericht.* Frankfurt/Main: Eichborn, 1994.

Winters, Peter Jochen. "Der Mielke-Prozess." In *Eine Diktatur vor Gericht: Aufarbeitung von SED-Unrecht durch die Justiz*, ed. Jürgen Weber and Michael Piazolo. Munich: Olzog, 1995.

Worst, Anne. *Das Ende eines Geheimdienstes. Oder: Wie lebendig ist die Stasi?* Berlin: LinksDruck, 1991.

Poland

de Weydenthal, Jan B. "Inquiry into the Murder of Father Popieluszko Reopened." *Report on Eastern Europe* (August 17, 1990): 2–15.

Centrum Badania Opinii Społecznej. Telewizyjno-radiowe wystąpienie premiera T. Mazowieckiego w opinii społecznej. BD/229/50/89. Warsaw: November 1989.

———. Oczekiwania i obawy związane z lustracją. BS/38/29/93. Warsaw: March 1993.

———. *Lustracja—Problem wciąż aktualny.* BS/34/34/96. Warsaw: February 1996.

Dubinski, Krzystof. *Magdalenka: Transakcja epoki.* Warsaw: Sylwa, 1990.

Dziewulski, Jerzy. Interview by author, July 19, 2000, Warsaw.

Ekiert, Grzegorz. *The State Against Society: Political Crises and Their Aftermath in East Central Europe.* Princeton, NJ: Princeton University Press, 1996.

Hall, Aleksander. *Pierwsza Taka Dekada.* Poznan: "W drodze," 2000.

Herzog, Aleksander. Interview by author, November 20, 1996, Warsaw.

Holzer, Jerzy. "The Communist Poland: The Role of a Concept of the Polish History for the Transformation to Democracy." In *After Communism: A Multidisciplinary Approach to Radical Social Change*, ed. Edmund Wnuk-Lipinski. Warsaw: Institute of Political Studies, 1995.

———. Interview by author, November 25, 1996, Warsaw.

Kieruj, Adam W. Interview by author, November 14, 1996, Warsaw.

Kubik, Jan. *The Power of Symbols Against the Symbols of Power: The Rise of Solidarity and the Fall of State Socialism in Poland.* University Park, PA: Pennsylvania State University Press, 1994.

Kurski, Jacek and Piotr Semka. *Lewy Czerwcowy*. Warsaw: Editions Spotkania, 1993.

Lityński, Jan. Interview by author, July 12, 2000, Warsaw.

Łoś, Maria. "Lustration and Truth Claims: Unfinished Revolutions in Central Europe." *Law and Social Inquiry* 19 (1995).

Mazowiecki, Wojciech. Interview by author, June 17, 1996, Cambridge, MA.

Niesiołowski, Stefan. Interview by author, July 11, 2000, Warsaw.

Ordyński, Jan. Interview by author, June 4, 1997, Warsaw.

Osiatynski, Wiktor. "Agent Wałęsa?" *East European Constitutional Review* 1, 2 (Summer 1992): 28–30.

———. "The Roundtable Talks in Poland." In *The Roundtable Talks and the Breakdown of Communism*, ed. Jon Elster. Chicago: University of Chicago Press, 1996.

Sabbat-Swidlicka, Anna. "Crisis in the Polish Justice Ministry." *Radio Free Europe/Radio Liberty Research Report* 2 (April 9, 1993): 14–18.

Sałkowski, Jan. Interview by author, December 18, 1996, Warsaw.

Skorzynski, Jan. *Ugoda i Rewolucja: Władza i opozycja 1985–1989*. Warsaw: Rzeczpospolita, 1995.

Słodkowska, Inka, ed. *Programy Partii i Ugropowan Parlamentarnych 1989–1991*. Two vols. Warsaw: Instytut Studiow Politycznych PAN, 1995.

Sokolewicz, Wojciech. "The Relevance of Western Models for Constitution-Building in Poland." In *Constitutional Policy and Change in Europe*, ed. Joachim Jens Hesse and Nevil Johnson. Oxford: Oxford University Press, 1995.

Stanowska, Maria. "Orzecznictwo Sądu Najwyzszego w sprawach rehabilitacyjnych w latach 1988–1991." *Archiwum Kryminologii* 19 (1993): 133–165.

Stefański, Jacek. *Polska 1988–1993*. Kolbuszowa: Biblioteka Publiczna Miasta i Gminy w Kolbuszowej, 1995.

Walicki, Andrzej. "Transitional Justice and the Political Struggles of Post-Communist Poland." In *Transitional Justice and the Rule of Law in New Democracies*, ed. A. James McAdams. Notre Dame, IN: University of Notre Dame Press, 1997.

Wasilewski, Jacek. "Towards new Political Elites in Poland." In *Post-Communist Poland: From Totalitarianism to Democracy*? ed. Jacques Coenen-Huther and Brunon Synak. Commack, NY: Nova Science, 1993.

Wójcik, Dariusz. Interview by author, July 13, 2000, Warsaw.

Russia

Afanasiev, Yurii. "Perestroika i istoricheskoe znanie." In *Inogo ne dano*. Moscow: Progress, 1988.

Alekseev, T.A. et al. "Kakovy ideologicheskie usloviia obshchestvennogo soglasii v Rossii?" *Polis* 3 (March 1997): 16–52.

Allensworth, Wayne. *The Russian Question: Nationalism, Modernization, and Post-Communist Russia*. Lanham, MD: Rowman and Littlefield, 1988.

Amnesty International. "Dokumenty! Discrimination on Grounds of Race in the Russian Federation." London: Amnesty International Publications, 2003.

Applebaum, Anne. *Gulag: A History of the Soviet Camps*. New York: Random House, 2003.

Aron, Leon. *Boris Yeltsin: A Revolutionary Life*. London: HarperCollins, 2000.

Bakatin, Vadim. *Izbavlenie ot KGB*. Moscow: Novosti, 1992.

Batalov, Eduard. "Chem zapolnim ideinyi vakkum?" *Svobodnaia mysl'* 11 (1996): 3–11.

Bialer, Seweryn. "The Changing Soviet Political System: The Nineteenth Party Conference and After." In *Politics, Society, and Nationality Inside Gorbachev's Russia*, ed. Seweryn Bialer. Boulder: Westview, 1989.

Chiesa, Giulietto. *Transition to Democracy: Political Change in the Soviet Union, 1987–1991*. Hanover, NH: University Press of New England, 1993.

Colton, Timothy J. *Transitional Citizens: Voters and What Influences Them in the New Russia*. Cambridge: Harvard University Press, 2000.

Colton Timothy J. and Michael McFaul. "Russian Democracy under Putin." *Problems of Post-Communism* 50, 4 (July/August 2003).

———. *The Harvest of Sorrow: Soviet Collectivization and the Terror-Famine*. New York: Oxford University Press, 1986.

Conquest, Robert. *The Great Terror: A Reassessment*. New York: Oxford University Press, 1990.

Davies, Robert William. *Soviet History in the Gorbachev Revolution*. Bloomington: Indiana University Press, 1989.

Dem'iachenko, Yu. A. and P.E. Stepanov. *Ne predat' zabveniiu: Kniga Pamiati zhertv politicheskikh repressii*. Pskov: 1996.

Devlin, Judith. *The Rise of the Russian Democrats: The Causes and Consequences of the Elite Revolution*. Hants: Edward Elgar, 1995.

Gorbachev, Mikhail. *Izbrannye rechi i stat'i*. Moscow: Izdatel'stvo politicheskoi literatury, 1987.

———. *Perestroika: New Thinking for Our Country and the World*. New York: Harper & Row, 1987.

Gosudarstvennaia Duma. *Stenogramma zasedanii* 11 (December 7, 1994).

Grimsted, Patricia Kennedy. "Russian Archives in Transition: Caught Between Political Crossfire and Economic Crisis." *The American Archivist* 56 (Fall 1993): 614–662.

Gromova, Tatiana. Interview by author, June 12, 1999, Moscow.

Hauslohner, Peter. "Politics before Gorbachev: De-Stalinization and the Roots of Reform." In *Politics, Society, and Nationality Inside Gorbachev's Russia*, ed. Seweryn Bialer. Boulder: Westview, 1989.

Herspring, Dale R. "Putin and Military Reform: Some First Hesitant Steps." *Russia and Eurasia Review* 1, 7 (September 10, 2002) at www.jamestown.org.

Hoffman, David E. *The Oligarchs: Wealth and Power in the New Russia*. New York: Public Affairs, 2002.

Hough, Jerry F. *Democratization and Revolution in the USSR, 1985–1991*. Washington, DC: Brookings Institution, 1997.

———. "Swept Under: Torture, Forced Disappearances and Extrajudicial Killings during Sweep Operations in Chechnya." February 2002.

Human Rights Watch. "Last Seen . . .: Continued Disappearances in Chechnya." April 2002.

Jowitt, Ken. "Undemocratic Past, Unnamed Present, Undecided Future." *Demokratizatsiya* 4 (Summer 1996): 409–419.

Juviler, Peter. *Freedom's Ordeal: The Struggle for Human Rights and Democratization in Post-Soviet States*. Philadelphia: University of Pennsylvania Press, 1998.

Katkov, N.F. "Vosstanovlenie istoricheskoi pravdy i spravedlivosti." *Voprosi istorii* KPSS 9 (1991): 83–92.

Knight, Amy. *Spies Without Cloaks: The KGB's Successors*. Princeton: Princeton University Press, 1996.

Kostinsky, Aleksandr. Interview by author, May 25, 1999, Moscow.

Kramer, Mark. "Archival Research in Moscow: Progress and Pitfalls." *Cold War International History Project Bulletin* (Fall 1993): 18–39.

Laquer, Walter. *Stalin: The Glasnost' Revelations*. New York: Macmillan, 1990.

Ligachev, Yegor. *Inside Gorbachev's Kremlin*. Translated by Catherine Fitzpatrick et al. New York: Random House, 1993.

Malaia entsiklopediia Rossiskoi politiki: Osnovnye partii i dvizheniia zaregistrirovannye Ministrom iustitsii. Moscow: Supreme Soviet, 1992.

Marsh, Rosalind. *History and Literature in Contemporary Russia*. London: Macmillan, 1995.

Mason, David S. and Svetlana Sidorenko-Stephenson. "Public Opinion and the 1996 Elections in Russia: Nostalgic and Statist, Yet Pro-Market and Pro-Yeltsin." *Slavic Review* 56 (Winter 1997): 698–717.

Mezhuev, B.V. "Poniatie 'nazional'nyi interes' v Rossiiskoi obshchestvenno-politicheskoi mysli." *Polis* 1 (January 1997): 5–31.

Petrov, Nikita. Interview by author, June 8, 1999, Moscow.

Ponomarev, Lev. Interview by author, May 27, 1999, Moscow.

Popkov, N.E. and V.N. Miasnikov. *Samarskaia oblast': Belaia kniga o zhertvakh politicheskikh repressii*. Samara: Samarsky Dom pechati, 1997.

Sakharov, Andrei. *Moscow and Beyond, 1986–1989*. Translated by Antonina Bouis. New York: Alfred A. Knopf, 1991.

Shentalinsky, Vitaly. *The KGB's Literary Archive*. Translated by John Crowfoot. London: Harvill, 1995.

Smith, Gordon B. *Reforming the Russian Legal System*. New York: Cambridge University Press, 1996.

Smith, Kathleen E. *Remembering Stalin's Victims: Popular Memory and the End of the USSR*. Ithaca: Cornell University Press, 1996.

Thorson, Carla. "Has the Communist Party Been Legally Suspended?" *Radio Liberty* 3, 40 (October 4, 1991): 4–8.

Tolz, Vera. "New Situation for CPSU and KGB Archives." *Radio Liberty* 3, 38 (September 28, 1991): 1–4.

van Goudoever, Albert P. *The Limits of Destalinization in the Soviet Union: Political Rehabilitation in the Soviet Union Since Stalin*. Translated by Frans Hijkoop. London: Croom Helm, 1986.

Vdovin, Yurii. "Grazhdansky kontrol." *Vestnik Memoriala* 1 (May 1993): 13–17.

Wheatcroft, Stephen G. "Glasnost' and Rehabilitations." In *Facing Up to the Past: Soviet Historiography Under Perestroika*, ed. Takayuki Ito. Sapporo, Japan: Slavic Research Center, Hokkaido University, 1989.

———, ed. *Reabilitatsia: Politicheskie protsessy 30–50–x godov*. Moscow: Izdatel'stvo politicheskoi literatury, 1991.

Yakovlev, Aleksander N. *A Century of Violence in Soviet Russia*. New Haven and London: Yale University Press, 2002.

Yanowitch, Murray. *Controversies in Soviet Social Thought: Democratization, Social Justice and the Erosion of Official Ideology*. Armonk, NY: M.E. Sharpe, 1991.

Yaroshevski, Dov B. "Political Paticipation and Public Memory: The Memorial Movement in the USSR, 1987–1989." *History and Memory* 2 (Winter 1990): 5–31.

Yurasov, Dmitry. "Hinter sieben Siegeln." *Deutschland Archiv* 26, 7 (July 1993).

Press

Die Andere
Associated Press
BBC Monitoring Europe
Current Digest of the Soviet Press
Deutsche Presse-Agentur
Economist, The
Financial Times
FBIS-EEU
Gazeta Prawnicza
Gazeta Wyborcza
Interfax
Izvestiia
Kuranty
Literaturnaya gazeta
Moskovskie novosti
New York Times
Nezavisimaya gazeta

Ogoniek
Pravda
Radio Free Europe/Radio Liberty
Reuters
Rossisskie vesti
Rzeczpospolita
Sovetskaya kultura
Der Spiegel
Times, The (London)
Washington Post, The

Government Documents

Akty Sekretariatu Posiedzen Sejmu
Biuleten' (Supreme Soviet RSFSR)
Biuleten' (Soviet of Nationalities)
Biuletyn
Bundesgesetzblatt
Dariusz Sejmowy
Dziennik Ustaw
Materialy parlamentskikh slushanii
Monitor Polski
Orzecznictwo Trybunalu Konstytucyjnego
Sprawozdanie stenograficzne Sejmu PRL
Sprawozdanie stenograficzne Senatu PRL
Sprawozdanie stenograficzne Sejmu RP
Vedemosti s'ezda narodnykh deputatov RSFSR i Verkhovnogo Soveta RSFSR
Verhandlungen des Deutschen Bundestages
Volkskammer der DDR

Index